THE PARADOX OF PARLIAMENT

The Paradox of Parliament

JONATHAN MALLOY

UNIVERSITY OF TORONTO PRESS
Toronto Buffalo London

© University of Toronto Press 2023
Toronto Buffalo London
utorontopress.com

ISBN 978-1-4875-5088-2 (cloth)
ISBN 978-1-4875-5099-8 (paper)
ISBN 978-1-4875-5100-1 (EPUB)
ISBN 978-1-4875-5102-5 (PDF)

All rights reserved. The use of any part of this publication reproduced, transmitted in any form or by any means, electronic, mechanical, photocopying, recording, or otherwise, or stored in a retrieval system, without prior written consent of the publisher – or in the case of photocopying, a licence from Access Copyright, the Canadian Copyright Licensing Agency – is an infringement of the copyright law.

Library and Archives Canada Cataloguing in Publication

Title: The paradox of Parliament / Jonathan Malloy.
Names: Malloy, Jonathan, 1970– author.
Description: Includes bibliographical references and index.
Identifiers: Canadiana (print) 20220487006 | Canadiana (ebook) 20220487103 | ISBN 9781487550882 (cloth) | ISBN 9781487550998 (paper) | ISBN 9781487551001 (EPUB) | ISBN 9781487551025 (PDF)
Subjects: LCSH: Canada. Parliament. | LCSH: Canada. Parliament – Decision making. | LCSH: Representative government and representation – Canada.
Classification: LCC JL136.M364 2023 | DDC 328.71 – dc23

We welcome comments and suggestions regarding any aspect of our publications – please feel free to contact us at news@utorontopress.com or visit us at utorontopress.com.

Every effort has been made to contact copyright holders; in the event of an error or omission, please notify the publisher.

We wish to acknowledge the land on which the University of Toronto Press operates. This land is the traditional territory of the Wendat, the Anishnaabeg, the Haudenosaunee, the Métis, and the Mississaugas of the Credit First Nation.

University of Toronto Press acknowledges the financial support of the Government of Canada and the Ontario Arts Council, an agency of the Government of Ontario, for its publishing activities.

Contents

Acknowledgments vii

1 The Paradox 1
2 Historical Foundations and the Competing Logics 12
3 Parties 39
4 MPs 67
5 House of Commons Business 102
6 Diversity 145
7 The Senate 182
8 Scrutiny 203
9 The Future of Parliament 233

Notes 249

Index 281

Acknowledgments

My interest in legislatures began in 1992 when I was accepted into the Ontario Legislative Internship Programme (OLIP), after completing my undergraduate degree in political science at the University of Waterloo. I entered OLIP because I was interested in politics. I left with a deep interest in legislatures, thanks especially to the guidance of then-director Graham White. I went on to do my MA at Queen's University on House of Commons committees under the supervision of the late C.E.S. (Ned) Franks. I remain grateful to these two mentors. From Ned I learned that legislatures were deeply complex places that could only be understood as whole entities. From Graham I learned that they were profoundly human places, populated by flawed but often still noble people.

Over the years my thinking on legislatures and representative democracy has been spurred by many other individuals, and I can only name a few here: David Docherty, Sylvia Bashevkin, Jennifer Smith, Peter Russell, Leslie Seidle, Alex Marland, Kelly Blidook, Royce Koop, Jean-François Godbout, Louise Cockram, Elsa Piersig, Jack Stillborn, and the late Gary Levy, among many more. Special thanks to Paul E.J. Thomas, scholarly colleague, legislative enthusiast, and friend. Thanks also to Jim Farney and Loleen Berdahl.

Over the years I received valuable additional feedback on the ideas and passages in this book from many people, including Bill Cross, Joanna Everitt, Kiera Ladner, Mario Levesque, J.P. Lewis, John

McAndrews, Jared Wesley, and Charlie Feldman. I want to thank former Member of Parliament Harold Albrecht for his feedback on chapter 4 on MPs, and Michael Donison on chapter 5 on House of Commons business. Most of all, this book is much improved thanks to the work of the Press's three anonymous reviewers, who posed important and careful questions and comments that forced me to reflect, rethink, and sometimes defend all aspects of the book. All the above people can take credit for making the book better, while I remain responsible for any deficiencies.

My greatest debt is to the University of Toronto Press, which patiently waited for this manuscript for a decade. I greatly appreciate the Press's forbearance and the work of its talented editors and staff in bringing this book to publication.

I am approaching thirty years of involvement with the Canadian Study of Parliament Group (CSPG), including a stint as its president. This book has been shaped by countless CSPG events, publications, and conversations, and I want to extend my gratitude to the House of Commons as well as the Senate and Library of Parliament for their longtime support of the Group, giving it freedom to engage in serious and often critical conversations about Parliament. It has been my privilege to work with a tremendous CSPG board and staff over the years, with far too many individuals to list here, though I do want to particularly thank the wise and savvy Dianne Brydon, the very capable Michel Bédard, and the multi-talented Charlie Feldman.

I also want to thank the School of Politics and International Relations at the Australian National University for hosting me as a visiting scholar in 2016, allowing me to spend plenty of time at both the current Parliament of Australia, observing its often raucous House of Representatives, and also the Parliament's former location, now transformed into the Museum of Australian Democracy, the happiest place on earth for parliamentary nerds. My time in Canberra was most helpful in giving me a new perspective on the Canadian Parliament and its strengths and weaknesses.

It has been my privilege since 2000 to be a member of the Department of Political Science at Carleton University, and to be surrounded by a truly excellent and supportive group of scholarly colleagues. Students, particularly in my PSCI 4006 Legislatures and Representation classes, have constantly spurred me to think about legislatures and their meaning in the twenty-first century. Since 2019 I have held the Honourable Dick and Ruth Bell Chair in Canadian Parliamentary Democracy in the Department. The resources and opportunity of the Bell Chair were crucial to completing this manuscript, and I am most grateful to the late Ruth Bell for establishing the Chair. I think she would have been pleased to see this book.

My final thanks are to my wife, Ruth, and my daughters, Alida and Emma, who have long indulged my interest in legislatures, including their physical settings, often patiently waiting as I snap one more "legislative selfie."

Living in Ottawa, I have the privilege of casual acquaintance with the Parliament buildings, sometimes passing them on a run or kayaking behind them on the Ottawa River, enjoying the view found on the cover of this book. But it is always profoundly satisfying to see visitors gathered on the parliamentary lawn, taking pictures and taking in the majesty of the setting. It reminds me that Parliament remains unique and special, and that it has been a privilege to write this book about it.

CHAPTER ONE

The Paradox

Parliament occupies an ambiguous place in Canadian politics. The parliamentary buildings in Ottawa stand in many pictures and images as the symbols of Canadian democracy. Yet the actual House of Commons and Senate embody frustration and cynicism.

Critics argue that Parliament is superficial and meaningless, and too dominated by party discipline and self-seeking behaviour. Equity-seeking groups see it as a patriarchal, colonial institution. Members of the House of Commons lament the ambiguity and futility of their roles. Senators struggle with the legitimacy of their entire chamber.

On the other side, defenders of Parliament assert that the institution is in need of understanding more than criticism. They argue party discipline is essential for the functioning of Parliament and, while it may be old, Parliament is also flexible and able to adapt with the times. Laments about Parliament may be based in misinformation, ignorance, and nostalgia for a golden age that never existed. And while Parliament may be messy and at times frustrating, defenders argue this is the nature of democracy.

The Paradox of Parliament does not take sides in these debates. It does not argue for, or against, reform. It does not condemn Parliament, nor does it defend the status quo. Instead it seeks to understand and analyse Parliament, and the many debates surrounding it. In this book we will look carefully at what Parliament does, the expectations surrounding it, the roles of parties and parliamentarians, the dimensions of gender and racial diversity, and other important topics.

Dissatisfaction with Parliament is not new, and expert observers have long noted this. "The list of indictments against the Canadian parliament is impressive," wrote Robert Jackson and Michael Atkinson in 1980.[1] David Docherty observed in 1997 that "[c]riticisms of Parliament, and the women and men who serve in it, come from all fronts."[2] "The House of Commons has a problem, and it knows it – no one is happy with its performance," said David Smith in 2007.[3] Claims of "the decline of Parliament" are long-standing, and not limited to Canada. Jackson and Atkinson also note that "scholars in parliamentary systems of the British type often refer to a 'classic' and harmonious period from which Parliament has declined."[4] If the Canadian Parliament has declined, it has been doing so for a long time.

Parliamentary reform is also not new. In fact, Parliament went through considerable institutional reform in the last decades of the twentieth century. Major reforms in 1968, 1982, and 1985–6 significantly changed the way the House of Commons worked, focusing particularly on concerns about party discipline and the role of the individual MP. Further adjustments continued after that. But none fundamentally changed the underlying concerns about party discipline, the concentration of executive power, and the overall efficacy and legitimacy of Parliament. As C.E.S. Franks argues, "reform of Parliament is not simply a technical matter ... although it is often presented in those terms."[5]

Debates about the House of Commons go through cyclical phases in which different concerns and dynamics are at work. Opposition parties are typically great champions of parliamentary reform. Yet they inevitably change their tune when they gain power. As the third-place opposition leader running in the 2015 election, Liberal Party leader Justin Trudeau promised to "make free votes in the House of Commons standard practice," to not use prorogation "to avoid difficult political circumstances," and to bring an end to the "undemocratic practice" of omnibus bills.[6] Each of these was in reaction to actions of the Harper Conservative government of 2006–15. Yet Prime Minister Trudeau broke all of these promises, along with his pledge that "2015 will be the last federal election conducted under the first-past-the-post voting system." (Trudeau did, however, deliver on his promise of Senate reform.) And this was merely the latest cycle, as nearly every incoming prime minister in recent memory has promised parliamentary reforms, but inevitably delivered far less than promised – which often precipitates entirely new calls for reform. It is little wonder that a 2008 study on parliamentary reform by longtime observer Thomas Axworthy was titled "Everything Old Is New Again."[7]

Concerns about the Senate are less cyclical and more evolutionary. As I argue in chapter 7, the Senate is a solution shopping for a problem to solve; the problem itself has changed over the years. In the 1960s and 1970s the Senate was close to death, criticized for its patronage appointments and ties to economic and business elites. But as concerns grew about national unity and the survival of the Canadian federation, interest turned to the Senate's role as a body of regional representation, especially for Western Canada. The "Triple-E Senate" (Equal, Elected, and Effective) became a slogan of the 1980s and 1990s, but was never realized. Instead, the Senate itself began to highlight its supposed value as the chamber of "sober second thought," serving as a check on majority governments and emphasizing its more thoughtful elements. Appointment also meant its membership was more diverse than the House of Commons. The Senate was then transformed in 2016 by a new appointment process that has left traditional partisanship behind. Throughout, the exact value and purpose of the Senate has shifted, as has the problem it is meant to solve.

The area where concerns are most perennially consistent is the diversity of Parliament. Monique Bégin, a woman MP first elected in 1972, writes that "I felt from the start that I was in forbidden territory where I was a tolerated exception."[8] Women continue to be under-represented in Parliament, as do racialized Canadians. Celina Caesar-Chavannes, a Black woman elected in 2015, said, "I was acutely aware that the space was not made for me as I signed my name into history under the ornately framed picture of the Fathers of Confederation on the day of my swearing-in."[9] Indigenous people have a particularly complex relationship with Parliament after centuries of colonialism. Mumilaaq Qaqqaq, an Inuk MP elected in 2019, did not run for re-election in 2021, and in one of her final parliamentary speeches said, "Every time I walk onto the House of Commons grounds and speak in these chambers, I am reminded every step of the way I do not belong here."[10]

Progress has been made over time, but slowly. Parliament is different and more inclusive than thirty or forty years ago; after Svend Robinson came out as the first open LGBT legislator in Canada in 1988, "when engaging on gay and lesbian issues, Robinson could now employ an important change in syntax; instead of saying 'they,' he could now say 'we.'"[11] Yet Indigenous people, women, racialized Canadians, people with disabilities, and openly LGBT people still remain underrepresented. And there is increasing recognition that the institution itself is not neutral terrain, but rather has deep privileged elements resistant to change. In the 2017 book *Turning Parliament Inside Out*, a team of MPs argues that change is necessary, "otherwise we will continue with what we have – a group of mainly old straight white males shouting scripted questions and answers across the House of Commons in order to retain their parliamentary seats and work their way up the party hierarchy."[12]

And there is much more. Parliamentary reform is perennial but its elements evolve. Different concerns and values come to the fore, and debates shift over time. Some issues ebb and flow; others evolve and expand. And throughout, there is an ongoing and multifaceted dissatisfaction with the institution itself.

EXPLANATIONS FOR PARLIAMENT'S PROBLEMS

Various reasons are given to explain why Parliament does not seem to work well. One is insufficient public understanding. Many popular and scholarly commentators lament the apparent decline in civic knowledge and familiarity with the rules and norms of Canada's political institutions. This can have different implications; some argue that Canadians do not understand that their parliamentary traditions are being undermined, while others suggest that they are too quick to assume so and misunderstand how the system really works. Regardless, a common lament is that Canadians no longer know enough about their own parliamentary institutions. But this presupposes that they once did.

A second explanation for parliamentary decline is the growth of the modern state. The argument here is that the sheer scope of government activity has overwhelmed the institution. This explanation has a certain resonance, but has been around a long time; in 1978, Robert Stanfield, former leader of the Progressive Conservative Party, argued that the state had expanded so greatly that legislators were unable to keep up either in scope or depth: "We must make a choice between all-pervasive government and parliamentary responsible government ... we cannot have both."[13] Indeed, the considerable reforms of the late twentieth century, including the expansion of MPs' offices, increases in legislator pay, expansion of committee powers, and much more, were in response to the growth of government and the need for Parliament to keep up.

A third common explanation is the influence of modern communications; first television, and then the internet and social media. Television cameras were introduced into the House of Commons in 1977, and for some, this is the key culprit in the decline of Parliament. Thomas Axworthy wrote in 2008 that "[t]his initiative has encouraged our politicians to perform in an exaggerated and unseemly fashion. Rather than debate, the quest is to find a 30-second clip that television will use, the more sensational and outrageous, the better."[14] Blaming television for parliamentary misbehaviour and increased partisanship has been accepted wisdom for many years. But at least some of this may be misplaced nostalgia. One early survey of MPs' reactions found that many believed television had *improved* decorum, since members were now conscious of being on camera.[15] More recently, social media is seen as a culprit in accelerating partisanship or simply bypassing parliamentary institutions altogether as places of deliberation and debate. But as with television, the effects are almost certainly more complicated, and at least some aspects of technology have buoyed and invigorated Parliament.

In short, many people talk about the deterioration and decline of Parliament. It is often taken for granted as an accepted fact, caused by a variety of well-worn reasons. But in *The Paradox of Parliament* I suggest we need to step back and consider the matter more carefully.

The underlying reason why there is so much perennial dissatisfaction with Parliament is because we don't agree what Parliament should actually do. "There would be some agreement about the House of Commons if we knew what its function was," J.R. Mallory observed in 1979.[16] David Docherty wrote in 2005 that "until we delineate what functions they should be performing, it is difficult to hold representative bodies up to any type of standard."[17] "The evaluation of all reforms is impossible in the absence of a coherent philosophy about the functions of the legislative system and the institutions which comprise it," wrote Jackson and Atkinson in 1980.[18] And yet, problems and reforms are often presented piecemeal, focusing on one aspect without considering the entire institution and its purpose. And to truly understand Parliament, we must recognize that Parliament is fundamentally a paradox.

PARADOX AND THE COMPETING LOGICS

Legislatures are intellectual puzzles.[19] Despite their well-documented and publicly accessible nature, they are perhaps the most complex of political institutions. Legislatures symbolize democratic governance, and deciding who sits in them is the focus of great struggles through elections and political parties. Yet once elections are over, many legislatures, including the Parliament of Canada, appear curiously unfulfilling and hollow at the centre.

Individual legislators in many systems seem to have little power, while real decision-making resides elsewhere in parties, government leaders, and the giant and often opaque institutions and processes of the modern state. The result can be a sense of disconnection and ennui about legislative proceedings and their purpose and effectiveness in a modern political system.

There are two broad types of legislatures in the democratic world: parliamentary systems and presidential systems. The above criticisms are particularly germane to parliamentary systems such as Canada's, in which governments are directly responsible to the legislature and are the dominant players in legislatures.[20] In contrast, there is a clearer separation of roles in a presidential system such as the United States, where Congress and the President are distinct, and Congress can operate independently with a great deal of autonomous power separate from the President. Yet the American system produces as much dissatisfaction as the Canadian Parliament; perhaps even more, with its increasingly perpetual deadlock between presidents and Congress.

In Canada, expectations of legislatures go two broad ways. One is based on legislatures as places of *representation*. Here the key criticism is typically about the dominance of political parties and the lack of opportunities for individual members to take autonomous legislative action. For many, legislatures are at the heart of what was once called a "democratic deficit," whereby citizens feel disconnected from government and unable to be heard through their elected representatives, because the system seems to stifle all but a few voices.

But another framing focuses more on legislatures as *decision-makers* and instruments of oversight. In this view, legislatures are in trouble precisely when everyone is trying to go their own way, more concerned with individual agendas and short-term political advantage than with good legislation and good government. This criticism may be particularly evident in times of minority government, where brinkmanship and short-term gain predominate. But even in majority eras, there is the same complaint that legislatures fail to play significant roles because of legislators' own amateurism, opportunism, and unrealistic expectations. Here it is less the fault of the system than the players in it.

In this book, I suggest the Canadian Parliament is best understood through two competing frames of understanding following from the above: a *logic of representation* and a *logic of governance*. The logic of representation focuses on Parliament as a representative body. It emphasizes Parliament as the voice of Canada – each member of the House of Commons tied to a specific electoral district which, when combined, comprises the whole of Canada. The logic of representation emphasizes MPs as independent actors. It may also draw attention to their gender, racialized identities, and other characteristics, here emphasizing their function as representatives of non-territorial communities. Similarly, the Senate, while not directly connected to the people by elections, follows a seat allocation formula designed to represent each region of Canada. And since 2016, senators have been recommended by an independent panel charged with identifying individuals that reflect and represent the diversity of Canada.

The logic of representation emphasizes MPs (and senators) as vehicles of representation from constituencies and other types of communities to Parliament. It may see political parties as interfering with this function, overriding legislators' individual roles as representatives through party discipline dictated from above. Or it may see parties as aggregators, bringing together members representing similar views and interests into a larger representative vehicle. Regardless, the primary emphasis is on representing the voices of Canada.

In contrast, the logic of governance emphasizes Parliament as a decision-making body. While recognizing the representative dimension, the logic of governance sees Parliament – and specifically the House of Commons – as the body to which government must remain responsible. Assuming that the government retains the House's support, the prime minister and cabinet then serve as the dominant actors in Parliament – controlling much of the agenda and pushing to get the government's bills and motions passed. Accountability is maintained daily through Question Period and more indirectly through legislative debate, as well as the scrutiny functions of committees, and is tested occasionally through votes of confidence.

The logic of governance sees MPs primarily as part of this larger process, forming into government and opposition teams in order to expedite or oppose government business, and to defend or to scrutinize government actions. This does not dismiss the individual roles of MPs. But it emphasizes their *collective* roles within these functions, which are closely linked to political parties and party leaders. Representation is an essential part of this dynamic, but the ultimate emphasis is on governance, decision-making, and the overall accountability of governments to the House of Commons and ultimately the Canadian electorate.

These dueling concepts of the logic of representation and the logic of governance both have strong roots in Canadian democracy and the Westminster model of parliamentary democracy that Canada inherited from Britain. Anthony Birch expresses them as the dual concepts of "representative government" and "responsible government," both of which developed slowly in British parliamentary tradition and Canadian colonial history.[21] C.E.S. Franks contrasts them as legislative-centred and executive-centred ways of understanding Parliament.[22]

But together they produce a paradox; a contradiction. Is the purpose of Parliament to represent and hear the different views of the nation? Or is it to make decisions and hold decision-makers accountable? The answer is both, and Parliament exists to integrate the two. Yet the two often clash against each other, and the institution is constantly pushed and pulled between them. This is the paradox of Parliament.

Paradox and contradictions are arguably a characteristic of all legislatures. Gerhard Loewenberg argues that "legislatures are paradoxical institutions."[23] For Loewenberg, paradox rises largely from the passage of time, producing a gap between historic and modern expectations. He suggests that the developmental paths of both presidential and parliamentary systems have "left contradictions between the inherited structure and the modern political environment, the source of persistent puzzles about the modern legislature."[24]

But as we will see in chapter 2, the Canadian parliamentary system was developed with awareness of the logics of both representation and governance, and was deliberately intended to reconcile them – to resolve the paradox. We also see in chapter 3 how political parties serve as the key modern mechanism for reconciling the logics. If there is a paradox in the Canadian system, it was arguably built into the design and can be, and is, reconciled.

But the two logics still clash against each other, and Parliament is constantly pushed and pulled between them. This is the problem of Parliament: not necessarily the paradox itself, but the challenge of balancing the two logics and reconciling them in practice.

This push and pull between the two logics is the key theme of *The Paradox of Parliament*. In chapter 4 we look at individual members of the House of Commons, and how MPs are often unprepared for the limitations of their role. Even though they campaign as members of political parties, they often do not fully grasp how much parties and the logic of governance determine and constrain their ability to act as individual representatives following the logic of representation. While many do develop ways to balance and reconcile the competing logics, others struggle to do so. Then in chapter 5 we will see how House of Commons proceedings operate primarily on the logic of governance, often as an escalating game between government and opposition as each tries to outmanoeuvre the other (and opposition parties also compete against each other). Again, individual MPs have long struggled to find sufficient independent roles within this game of tightly organized teams.

In chapter 6 we look at the increasing diversity of Parliament, particularly in gender and race, and how the push for better group and identity representation primarily follows the logic of representation. This sits uneasily with the logic of governance and the adversarial government-opposition divide that often operates, in the words of former MP Libby Davies, "like boys in a sandbox."[25] Chapter 7 looks at the Senate, which has recently taken a radical tilt toward the logic of representation, creating a chamber of mostly independent and at most semi-organized senators. While this experiment has generally worked so far, the long-term result remains unknown. With no one truly in charge of the Senate anymore, it lacks the organizing discipline fundamental to the logic of governance. In chapter 8 we look at Parliament's role in scrutiny, particularly over money, and how this role is built on the logic of governance, especially the principle that Parliament's primary role is to hold the government accountable for its decisions, not necessarily make the decisions itself.

Again, the paradox of Parliament can be reconciled. The problem is not necessarily the paradox itself. Rather it is the lack of recognition that Parliament has many dimensions and serves complex purposes. Discussions of the purpose of Parliament, and evaluations of its performance, often stumble or see only part of the picture because they are based too much in one logic over the other.

Opposition parties inevitably tend toward the logic of representation – of voice, of grievance, of individual concerns. But governments follow the logic of governance – of making decisions and standing by them. It is only natural that parliamentary actors switch their rhetoric as they move from opposition to government (and back to opposition), so that where one stands on these concepts literally depends on where one sits in the chamber.

Discussions of decline may follow the logic of either representation or governance, and may contradict each other. They may focus on the alleged decline of ordinary members of Parliament and their ability to act independently of their party. This reflects the logic of representation: MPs are there to act as voices. But others may argue that decline has occurred because Parliament has eschewed its mature role of scrutiny and holding government to account, and is too busy trying to be involved in the details of policy and blurring accountability. This is the logic of governance.

The Parliament of Canada, then, co-exists according to two separate logics: the logic of representation and the logic of governance. While compatible and intertwined in parliamentary history and institutional design, they are often in tension with one another, especially over the role of individual MPs. Parliament simultaneously functions according to both logics, is evaluated by both logics, and often falls short of expectations on both. This paradox, and the difficulties of reconciling it, is at the heart of the dissatisfaction about Parliament.

CHAPTER TWO

Historical Foundations and the Competing Logics

In chapter 1, I developed the idea of Parliament as a paradox, understood in one sense through a logic of representation and in another by a logic of governance. This chapter develops these ideas further by examining the historic evolution of Canadian parliamentary institutions. I begin with the estrangement of Indigenous peoples from that historical process. The chapter then looks at the early development of Canadian legislatures, and key thinkers and ideas about parliamentary government. We see how the parliamentary system was designed to accommodate the paradox, but also that the accommodation has not always worked in practice, and how reform efforts over the years have tended to prioritize one logic over the other. I conclude with why Canada seems to struggle with reconciling the paradox more than other countries.

INDIGENOUS PEOPLES AND LEGISLATIVE REPRESENTATION

A discussion of governing institutions in Canada should begin with reference to the Indigenous peoples that have occupied the land for thousands of years. While Indigenous nations historically did not have large-scale legislative institutions in the sense understood today, they certainly had, and have, structures of representation and governance.

We cannot explore here the full range and diversity of Indigenous political structures, which may be based on heredity, elders and knowledge keepers, patriarchal or matriarchal structures, and other sources of authority and places of deliberation.[1] But while there are many different types of decision-making processes and structures in Indigenous nations, a widespread principle is a preference for *consensus*, as opposed to the adversarial decision-making, with winners and losers through majority vote, that characterizes most Western legislative systems.

Historically, the stark contrast between the colonial parliamentary system and Indigenous political institutions was merely part of the overall colonization of Indigenous peoples in Canada. The signing of early treaties and issuance of the *Royal Proclamation of 1763* by George III of Britain established a direct relationship between the Crown and Indigenous nations, separate from the fledgling legislative assemblies and political systems developing for settler populations in the Canadian colonies. Instead, treaties were the primary political institution governing Indigenous-settler relations.

There is little evidence of Indigenous participation in colonial legislatures, either as representatives or voters. In general, Indigenous persons could only vote if they were not considered Indigenous under Canadian law, or if they surrendered their Indigenous rights and identity, an assimilation process known as "enfranchisement." For example, in 1857 the pre-Confederation Parliament of Canada (today's Ontario and Quebec) introduced an enfranchisement law that would allow men with Indigenous status (all women being excluded from voting at that time) to vote in elections and potentially participate in legislative assemblies; the racist title of the law was the *Gradual Civilization Act*.[2] Very few individuals voluntarily sought enfranchisement under this system.

Restrictions continued following Confederation in 1867. While the statutory basis varied over time, effectively all First Nations and Inuit could not vote nor stand for office. The *Indian Act* of 1876 also introduced "compulsory enfranchisement" in which any First Nations member with educational or professional qualifications was automatically enfranchised, losing their status and rights.[3] While they gained the right to vote, it came at a very high and often involuntary price and was part of the general attempt to assimilate and erase First Nations entirely. Unsurprisingly this did not build a positive relationship between First Nations and the Canadian parliamentary system.

However, one notable Indigenous figure was elected to Parliament in early Canadian history: the Métis leader Louis Riel, who was elected to the House of Commons in 1873. A wanted man after the Red River Resistance of 1870 in Manitoba, Riel never formally sat in the House and only once came to Ottawa, in disguise, to sign the register roll to retain his eligibility. After a motion by a hostile Ontario MP, Riel was nevertheless stricken from the rolls for non-attendance, but was re-elected in a by-election.[4] Thus, despite being elected to the House of Commons, Riel was unable to engage in the institution and turned to more confrontational political mobilization, culminating in the Northwest Resistance of 1885 and his execution. And while a few other Métis individuals were also elected to Parliament, Canada's first century generally saw an estranged and often poisoned relationship between Parliament and Indigenous peoples.

Voting rights without giving up other rights were finally extended to Inuit in 1950 and First Nations in 1960. In 1968 Len Marchand of the Okanagan Nation was the first First Nations person to be elected to the House of Commons. (Peter Ittinauar was the first Inuk, in 1979.) Marchand writes that when he gave his first speech in the House of Commons:

> I was more than a little nervous. My nerves weren't just because I was personally shy; this was the first time, in all the centuries since the Europeans had begun arriving in what would one day become the Dominion of Canada, that any of us, the original inhabitants, had had the right to stand up in the centre of government and speak. Whatever I might think of my own qualities, this was history, and it was all up to me.[5]

Marchand went on to serve eleven years in the House and as a cabinet minister, and was later appointed to the Senate. But Indigenous representation in the House as well as the Senate grew very slowly, only accelerating in the twenty-first century.

Furthermore, some Indigenous nations and people continued to not vote or seek participation through Parliament.[6] This is partly because of the long history of estrangement between Indigenous peoples and parliamentary institutions. It also reflects the importance of Indigenous sovereignty and the primacy of the direct treaty relationship with the Crown. Indigenous voter turnout remains below the Canadian average (though varying considerably between different nations and communities). This may partly reflect other factors, such as low socio-economic status, that depress voting for both Indigenous and non-Indigenous people, but it also surely reflects the negative historic relationship between Parliament and Indigenous peoples.

In chapter 6 I will focus more directly on the modern relationship between Indigenous peoples and Parliament, including the slowly growing number of Indigenous MPs and senators. Later in this chapter we will also discuss the unique legislative assemblies of the Northwest Territories and Nunavut, which adapt the Westminster system into a more consensus-oriented, non-party model reflecting Indigenous principles. The key point to recognize here is the absence and estrangement of Indigenous peoples from the historic development of parliamentary government in Canada, and the deep divide in political values and decision-making norms between typical Indigenous values of consensus decision-making and the traditionally adversarial nature of the parliamentary system.

THE EARLY DEVELOPMENT OF CANADIAN LEGISLATURES

The Parliament of Canada owes its origins to the Parliament of the United Kingdom, an institution that traces its own evolution back over nine hundred years based on struggles between the monarch and nobility. This concept of *evolution* is crucial. Unlike many modern legislatures, the rules and parameters of the UK Parliament and its predecessors were not laid out at a single starting moment.[7] Instead it evolved through both key events, such as the signing of the Magna Carta of 1215 and the Glorious Revolution of 1688, and more gradual changes over decades and centuries, often through the development of unwritten customary conventions rather than written rules. This principle of gradual evolution, especially the concept of unwritten conventions, was inherited by Canadian legislatures. We cannot understand the Parliament of Canada without understanding its roots in the evolutionary British model that developed in London in the Palace of Westminster (hence the "Westminster Model").

As Canada began to be settled by European colonizers, governing institutions gradually developed. Legislative assemblies were created, with representatives elected by wealthier male landowners, in Nova Scotia in 1758 and Prince Edward Island in 1773, in New Brunswick when it became a separate colony in 1784, in Upper and Lower Canada (Ontario and Quebec) in 1791, and in Newfoundland in 1832.

But these early colonial assemblies were only minor players in the governing of the colonies. They embodied a form of "representative government," but not "responsible government." Each colony had an executive council and also a legislative council, both of which were appointed by the colonial governor, who in turn was appointed by the British government. The executive council was the forerunner to today's cabinet and oversaw government affairs; the legislative council was similar to the modern Senate – an appointed body that passed laws in conjunction with the elected legislative assembly. The governors remained in control of the colonies; while the elected assembly passed laws, the governor did not need its support to stay in power. There was no concept of a premier or prime minister drawn from the assembly who would directly lead the government.

This was different than in London, where Parliament had asserted its authority over the monarch after a long struggle culminating in the 1689 *Bill of Rights*, which placed restrictions on the monarchy, most notably the Crown's right to impose taxes without approval from Parliament. Parliament further asserted its autonomy in the 1700s, as ministers began to be drawn exclusively from it and met separately from the King, increasingly led by a "prime minister."

Not surprisingly, nineteenth-century colonists in British North America took the Parliament at Westminster as their example and lobbied for similar reforms that gave primary power to the elected legislative assembly, making government responsible to the assembly. For reformers, representation without truly "responsible" government was insufficient. Yet the representative assemblies did fulfil many functions similar to the UK Parliament: passing laws, expressing grievances, and offering a chance for the colonial state to gauge opinion within the propertied elite of the colonies.

The push for reform continued, leading to the brief 1837 Rebellions in Upper and Lower Canada and the resulting investigation and report by Lord Durham, who recommended (1) the union of the two colonies and (2) the establishment of responsible government. As we explore in the next section, the Durham Report contained key principles for the design of legislative institutions in Canada. However, these were not immediately acted on, although the other recommendation of union was, largely as an attempt to assimilate the French-speaking population of Canada.

When "responsible government" was enacted in the Canadian colonies in 1848, it was done in a very undramatic fashion. It was a slow rather than an immediate response to the Rebellions and the Durham Report, and in the long tradition of gradual evolution of Westminster parliamentary institutions.

In 1846, the British Secretary of State for the Colonies, Lord Grey, instructed the colonial governor of Nova Scotia, in a confidential letter, to conform to the new imperial policy that colonial governors should select their ministers from the assembly and ensure those ministers had the support of a majority of the assembly. The motivations behind this policy change remain obscure, but it was likely a combination of recognizing that the colonies would continue to agitate – to not respond was to risk further rebellion and revolution – and a more pragmatic decision to grant new powers to the colonies at a time when Britain was embracing free trade and no longer gave imperial preferences to its colonies.[8] Regardless, the change in policy meant that in January 1848 a new government was formed in Nova Scotia from the assembly alone. Similar developments followed in the unified Province of Canada and eventually the other colonial assemblies.

These moments are a crucial part of Canada's parliamentary and constitutional history. But they understandably remain little known or celebrated, because the story is complicated, lacking in drama, and only one step in the continuing evolution of Canada's parliament. Yet 1848 was the crucial crossover, in which Canadian assemblies became no longer merely places of representation – but also of governance.

Premiers (i.e., prime ministers) on the British model immediately began to arise in the colonies, eclipsing governors and providing the necessary leadership to ensure executive councils (cabinets) had the support of the assembly. These individuals gradually extended their control of the assemblies, with their supporters coalescing into groups that were the forerunners of today's political parties. In doing so, the Canadian assemblies closely followed the developments in Britain of a century earlier. By the time Confederation took place in 1867, responsible government, and not just representative government, was fully established in Canada.

THE LOGIC OF GOVERNANCE

Unlike the evolutionary British Parliament, the Parliament of Canada was designed at a specific point in time in the run-up to Confederation in 1867. This Parliament was naturally based on the British model, and the *Constitution Act, 1867* (at the time the *British North America Act*) states that Canada will have "a Constitution similar in Principle to that of the United Kingdom." But the British Parliament was a template, not a straight transfer, and some aspects, such as the Senate, were specifically designed for Canada. Consequently, the intentions of the designers of the Canadian Parliament and their antecedents have attracted significant study.[9]

Janet Ajzenstat is perhaps the most prominent modern scholar of those discussions. She calls particular attention to the earlier Durham Report, and what she calls Durham's idea of "mixed government"[10] – a balance of power between the executive and legislative, rather than giving power wholly to one or the other. Ajzenstat suggests that while some reformers of the era argued that the executive – the government – should be completely subordinate to a legislature elected by "the people" and which held all the power of initiative, "Durham proposed a form of government for the colonies in which a strong executive was to balance a representative assembly."[11] Most notably, the executive was to have power over introducing bills related to taxation and spending – "money bills." This strong executive would then be able to pursue collective projects and the national interest, rather than simply reacting to shifting initiatives and opinions in the legislature. This executive would still be accountable, but on a long-term basis, most notably through elections.

This "strong executive" model was clearly chosen intentionally by the designers of the Canadian Parliament. It concentrated power and initiative in the executive, most notably for money bills as described above. And by designating a clear executive in charge, the design also created a natural opposition of others who wished to replace it. Ajzenstat points out how this system channels self-interest and ambition into opposing forces, forcing parliamentarians to take sides and preventing any one person from claiming they speak for "the people." It ensures "that no political leader may govern in the name of all"[12] and creates a natural, if self-seeking, opposition that is always present to scrutinize the government's mistakes and hold it to account. This is a core principle of the logic of governance – a Parliament in which a strong executive dominates the proceedings, but then is held accountable through scrutiny and elections.

Another articulation of the "strong executive" idea, though published too late to influence Canadian designers, is Walter Bagehot's *The English Constitution*, which appeared in 1867. Bagehot emphasized the fusion between the executive and the legislature in the Westminster system of government, with the prime minister and cabinet expected to hold seats in Parliament: "The efficient secret of the English Constitution may be described as the close union, the nearly complete fusion, of the executive and legislative powers."[13] "Cabinet," he famously noted, is "a hyphen which joins, a buckle which fastens, the legislative part of the state to the executive part of the state."[14] Bagehot contrasted this to the United States with its separation of powers between the President and Congress, suggesting that this separation weakened and "enfeebled" both. In contrast, he argued, the fused Westminster system meant a stronger and consequently more responsive system that could provide clear decisions and actions.

Ajzenstat and other Canadian scholars like Dennis Baker disagree with Bagehot's concept that the executive and legislature are "fused" together, and argue instead that they remained separated powers.[15] We do not need to resolve that debate here, but this is arguably an even stronger articulation of the logic of governance and the idea of a strong executive that is not simply subject to the day-to-day shifting whims of the legislature. In Ian Brodie's words, "The populist dream of parliamentary government with 300 free agents sitting in the House of Commons has been proven impractical here and around the world."[16] Under the logic of governance, the executive needs room to properly lead and govern, and then be held to account.

The ideas of Bagehot and others also articulated the relationship of the Crown to the rest of Parliament. The Crown is a complex and subtle concept, and while it is a fundamental constitutional component of Parliament, this book will not explore the Crown itself in depth as a separate entity.[17] But constitutionally, Parliament has three formal parts: the House of Commons, the Senate (equivalent to the House of Lords in the United Kingdom), and the Crown. All legislation passed through the two houses of Parliament must receive Royal Assent, after which it formally becomes law. Royal Assent is normally performed in Canada by the Governor General, representing the monarch, who in turn embodies the entity understood as "the Crown."

Canadian scholar David Smith refers to "the invisible Crown."[18] Using a modern computing metaphor, the Crown can be thought of as the underlying and largely hidden operating system of Canadian parliamentary government, while the Senate, House, and government institutions are programs or applications relying on it. The Crown is thus "invisible" and yet fundamental to the functioning of everything else.

From a day-to-day viewpoint, "the Crown" may seem to have little relevance to the rest of Parliament, even though it is represented by the prime minister and cabinet in Parliament. The Governor General reads the Speech from the Throne at the beginning of each parliamentary session. But the Speech is written by the government and reflects its key priorities (though the Governor General may have an opportunity to add an introduction of their own).[19] Royal Assent is a routine activity that may occur in batches, with the Governor General visiting Parliament Hill to approve several bills at once. The Governor General plays no part in parliamentary struggles except in extreme circumstances, and even then their decisions are highly prescribed, with the last refusal of a Canadian prime ministerial request in 1926. (We discuss the unusual 2008 prorogation of Parliament later in this chapter.)

Writing in the nineteenth century, Bagehot distinguished between the "dignified" and "efficient" parts of the parliamentary system in a way that still resonates today. The "dignified" parts, most notably the monarch, he argued, provided essential symbolism and unity even though they had little or no actual decision-making power. Referring to the monarch of the time, Queen Victoria, Bagehot writes: "The use of the Queen, in a dignified capacity, is incalculable. Without her in England, the present English Government would fail and pass away."[20] He again contrasted this with other European countries in which monarchs had attempted to exercise power in a manner that led to division and often revolution. The "dignified" monarchy, however, appealed to all because of its universality, and provided the necessary legitimacy and authority for the decisions made by the "efficient" parts – especially cabinet and the House of Commons itself. (Bagehot placed the upper British house, the House of Lords, somewhere between dignity and efficiency.) Note Bagehot's arguments based on *efficiency* – a system that can provide decisiveness and accompanying responsibility, in line with the logic of governance.

The ideas of Durham, Bagehot, and others recognized but did not necessarily rest on organized political parties as we understand them today. But over the course of the nineteenth century, in both Britain and Canada, government and opposition became more and more synonymous with two opposing political parties, each with their own leader; one in and one out of office (and sometimes with additional opposition parties). Elections gradually evolved from local and largely autonomous affairs into national campaigns with party platforms and leaders, and parliamentary voting itself became increasingly tight along party lines. Parliamentary government became synonymous with party government.

Nevertheless, the rise of modern parties did not negate the basic design of Parliament. Parliament was, in fact more than ever, characterized by a "strong executive" and the MPs supporting that executive, faced by an equally organized opposition criticizing it and hoping to replace it. Party government clarified accountability, as voters were given increasingly clear choices between approving or rejecting the performance of government. This was quite different from the United States, where Presidents and Congress were (and are) often in conflict with each other, creating messy compromises and blaming each other for shortfalls. In contrast, the logic of governance combines power and accountability in an elegant design, at least in theory.

THE LOGIC OF REPRESENTATION

The logic of governance explains how Parliament works as a collective body. But what does this mean for individual MPs and *representation*? Individual MPs are the link between Parliament and tens of thousands of individual voters. How should that link be navigated? How can MPs best act in the interests of both their constituency and the country as a whole, and exercise their own judgment?

For the theorists and designers of Parliament, this was precisely the job of MPs within the overall system; to figure out how to bridge the individual and local with the collective and national. For this reason, Durham advocated what Ajzenstat calls "mixed government" – a system with built-in balance. To get anything done, MPs had to work together within their government and opposition teams, which meant sometimes setting aside their own priorities and preferences, or those of their constituents. This follows from the overall logic of governance.

But what does this mean in concrete, everyday terms? This is the challenge raised by the logic of representation. MPs have wrestled with the question of their individual roles for a long time, and how it relates with the logic of governance that places so much emphasis on collective decision-making. Concepts such as "mixed government" and the "efficient secret" provide an elegant grand framework. But they have less to say about the autonomy and individual agency of MPs, especially in modern, highly disciplined political parties. Parties do have internal mechanisms for consultation and discussion, and party discipline is not necessarily always oppressive or despised, as I explore in chapter 3. But few would disagree that most Canadian MPs are at least somewhat unhappy with their limited roles, as we will explore at length in chapter 4.

In the late twentieth century, it was common to suggest that the supposed plight of the ordinary MP in Canada was partly influenced by confusing its "strong executive" system with the different system in the United States, where American legislators exercised considerably more freedom. Franks suggested in 1987 this "legislature-centred conception" of Parliament "has special force in Canada because of the proximity of the US example"[21] and Jennifer Smith argued in 1999 that "radical reformers" in Canada wanted to institute "the American congressional model."[22] American influence was also evident in scholarship, as the bulk of comparative legislative studies was dominated by American conceptions and theories that took the individual member of Congress as the basic unit of legislative behaviour.[23]

Indeed, the mid and late twentieth century saw a very sprawling American congressional system, in which legislators regularly crossed party lines and operated with considerable freedom, because the executive did not dominate the legislature as in a parliamentary system. It was thus possible to argue that any discussion of greater freedom for Canadian MPs was built on an erroneous envy of American legislator power, without recognizing the very different legislative systems and the advantages of the strong-executive model and the logic of governance.

However, the twenty-first century has seen a hardening of party lines in the US Congress, with highly disciplined voting and only a small number of centrist swing legislators. Presidents of both parties struggle to pass their budgets and legislative programs against congressional opposition, repeatedly leading to gridlock and paralysis, including entire shutdowns of government. This hard-core partisanship was also evident earlier in American history as well; the mid- and late-twentieth-century cross-partisanship was arguably an aberration. If anything, twentieth-century Canadian envy of the freedom of American members of Congress may be turning to admiration in the twenty-first century of the stability and efficiency of the parliamentary system, and implicitly a new admiration for the logic of governance.

Still, the perennial question of MPs' roles continues, in a search for a coherent logic of representation that is as clear as the logic of governance. Parliament was designed and built to accommodate both – to bring MPs together to represent constituents while working collectively in government and opposition teams under a strong executive. But while this makes big-picture sense, many MPs, and Canadians, clearly find it insufficient. A majority of parliamentary reform efforts push for a stronger role for individual MPs, and for a more concrete articulation of how they can be effective representatives within a system that emphasizes their team rather than individual roles.

This is the paradox of Parliament – operating primarily on a logic of governance, but also animated by a less coherent but very tangible logic of representation. The logic of representation targets the vulnerabilities of the logic of governance, especially the unclear individual agency of MPs, and the elaborate theatre of parliamentary debates and votes that are largely predictable. C.E.S. Franks wrote in 1987: "Nowhere else do all the contradictions and problems of Canadian parliamentary government come together so powerfully as they do in policy-making. The parliament-centred rhetoric of reform demands a strong role for the House of Commons, while the executive-centred reality puts parliament on the sidelines."[24]

As mentioned in chapter 1, Gerhard Loewenberg considers that "[all] legislatures are paradoxical institutions"[25] because they are old designs in a modern political environment. But the Canadian paradox is not because of the passage of time. Rather, the paradox was anticipated by designers and can be resolved, particularly through political parties. Defenders of the logic of governance argue that reconciliation of the individual and the collective is built into the system, essentially arguing that the logic of representation was anticipated and incorporated.

But it is an imperfect reconciliation that leaves many gaps. And the gaps may be growing. One of the key challenges is the increasing importance of non-territorial representation, most notably women and racialized Canadians. As I explore in chapter 6, many women in particular have wrestled with how to reconcile their values with the seemingly relentless zero-sum combat between government and opposition that characterizes most parliamentary business. As well, the Senate has lurched heavily away from the organizing logic of governance toward a pure logic of representation of largely independent members with the changes of 2016.

The logic of representation is far less coherent than the simple elegance of the logic of governance. Yet it is very real, and beats in the heart of every frustrated MP who feels they have no real power; every citizen wondering why their MP seems more accountable to their party leader than to their constituency; every individual appearing before parliamentary committees only to realize outcomes are predetermined; and it hovers over parliamentary debates that are poorly attended and largely ignored because only the debate itself matters, not the words actually spoken. The logic of representation finds that the logic of governance and "strong executives" is not enough, and that MPs exist to actively *represent*, rather than simply act as instruments of party and "efficiency" according to the logic of governance.

This clash is why Parliament is fundamentally a paradox. As we have seen, parliamentary designers anticipated that the institution must accommodate different and contrary impulses, of both representing and deciding. The fundamental problem is the failure to recognize that Parliament operates under two competing logics, often with a gap between theory and practice.

"EVERY REFORM CREATES A NEW PROBLEM"

The competing logics of governance and representation have driven parliamentary reform efforts over the last half-century – but rarely both at the same time. Canadians have debated whether party discipline is too strong, and a variety of reforms have been proposed and sometimes implemented. Others have defended the system, saying it is in need of understanding more than change. And solutions to one issue have at times precipitated new problems as the balance shifts between the two logics; as J.R. Mallory wrote in 1979, "every reform creates a new problem."[26] In this section, I review the history of Canadian parliamentary reform since the 1960s and how its cyclical patterns have been driven by the competing logics.

Reforms of the 1960s–1980s

The 1960s, 1970s, and 1980s saw significant changes to the House of Commons. Some of these changes were clearly in relation to the logic of representation, attempting to produce more autonomy for individual MPs. Others were more in line with the logic of governance – streamlining parliamentary business and decision-making to increase clarity and efficiency.

In 1968, the Pierre Trudeau government introduced major Commons reforms, establishing a comprehensive system of standing committees and ending Parliament's traditional veto over government spending plans – the power of "supply" – in return for a series of days on the House schedule when the opposition controlled the agenda. Television was introduced to the House of Commons chamber in 1977. And in 1982 and 1985–6, two major waves of reforms recommended by the special Lefebvre and McGrath committees standardized the parliamentary calendar, attempted to make debates shorter and more lively, empowered committees to set their own agendas, and provided for the election of the Commons Speaker, among other changes.

These reforms were widely hailed at the time as transformational. And indeed, they were significant: David Docherty wrote in 1997 that "the House of Commons in the 1990s is a much different legislature than it was thirty years ago. The opportunity structure of office is far more welcoming, providing backbenchers with more openings for advancement and meaningful work."[27] But, he added, "at the same time, members of parliament are still beholden to party leaders for promotion and to the party label for re-election." Paul G. Thomas observed in 2010 that "during the three decades from the 1960s to the 1990s, the House of Commons underwent more study and reform than any previous time in its history."[28] "But," Thomas continues, "the payoffs in terms of enhanced parliamentary influence were marginal at best."

Efficiency reforms driven by the logic of governance, such as the shortening of debates and timely approvals of spending, were generally more successful than those driven by the logic of representation. This is because while the latter tended to know what it was against – excessive party discipline – it was less clear precisely what it was for. Lacking a clear underlying theory, many reforms were reactive and piecemeal and caused new complications.

For example, the ending of Parliament's veto over "supply" in 1968 in return for opposition days and a full standing committee system provided more fixed opportunities for influence. But the committees have never proved entirely satisfactory; as early as 1971, Franks identified the "dilemma"[29] of the new standing committees that already appeared not to be living up to their perceived potential. Rather than becoming independent and autonomous vehicles for the logic of representation as some had envisioned, they polarized along party lines and were plagued by amateurism and indifferent members. And we saw in chapter 1 (and will again in chapter 9) that the introduction of television in the House of Commons caused consternation and concern from the start.

Perhaps the most interesting example of changes leading to new problems is the informal decision by opposition party leaders in the early 1980s to begin drawing up designated lists of speakers for Question Period, which were then given to the Speaker to follow. This created a smoother-running operation rather than the previous practice of MPs randomly standing to catch the Speaker's eye.

But over time this created an entirely new power of party leaders over backbenchers – the power to decide who gets to speak. By 2010, eliminating this practice was a key focus of unsuccessful reforms promoted by MP Michael Chong. I discuss this further in chapter 5.

Other reforms, in and outside Parliament, also had unintended consequences. One was the 1972 Elections Canada reform requiring the signature of party leaders on every local nominee's candidate papers. Meant to eliminate local confusion if two candidates claimed to be the party nominee, it serves as a potent (if rarely used) power for party leaders over their backbenchers who fail to toe the party line. And Peter McLeod argues that the gradual introduction of constituency offices in the 1960s and 1970s, intended to assist MPs in dealing with constituent matters, was not by design, and that "the advent of constituency offices may be the country's most dramatic if accidental parliamentary reform – wholly reshaping the role of MPs and their relationship to Canadians" in ways that prioritized MPs as local service delivery agents rather than national parliamentarians.[30]

While many reforms were driven by the logic of representation, some argued that the true problem was Parliament's failure to live up to the logic of governance, and particularly to draw a clear line between the executive and legislative that ensured proper accountability. Some argued that MPs themselves were the problem, showing indifference and a lack of interest in playing a scrutiny function, and wanting to engage in policy-making roles that were properly the role of the government.[31] Sharon Sutherland decried the growth of parliamentary committees "bearing only certain superficial resemblances to the American congressional system" undertaking American-style investigations that only blurred responsibility and accountability.[32] Many believed the root problem was "amateurism," with too many inexperienced MPs who failed to properly understand their roles.[33]

Parliamentary reform debates continued along these two tracks. For some, the problem was a need for further reforms based on a strengthened logic of representation. For others, it was misplaced reforms and attitudes that failed to recognize and conform to the logic of governance.

The 1990s and 2000s: The Reform Party and Paul Martin's "Democratic Deficit"

The reforms of the 1960s to 1980s were, in the end, adjustments within the existing parliamentary world. They did not target parliamentary culture itself. But in the 1990s, a stronger critique of Parliament arose, embodied in the rise of the Western-based Reform Party. Formed in 1987, Reform vaulted into the House of Commons in 1993 with fifty-two seats, after previously having only a single MP. Under its leader Preston Manning, Reform pledged to play a "constructive" role in the Commons, with substantive contributions rather than partisan potshots; a strict code of orderly behaviour in the chamber rather than the usual heckling; a preference for "clusters" of subject MPs rather than a shadow cabinet of specialized critics; and oddities like an alphabetical seating arrangement that played no favourites and left Manning in the third row rather than the typical leader's front seat.

Reform's ideas clearly reflected the logic of representation and a "delegate" model that required MPs to act according to constituency opinion rather than relying on their own, or their party's, judgment. Many of their ideas echoed the earlier Progressive Party, which also suddenly entered in large numbers into the House in 1921, and declined to name a single parliamentary leader or to play many of the traditional opposition roles. These ideas all challenged basic tenets of parliamentary culture and according to Jennifer Smith even "undermined responsible government"[34] – especially the clear division between government and opposition on which the logic of governance was based.

But many of the Reform practices faded away within a few months or years, as the party conformed to the existing institutional culture and practices of the Commons. Manning and other Reformers initially had an unrealistic idealized view of Parliament, and in particular showed limited grasp of the strengths of the logic of governance.[35] They overestimated the degree to which "constructive" suggestions could substitute for the realities of deep ideological and policy disagreements. Their gentle tactics meant they could not gain traction in the highly competitive world of Parliament and media coverage as each party grappled for advantage. And while the delegate model was admirable, it was more difficult to apply consistently in practice. We will examine the evolution of Reform's ideas further in chapter 3 on parties. The main issue here is that Reform's ideas on how to change parliamentary culture and practices were deeply rooted in one logic, the logic of representation, with limited reflection about the other equally important logic, of governance.

In the early 2000s, another critique of parliamentary culture arose. The "democratic deficit" became a widespread term to describe the alleged weaknesses of Parliament as well as other political institutions, and was embraced by Paul Martin as he challenged Jean Chrétien for leadership of the Liberal Party and the prime ministership. As a leadership candidate Martin proposed a six-point plan of parliamentary reform, including lessening party discipline and increasing backbenchers' opportunities to influence legislation.

But in a perceptive 2003 commentary on Martin's proposals, Peter Aucoin and Lori Turnbull argued that it was not entirely clear what the alleged "democratic deficit" really was, and whether it could be solved by institutional solutions like Martin's. They wrote: "The conundrum here is that there is as yet no generally accepted political science explanation for the democratic-deficit phenomenon as it applies to the institutions and processes of representative democracy."[36] In other words, while there was certainly evidence of public discontent and disconnection, it was not clear whether or to what extent "parliamentary reform" was the answer, or exactly how the reforms conceived the purpose of Parliament. While rooted in aspects of both the logics of representation and governance, Martin's ideas were, like many reforms, better at targeting what they were against rather than exactly what they were for. In any event Martin's reform agenda was derailed by larger problems as the government slid to a minority in 2004 and then lost power in the 2006 election.

The 2004–2011 Minority Era and Beyond

The minority governments of 2004–11 changed the nature of parliamentary reform debates yet again. The issue moved from the long-standing primary concern with individual MPs and party discipline – mostly revolving around the logic of representation – to deeper and more fundamental debates about the logic of governance itself.

In this period the House of Commons itself became in some ways more relevant than ever, or at least the centre of attention due to a number of narrow votes. This included a 2005 confidence vote attempting to bring down the government, which resulted in a tie broken by the Speaker that kept the government alive. But concern arose about Parliament's bitter and combative environment in which the government could fall at any time. This instability was, for some like Peter Russell, outweighed by the invigorated overall importance of the institution, since a minority parliament was much more able to constrain governments.[37]

Yet some incidents raised questions about the basic foundations of the logic of governance. The most important was in 2008, when the opposition parties formed an agreement to try to defeat the Conservative government of Stephen Harper in a vote of non-confidence, replacing it with a Liberal-NDP coalition government that would also have the parliamentary support of the Bloc Québécois. Harper fought against the plan, successfully asking Governor General Michaëlle Jean to prorogue Parliament for seven weeks, denying the opposition the chance to hold its motion of non-confidence. By the time Parliament reconvened, the opposition deal had collapsed and the government continued. The crisis was short-lived but triggered a tremendous debate over the constitutionality of the various actions.

Harper claimed that "[t]he opposition has every right to defeat the government, but [Liberal leader] Stéphane Dion does not have the right to take power without an election."[38] This claim was false, as parliamentary convention clearly permits another leader to form a government without an election if they can show they have the confidence of the House. This is fundamental to the logic of governance, which rests power in governments being responsible to the House. Prime ministers are not elected directly. But a transfer of power between parties without an election had not happened federally since 1926 – that new government soon collapsed – and was not written down as a rule. Instead, in the British evolutionary tradition, it was merely an unwritten convention.

The counterargument that governments should possess an electoral mandate, even if not technically constitutional, can seem democratically reasonable; as Tom Flanagan argued at the time, "Gross violations of democratic principles would be involved in handing government over to the coalition without getting approval from voters."[39] This is closer to the logic of representation by suggesting that power rests directly in the people. Furthermore, the three-party opposition deal was shaky; Dion had earlier announced plans to step down as Liberal leader, and Ian Brodie asserts that "there was never any clear evidence that the three parties were really behind the non-confidence motion."[40] The collapse of the deal by the time Parliament returned a mere seven weeks later does suggest the opposition was not seriously ready to govern. Regardless, the controversy demonstrated a continuing ambiguity and confusion about a very basic aspect of Parliament.

As Aucoin et al. observe, the long period of majority government may have given scholars and others a sense of "false security"[41] about the extent to which the logic of governance and basic design of Parliament was itself accepted and understood. Consequently, the most important discussions of parliamentary reform in the early 2010s were no longer about the search for a sustainable logic of representation and finding things for MPs to do, but a reassertion of the underlying principles of the logic of governance stemming from the 2008 crisis and a search to clarify the rules to avoid another similar incident. This led to new reform proposals, now focused less on the logic of representation and empowering individual MPs and more on establishing written rules and guidelines for the logic of governance.[42]

These concerns about the basic stability of the system then diminished with the election of a majority Conservative government in 2011 under Stephen Harper, and then a Liberal majority under Justin Trudeau in 2015. Instead, the traditional concerns of government arrogance, backbencher impotence, and the stifling weight of party discipline returned to the forefront. These continued under the Trudeau minority governments of 2019 and 2021, both more stable than the minorities of 2004–11.

Thus the history of parliamentary reform in recent decades has been a constant seesaw between different conceptions of reform and the purpose of Parliament. Some are rooted in the logic of governance, others in the logic of representation; some call for change, and some call for better understanding. Yet most are not rooted in a clear and comprehensive conception of Parliament's purpose and role that incorporates both logics. Instead, many reformers emphasize one logic over the other, often failing to recognize the paradox and the need to accommodate both.

CONSENSUS LEGISLATURES

While the Parliament of Canada struggles to reconcile the logics consistently in practice, there are legislative institutions in Canada that have arguably done so: the legislative assemblies of the Northwest Territories and Nunavut. Neither has formal political parties, and members of the legislative assembly are elected and sit as independents. MLAs together select one of their number to be the premier, and then also elect individuals to form the cabinet. The remaining MLAs are known as "regular members." While they ask questions and hold the cabinet to account, and some may be consistently critical of the government, they do not play the traditional role of a rigidly organized, disciplined opposition. In doing so, the assemblies display the core logic of governance – a strong executive that makes decisions and is accountable for them – yet also give considerable rein for legislators to play their representation roles as they individually see fit, in the logic of representation.

Sometimes known as "consensus legislatures" or "consensus government," these institutions are deeply reflective of Indigenous values and reflect the strong Indigenous populations in both territories. The NWT assembly has operated on this principle since its modern establishment in the 1970s; when Nunavut was created as a territory in 1999, it also adopted the model. Noticeably the other territory of Yukon has a smaller proportion of Indigenous peoples and its legislative assembly operates with traditional political parties, similar to provincial legislatures. While some have tried to introduce parties into NWT elections, this has been consistently resisted.[43]

In some ways, the consensus legislatures reflect the ideal of many reformers: one that combines clear government accountability with representation that is not dominated by party discipline.[44] However, part of their successful endurance is the very small and intimate nature of the polity – vast in space, but with entire territorial populations smaller than a single House of Commons electoral district. A typical NWT electoral district has less than 2,500 people; Nunavut districts have even fewer, allowing for reasonably close and personal constituency connections.

The legislatures are by no means perfect. Their intimate nature means that politics and disagreement can get highly personalized. They may struggle for legitimacy amid parallel Indigenous self-governing structures, especially in the NWT. No one has seriously advocated attempting to import the consensus practices to southern legislatures. However, their continued resilience demonstrates the flexibility of the overall Westminster model, and is an example of resolving and balancing the competing logics.

CANADA IN COMPARATIVE PERSPECTIVE

Canada appears to struggle more than other similar parliaments with the paradox between the logics of governance and representation. To be sure, parliamentary reform is a perennial discussion in other countries as well. Yet dissatisfaction with the Canadian Parliament appears deeper and more fundamental.

The Westminster model has evolved differently in each of the dozens of countries that emerged from the British Empire, leaving a somewhat fluid set of common characteristics but no single definition.[45] However, if we focus on English-speaking settler societies similar to Canada like Australia and New Zealand, as well as Britain itself, we can see both very familiar similarities and important distinctions.

There are several differences between the British and the Canadian House of Commons, covered in greater detail later in this book. British MPs are more likely to vote against their own party; British parliamentary committees are generally considered stronger; British Question Time (the equivalent of Question Period) gives more meaningful opportunities for government MPs; and British MPs behave in a more orderly fashion than in Canada. These have all attracted much attention and sometimes envy by Canadians. Yet attempts to adopt British practices in Canada have generally failed. While there is no shortage of complaints about party discipline and parliamentary dysfunction in the UK Parliament, it appears to have found a better balance and reconciliation between the two logics.

Australia provides a different contrast. Australian party discipline is closer to Canada's, and Australian parliamentary proceedings are more raucous than either Canada or the UK, with ejection of members a regular occurrence. The largest institutional difference is the elected Australian Senate, which has occasionally drawn great interest from Canadian Senate reformers. Another major difference is the internal dynamics of political parties. As discussed in chapter 3, until very recently Australian party leaders were selected – and can still be deposed – solely by their parliamentary caucuses, leading to four successive prime ministers being overthrown by their own parties from 2010 to 2018. Australian internal party politics are more intricate than Canada, especially the complex factions of the Australian Labor Party; the country also has different electoral systems than Canada as well as compulsory voting. Still, Australians do not seem to question the basic purpose of their legislative institutions in the same way as Canadians.

A third country of comparison is New Zealand. As both a unicameral legislature (no upper house) and a unitary rather than federal state, power is concentrated in the New Zealand House of Representatives more than the lower houses of Canada or Australia. However, New Zealand's 1996 move to a mixed-member proportional (MMP) electoral system has established a new norm of minority or coalition governments. Only one majority government has been elected since the 1996 MMP reforms, in 2020. Another feature of New Zealand worth noting is its greater reliance on written rules for much of its constitutional parliamentary functions, rather than Canada's reliance on unwritten conventions that partly led to the crisis of 2008. Like the other two countries, New Zealand does not seem to wrestle with reconciling the logics of representation and governance in the way Canada does.

These comparisons are admittedly subjective. Still no comparable country seems as ambivalent about the basic purpose and performance of its parliamentary institutions as Canada. The Parliament of Canada appears weak and timid compared to its closest counterparts, more dominated by political parties and their opportunistic cycles, and less able to stand up for itself as an institution or to be supported by the rest of the political system in doing so.

A vivid example of the Canadian Parliament's feebleness is the increasing tendency of governments to prorogue Parliament abruptly with no notice – ending the current legislative session and cancelling all bills and committee activities – in order to escape difficult political circumstances. Jean Chrétien did this in 2003, as did Stephen Harper in 2008 and 2009 and Justin Trudeau in 2020, despite the latter's 2015 election promise to end the practice. In contrast, in 2019 British prime minister Boris Johnson tried to do much the same to get out of a tricky political situation in the Brexit debate, but was rebuffed by the British Supreme Court. The court found such an action unconstitutional, as prorogation in Britain normally follows a predictable annual cycle. Prorogation has been abandoned almost entirely in New Zealand (last used in 1991) and in Australia (once since 1977). Yet prorogation-by-surprise has become a common manoeuvre in Canada, allowing governments to abuse Parliament and its activities for their own ends. It is a prime example of the weakness of the Canadian Parliament and its inability to stand up for itself against short-term partisan forces. This weakness means it is less able to reconcile the competing logics, and instead is tugged back and forth between them.

Why can't the Canadian Parliament stand up for itself and develop a stronger ability to resolve the paradox? Why can't it reconcile the two logics and guide its own evolution and reform, rather than being buffeted back and forth by political parties?

We have already seen explanations such as American proximity, and the gradual, uninspiring development of responsible government in Canada that lacks a strong and dramatic founding story. But another and perhaps the greatest reason is the importance of regionalism in Canada. The overriding priority of national unity and the long-standing prominence of federalism and other constitutional institutions in Canada means that Parliament has both greater pressures on it and more institutional competitors than in other countries.

Canadian parliamentary reform debates arose in the twentieth century at the same time as the "mega-constitutional" reform discussions of the 1960s–90s, when Canadians argued over the basic parameters of Confederation and Canadian political institutions. Senate reform in particular has long been presented as a solution to constitutional, more than strictly parliamentary, problems. Given the occasional fragility of the entire Canadian federation, it is unsurprising that its parliamentary institutions are constantly questioned and rethought as well. David Smith suggests that "[t]he habit of criticism of government, promoted in civics literature as a strength of democracies, has been broadened in Canada since the 1980s into an institutional critique."[46]

Canadian parties and parliamentary institutions struggle to bridge linguistic and regional tensions more than in comparable countries. As I explore in chapter 3, this has led to the long-standing Canadian phenomenon of the "brokerage party" that brings together disparate elements of the country, along with other breakaway, regionally based parties. The jumbled nature of brokerage parties can mean they operate through tough, top-down enforcement and strong party discipline, in the service of both political and national unity. In the First World War an English-French division over conscription tore apart the Liberal Party, but the same potential split in the Second World War was successfully and carefully managed by Liberal leader W.L.M. King through very skilled brokerage management.

All this may encourage a more extreme practice of the logic of governance in Canada, enforcing tight party discipline and executive dominance to keep a lid on the boiling pot of regional grievances. And yet it also precipitates counterreactions and frustrations, voiced through the logic of representation. The result is cyclical, undermining the independent strength of Parliament as an institution that can reconcile the two logics within itself. Donald Savoie argues that Parliament and other central institutions are insufficient to properly accommodate the regional nature of Canada, except through blunt top-down control. For Savoie, this is a basic system fault in the Westminster template. He says, "Canada imported a constitution and political institutions from a country where geography never dominated politics to the extent that it always has in Canada"[47] and that "[d]esigned for a unitary state, Canada's national political institutions past and present continue to deny the country's geography."[48]

Federalism and intergovernmental relations also play a role as rivals to parliamentary supremacy. While Australia is also a federation and Britain has devolved power to Scotland, Wales, and Northern Ireland, Canada has long had the most powerful sub-national governments. The rise of "executive federalism" in Canada in the 1960s and 1970s placed an increasing spotlight on provincial premiers as national political players alongside the prime minister, away from the House of Commons. In the 1970s, Donald Smiley observed that in Canada interaction between federal and provincial governments ("interstate" federalism) was much stronger than regional interaction within national political institutions such as Parliament ("intrastate" federalism).[49] Indeed, the greatest and most important regional interactions and discussions in Canadian politics are often in federal-provincial meetings between the prime minister and premiers, rather than in Parliament.

Canadian political parties also operate very separately between federal and provincial levels. They are normally entirely different organizations (except for the NDP) and sometimes have little in common, such as the federal, Quebec, and BC Liberal parties, which are distinct from one another despite their common name. This is not the case in Australia, where parties are far more unified between the Commonwealth and state level and reinforce each other's efforts. In contrast, Canadian parties operate in separate federal and provincial worlds and are rarely of direct help to one another. This again undermines Parliament's claim to be the undisputed apex of national political efforts.

A final reason for Canadian parliamentary weakness compared to similar countries is what David Smith calls Canada's tendency toward "constitutional democracy" separate from "parliamentary democracy."[50] Since the nineteenth century, Parliament has had many of its enactments struck down by the courts as violating the federal-provincial division of powers, again diluting any notion of "parliamentary supremacy." Indeed, at the time of Confederation, some thought it contradictory to even combine a parliamentary system of concentrated power with a federal system that deliberately divided power. The enactment of the *Charter of Rights and Freedoms* in 1982 has led to further competition in which Parliament has had to adapt to court rulings. Compared to the above-mentioned countries, Canada has been a leader in the adoption of entrenched constitutional rights enforced by the courts. This may be good for the rights and freedoms of Canadians, but again means the Canadian Parliament must share power and the spotlight with other national and constitutional institutions.

Throughout this book we will return to international comparisons, including sometimes finding that the grass is not actually greener on the other side. Each country and system is unique and has its own strengths and weaknesses. Still, Canada appears to particularly struggle to reach full parliamentary maturity in a way that allows it to reconcile the two logics.

CONCLUSION

The competition between the logic of governance and the logic of representation is the paradox of the Canadian Parliament. The logic of governance is more developed, elegant, and rooted in historic tradition and the original design of the institution. The logic of representation is more vague and aspirational, but has momentum on its side. The paradox can be reconciled, but throughout its history, Parliament has gone through waves of reform as it struggles to do so. In the next chapter, we focus on political parties and how they act as reconcilers of the logics, imperfectly.

CHAPTER THREE

Parties

Political parties are a central aspect of Parliament, and they embody the tension between the logics of representation and of governance. As I argued in chapter 2, legislatures depend on competition between parties to animate the entire system. Without parties, most legislatures would be unwieldy cacophonous messes in which little got done. Parties are not absolutely necessary in the Westminster system, as the consensus legislative assemblies of the Northwest Territories and Nunavut demonstrate. But it is unrealistic to imagine larger jurisdictions proceeding without the organizing and disciplining influence of parties. Accordingly, this chapter looks at parties in Parliament and how they reconcile the two competing logics, though imperfectly.

Parties allow governments to enjoy stability, to plan ahead, and to have reasonable confidence that their legislative plans will be successful. Parties also ensure that the opposition will always hold the government to account, if only to advance its own self-interest. This is of course the heart of governance: governments decide, and are then held accountable for those decisions.

Parties also bring many benefits to MPs and to voters. While party discipline is sometimes criticized as excessive in Canada, most MPs find considerable value in parties. Parties allow them to be part of a team. It gives them allies and support. Parties provide a division of labour, giving latitude to MPs to specialize in particular areas and to rely on the party for direction in others. They also provide guidance for voters, the vast majority of whom do not follow politics closely, by providing a clear label and brand by which to select between candidates. Very few independent MPs have been elected without a party designation, and there is usually an exceptional story behind each one that allows them to be distinctive to voters.

Yet parties can also be confining. MPs chafe at the need to always follow the leader and stick with the team. They lament their inability to work more with other MPs across party lines. Indeed, much of the competition between parties can seem artificial and contrived, with instant outrage from the opposition over every government misstep, no matter how minor, and a similar stubborn refusal by the government side to admit even a hint of error. Parties and party discipline rub against the logic of representation, with its ideas that promote the independent judgment and voice of each MP and/or extol the primacy of constituency, region, and other collective representation beyond party labels.

As noted earlier, Canadians seem to particularly struggle more than other countries with the place of parties in Parliament. There is widespread dissatisfaction with the level of party discipline in the Canadian House of Commons. Yet Canadian discipline is not unusual by the standards of other parliamentary democracies. Furthermore, party discipline is not a new thing. In the reforming decades of the 1970s and 1980s, it was sometimes assumed that MPs in earlier times had more freedom. But more recent research, notably by Jean-François Godbout, shows conclusively that Canadian MPs have been voting in unison since the early twentieth century.[1] While some free-operating MPs did exist in the early Confederation era, they were gone by the 1920s. Senate voting was not quite as much in lockstep, but has also long been very high until the profound changes in 2016. Party discipline is a long-standing feature of Parliament and parliamentary democracies generally, not a recent or unique perversion of the system.

In fact, the great mystery of party discipline in Canada is what exactly causes, drives, and perpetuates a phenomenon that so many people decry. Why do so many MPs complain about party discipline, and yet stay in lockstep with their parties? Why do voters express dissatisfaction with parties, and yet almost never elect independent candidates? And why do the media and outside observers lament the opaque nature of party discipline, and yet commonly exploit any hint of a crack in the armour?

The role and place of parties also shifts in times of minority government. When the governing party does not hold a majority of seats, it is forced to bargain and to a degree share power with other parties; it can also play parties off against one another. Some argue that Parliament and democracy are better off with minority parliaments; this in turn prompts calls for electoral reform to the entire voting system that might lead to more minority governments, as in New Zealand.[2] This chapter addresses these arguments but also points out that, like all reforms, there can be unwanted consequences. In particular, minority government typically stiffens party discipline rather than diluting it.

Parties thus form part of the overall paradox of Parliament. Central to the logic of governance and making the entire system work, they also serve as primary vehicles for the logic of representation. Ideally they reconcile the two logics, but the reconciliation in practice is imperfect. In this chapter I sort out the place of parties in Parliament.

CANADIAN POLITICAL PARTIES: AN OVERVIEW

Political parties consist both of party MPs in Parliament (called the party "caucus" in Canada) and the larger organization of members and activists across Canada. Political parties together comprise a "party system," and the Canadian party system has evolved considerably over time. Kenneth Carty has identified three distinct eras of the Canadian party system up to 1993.[3] However, since 1993, the system has been in a near constant state of change. Looking at the evolution of the party system gives us insights into how parties' roles in Parliament have evolved as well.

In the first era, from 1867 to about 1921, Canadian parties were both loosely organized and significantly driven by patronage and local concerns. Active party involvement was often crucial for securing government employment and contracts, whether for menial jobs or senior positions and judicial appointments. But parliamentary party caucuses themselves were not as fixed and dominant in Parliament in the way that we understand it today. The bulk of parliamentary time was open for private members' business, including minor "private bills" for commercial or personal purposes. Patronage was central to greasing the wheels and ensuring MPs' support. This system gave at least some MPs, commonly referred to as "loose fish," freedom to represent local and patronage interests and to bargain with governments to give their support for necessary bills.

In the 1920s a second era arose with new political parties – first the Progressives and later the Co-operative Commonwealth Federation – that challenged the previous hegemony of the Liberals and Conservatives. Government was also growing more and more complex and party caucuses solidified, with an end to "loose fish." While the majority of parliamentary time in the 1800s was devoted to private members' business, by the early 1900s governments and government bills began to dominate the agenda.

The rise of a merit-based civil service in the early 1900s slowly reduced the emphasis on patronage, and parties developed broader mechanisms of engagement. Most significantly, leadership selection in Canadian parties was transformed, moving decisively from the caucus to the broader party.

In the first party system, parliamentary caucuses selected their own leaders, usually in opaque ways dominated by the most senior figures. But, beginning in 1919 with the Liberals, Canadian parties began to meet in convention to select the leader, with individual constituency delegates voting alongside the caucus and other party elites. In contrast, British, Australian, and New Zealand parties all continued to rely on party caucus selection, sometimes even now. (I further discuss these differences in leadership selection below.) There are several reasons why Canadian parties moved to leadership selection by convention rather than the caucus alone, but the most important is probably the primacy of regionalism in Canadian politics. Caucuses, especially when smaller in opposition, could be regionally imbalanced and unrepresentative of Canada. Conventions drew from a broader base, including regions where the party had few MPs but wished to grow.

Critically, this era was also when party discipline solidified in Parliament. As Godbout has shown, about 80 per cent of House of Commons votes fell along partisan lines in the first years of Confederation; this steadily rose, and by the 1920s over 90 per cent of voting was along party lines.[4] Parties were particularly divided along religious and linguistic lines; Godbout and Høyland suggest that while parties and their supporters were originally somewhat heterogeneous in this respect, a good deal of "partisan sorting" took place and in particular led Catholics to strongly favour the Liberal Party, especially after the hanging of Louis Riel in 1885 and the imposition of conscription in 1917.[5]

The third party system arose in the 1960s and is associated with several characteristics: the solidification of the New Democrats as the small but permanent "third" party, the growth of the modern welfare state and the ballooning size of government, and the importance of television and national campaigns focused on the party leader. This is the era when discontent over party discipline and the role of individual MPs became a more organized lament, even if the actual issues were long-standing.

This system was shattered in 1993, though it remains unclear what replaced it. 1993 saw the collapse of the Progressive Conservatives to two seats, the drop of the NDP to a distant fourth place, and the rise of the Bloc Québécois and Reform Party along with a continuing strong Liberal Party. The PCs and NDP fell so far that they did not qualify as officially recognized parties in the House of Commons, which requires twelve seats and qualifies parties for speaking opportunities and committee assignments. Things became even more complicated when the PCs and NDP regained party status in the 1997 election and created an unprecedented House of Commons with five officially recognized parties.

The reunification of the Reform Party (renamed the Canadian Alliance in 2000) with the Progressive Conservatives in 2003 to create the Conservative Party of Canada appeared to produce a more permanent four-party Parliament. After a series of minority governments from 2004 to 2011, the 2011 and 2015 elections returned traditional majority governments for the Conservatives and then Liberals, followed by strong Liberal minorities in 2019 and 2021. Meanwhile the Bloc and NDP remained permanent fixtures but with dramatically up and down fortunes, while the Green Party has won seats since 2011 but remains well below recognized party status. There is consequently little consensus on exactly what constitutes the post-1993 party system from a parliamentary standpoint, other than fluidity and change. But the two historic parties have clearly regained their traditional pre-eminence.

THE WEAKNESS OF CANADIAN PARTIES

Regardless of the historic era, Canadian parties have often been criticized as organizationally weak and immature, with implications for their performance in Parliament. Two noted authorities, Kenneth Carty and William Cross, observe that Canadian political parties are "by comparative standards, among the most organizationally weak and decentralized of parties in established democratic party systems."[6] Let's examine this further, through *membership, policy,* and *leadership selection.*

Only a small fraction of Canadians have ever taken out *membership* in a political party, and perhaps 1–2 per cent are ongoing, long-term members of a party.[7] Yet party membership is easy to obtain in Canada, and both local nominations and national leadership selection have long depended primarily on signing up new party members as the chief route to victory. Membership numbers can thus rise and fall dramatically as contested races come and go, and there are typically few restrictions to joining a party but then letting membership lapse after the race. For its 2013 leadership contest, the Liberal Party even ended its dependence on paid "membership" in favour of a looser "supporter" category. This phenomenon of "instant members" determining the local nomination and leadership races is much less prevalent in other similar systems like Britain or Australia. It has been identified as helping to invigorate parties, breaking up encrusted elites and mobilizing underrepresented groups such as ethnic and racial minorities. But it can also mean a lack of institutional continuity, especially for the parliamentary element of the party. An MP's loyalty and long service can be swamped at nomination time by an influx of new members supporting a rival candidate.

Canadian political parties also generally offer limited opportunities for *policy* influence by the general membership. While parties hold regular policy conventions that set official policy resolutions, policy direction is ultimately determined by leaders, sometimes ignoring or even contradicting convention resolutions. Canadian parties have historically had almost no substantive policy apparatus outside the parliamentary resources controlled by the leader, with central party offices devoted largely to fundraising and campaign preparation. In contrast, British parties, for example, have modest policy offices and foundations, and many European parties (such as in Germany) have significant institutional systems separate from their parliamentary and electoral operations. While the strength of these international examples should not be exaggerated, they suggest at least some counterweight to the dominance of Canadian leaders in setting party policies and direction.

Finally, *leadership selection* has long been decentralized in Canada. The adoption of the delegated leadership convention model by the 1920s further evolved at the end of the twentieth century to direct voting by every party member. Both conventions and then direct voting have given more power to ordinary party members, but at the expense of the party caucus. In contrast, the British Conservative Party did not even develop a full caucus selection mechanism until the 1960s, previously relying on elites alone to pick the leader. (However, the British Labour Party has long had broader selection mechanisms somewhat similar to Canada.) Australian party leaders in both major parties continued to be selected by the parliamentary caucus alone until the 2010s and still are in the Australian Liberal Party, and parliamentarians in the British Conservative Party and New Zealand National Party also have considerable power over selection today.

Historically, processes to *remove* Canadian leaders were almost as complex as selecting them, typically requiring a formal leadership review vote at a party convention. Only recently has this changed through the *Reform Act* of 2014, which provides an optional mechanism for leaders to be removed by a simple vote of their party caucus. This mechanism allowed the Conservative caucus to overthrow its leader, Erin O'Toole, in 2022. O'Toole's swift removal was an important change for Canadian political parties, which otherwise have sometimes struggled to get rid of their leaders. The most prominent example was in the early 2000s when a large number of Liberal MPs sought to depose their leader, Prime Minister Jean Chrétien, in favour of Paul Martin. The dissenters had no mechanism to actually remove Chrétien; neither did Chrétien have a way of forcing a vote to ratify his leadership, though he eventually did resign with Martin winning the resulting leadership convention.

O'Toole's removal was thus a striking change, and possibly an important shift in Canadian party dynamics. It brings Canadian parties closer to some of their counterparts in the above countries, where the party caucus has the power to remove its leader, though not necessarily to choose the permanent replacement. Australian parties have been the most active users of this mechanism; since 1971, six sitting Australian prime ministers have been challenged and removed as leaders, including four in a row from 2010 to 2018, as well as numerous opposition leaders. The swift demise of so many Australian prime ministers in the 2010s might suggest things got out of hand, and the Australian Labor Party has now adjusted its mechanisms to place selection of the new leader in the broader party, though they can still be removed by the caucus alone. While the Australian Liberal Party still selects its leader by caucus vote, the Labor changes and the demise of Erin O'Toole suggests that Australian and Canadian practices are coming closer together – one restricting caucus's exclusive role, and the other giving more power to the caucus.

Overall, though, the historic weakness of Canadian parties outside of their leaders' offices and control has been a major impetus to calls for parliamentary reform. Caucuses are seen as weak players caught between the leader and the broader membership. Critics argue that MPs lack either independent or collective power to set their own course. These ideas can be tested in the next section that examines how caucuses operate in Parliament and the key issue of party discipline.

PARTY DISCIPLINE: IS CANADA EXCEPTIONAL?

It is widely held that party discipline is unusually strong and strict in the Canadian Parliament. "Canadian political parties have more control over our politics than parties in any other democratic country," wrote former New Democrat MP Kennedy Stewart in the 2017 book *Turning Parliament Inside Out*.[8] Leslie Seidle stated in 2013 that "in the advanced parliamentary democracies, there is nowhere that has heavier, tighter party discipline than the Canadian House of Commons."[9] Alison Loat and Michael MacMillan wrote in their 2014 book *Tragedy in the Commons* that "Canadian party leaders today enjoy a remarkable amount of power when measured against their peers in Canadian history, or against leaders in similar parliamentary systems around the world,"[10] and Royce Koop echoed this in 2020, saying "Canada has one of the highest rates of party discipline in the democratic world."[11] Summing up these and other views, Alex Marland, while reserving his own judgment, wrote in 2020 that "some believe that Canada has the most rigid party discipline of any liberal democracy."[12]

Comparative evidence presents a more mixed picture. Now, comparing party voting across political systems can be methodologically challenging because of the need to ensure consistent measurement across different systems and contexts; for example, whether voting on private members' bills is included, or the extent to which all votes are formally recorded. Comparative studies also tend to focus on party *cohesion* rather than *discipline* – that is, a more positive framing of how much party members stick together, with party discipline referring to negative actions taken against dissenters. Party cohesion and party discipline are closely related but not the same thing, and I return to this point shortly.

Limited, rigorous cross-national studies suggest Canada is not as exceptional as many claim. In a 2006 study of patterns of party cohesion in eleven parliamentary democracies in the 1990s, Ulrich Sieberer found Canadian MPs voted with their party 98.25 per cent of the time – but this placed them only in the middle of the pack.[13] Ten of the eleven countries were at 94 per cent or above and, significantly, both the UK and Australia placed *higher* than Canada (at 99.31 and 99.0 respectively). A similar study of 1990s data by Depauw and Martin of sixteen countries (over shorter and different time periods) also found Canada in the middle, again behind the UK and Australia, at 97.6 per cent.[14]

On the other hand, considerable evidence exists to suggest that cohesion is indeed weaker in Britain than Canada. Government bills are regularly defeated in the UK House even in majority governments, a practice virtually unheard of in Canada except in minority situations. (Canadian governments may not proceed with a vote at all if they are unsure a bill will pass.) Party cohesion particularly broke down in Britain during the Brexit crisis in late 2019, when both the Conservative and Labour parties were in disarray over the issue and the House struggled to pass any of the proposals brought to it. More generally, British parliamentary parties have long followed a "three-line-whip" system that ranks the importance of bills, allowing MPs more leeway to vote against the party line on lower-priority bills while signalling which ones do require strict support.

Still, setting Britain aside for the moment, the evidence certainly casts considerable doubt on assertions that Canadian party *cohesion* is wildly exceptional or aberrant by international standards, at least for parliamentary voting. While Canadian MPs may vote in lockstep more than in Britain, this is not necessarily the case elsewhere, including other Westminster-model countries like Australia.

In fact, as the above figures show, high party cohesion is *normal* in parliamentary systems, where governments must retain the confidence of the legislature. This norm is captured by the phrase "party cohesion" – implying it is normal for legislators to stick together. Observers from other countries may even be a bit puzzled why Canadians focus so much on the issue at all, and might be mystified by arguments that MPs should be allowed to, or would even want to, vote against their party.

However, there is more to the picture than just recorded votes. In parliamentary systems, it is often the norms and practices behind the scene that are more crucial. This includes the ability of MPs to influence policy and decisions in private; what they are allowed to say in the legislative chamber or anywhere else; the distribution of opportunities and incentives for loyalty; and the degree of punishment for stepping out of line. Most of all, it is the extent to which MPs accept and abide by these norms, rather than defying them.

This is the real challenge, because regardless of how it compares statistically with other countries, there is clearly a disconnect in Canada between the reality of party control of Parliament and the expectations of many MPs as well as the public. This is why Canadians focus on party *discipline* rather than *cohesion*. MPs may vote in disciplined lockstep, but the true cohesion of the caucus behind the scenes may be much lower.[15]

This disconnect between cohesion and discipline is rooted in the two competing logics of governance and representation. The logic of governance requires strong cohesive parties for Parliament to properly operate. But this collides with the logic of representation that valorizes individual voices, and resents the force of discipline.

PARTY DISCIPLINE IN PRACTICE

Party discipline may be seen as a problem for MPs. But Alex Marland's study of party discipline in Canada establishes how it serves multiple functions, many of them beneficial to MPs.[16] Party discipline provides a powerful collective feeling and ecosystem of support for MPs – that they are colleagues on the same team, sharing deep feelings of trust and loyalty. In this mindset, it is selfish to break with the party, especially over a short-term controversy, rather than stick together over the long term and the bigger picture. Party discipline may mean occasional sacrifices by MPs, who sometimes must vote differently than they would prefer, but they then reap the rewards of collective solidarity and achieving larger goals.

One of the most famous and stark examples of this tradeoff was in 1998 when Carolyn Bennett, a newly elected Toronto Liberal MP, voted against an opposition motion that would extend benefits to individuals who acquired Hepatitis C through tainted blood transfusions. A physician who had worked with Hepatitis C victims, Bennett wanted to support the motion but was ordered to vote against it, in favour of the Liberal government's more limited benefit package. She did so, reportedly crying as she stood to vote, and "remain[ed] pained" by the vote two decades later.[17] But in doing so Bennett showed her loyalty, earning her gratitude and standing in the party, and ministerial positions in both the Paul Martin and Justin Trudeau governments.

The Bennett vote captures the clash between the logics of governance and representation. It is an exceptionally clear case of an MP who had multiple reasons to vote a certain way based both on their own expert judgment and widespread public feeling. Yet the government and party, for their own purposes, determined a different course of action. They made a tough decision for which they were then accountable – the basic logic of governance – and demanded that Bennett fall in line with that decision. She did, arguably trading short-term pain for long-term influence, both for herself and the other causes and issues she wanted to represent.

MPs that do not fall into line like Bennett can pay a price. Sometimes this can be highly visible, such as removal from a committee or critic role. At other times it is more subtle and behind the scenes, especially if the MP does not complain publicly. For example, in 2017 Conservative member Scott Reid voted against his party's position opposing cannabis legalization. A six-time elected senior MP, Reid reported that a survey of his constituents found a majority supported legalization; it fit with his own libertarian instincts, and a major cannabis producer was beginning operations in his eastern Ontario riding. But his vote went against his party's position opposing the bill, and as punishment, Reid was removed from his role as critic for democratic institutions, though he remained silent about this punishment for two years.[18]

The level of "acceptable" dissent in the House is unclear, and most MPs appear reluctant to test it. Even the greatest dissenters vote with their party the vast majority of the time. For example, in the majority 42nd Parliament from 2015 to 2019, the biggest dissenter, Liberal MP Nathaniel Erskine-Smith, voted against his party's position 3.4 per cent of the time; the next highest Liberal voted 1.8 per cent of the time against the party. Three Conservative MPs also voted at least 1 per cent of the time against their party.[19] These are not dramatic numbers, though they show that at least some MPs feel they have some leeway to go against the party line on certain issues. The price is a likely lack of promotion and other opportunities for MPs like Erskine-Smith.

Parties and MPs themselves have often justified party discipline *in public* by noting the internal *private* tools and mechanisms available for parliamentarians to raise dissent and concerns. Most notable are party caucus meetings, usually held weekly. Strictly limited to parliamentarians and considered confidential, these meetings allow MPs to ask questions and express disagreement with party leaders. Regional caucuses may also be held. The exact value of national caucus meetings is unclear; time is limited and there are far too many people in the room for any truly robust discussion. Some MPs consider them to be mostly pep rallies for the leader to get MPs on board with existing policy, rather than an opportunity to change policy. However, there is general consensus that leaders, including prime ministers, do take caucus meetings seriously, listen carefully, and will change direction if enough concern is raised in caucus.

Leaders and senior party figures also have other systems of consultation and listening. Former prime minister Brian Mulroney (1984–93) was particularly famed for his skilful management of MPs, taking care to be seen as listening carefully to backbencher concerns and rewarding them with praise and active promotion of the

MP back home. Alex Marland describes this systematic approach at length:

> On Wednesdays when the caucus met, a handful of PC MPs attended a breakfast meeting at 24 Sussex Drive, the prime minister's official residence. Mulroney took notes while listening to a rotation of three to five of his party's backbenchers from different parts of Canada who might have been steered to a seat next to a caucus adversary. Around 9 am, he met in his parliamentary office with the PMO chief of staff (who oversees political staff) and the clerk of the Privy Council (who oversees public servants). As Mulroney tells it, he raised the problems voiced over breakfast and directed that the MPs' concerns be addressed immediately, especially if something involved a localized campaign promise.... [After the Wednesday caucus meeting] the prime minister met again with the chief of staff and clerk, and once again relayed concerns from backbenchers. If a PC backbencher complained about an inaccessible minister, then the prime minister arranged for the minister to receive a message that others were interested in the position.
>
> There was more. After Question Period at 3:00 pm, backbenchers brought people from their electoral districts to meet the prime minister for a short chat and a photograph. On Wednesday evenings, Mulroney placed approximately ten telephone calls across the country to praise his caucus members. The president of a PC electoral district association would field a phone call about how the area's MP had spoken forcefully in the caucus that morning. If the MP's concern was about the need for a new bridge, then the prime minister instructed PMO staff to get the minister of public works to travel to the riding with the member to look into getting the bridge built. Mulroney encouraged the electoral district president to share this information with others. He propped up these types of private remarks by telling journalists about a member's passionate advocacy for local issues.[20]

In contrast, leaders like Jean Chrétien and Justin Trudeau were accused of indifference and inaccessibility toward backbenchers. It is unlikely that they were dismissive, but they were less systematic than

Mulroney, who was very overt in his caucus management techniques. Mulroney's efforts paid off when his caucus stuck by him in the early 1990s despite the deep unpopularity of him and his government. In contrast, Jean Chrétien faced increasing dissent and internal opposition even when he and his government were doing well in the polls, which led to him being overthrown by Paul Martin.

Each parliamentary party also has a "whip" – a senior MP reporting to the leader who is responsible for maintaining party discipline. The name itself implies a harsh and punitive function. But Marland notes how party whips serve as crucial intermediaries with "human resource functions" whose role is not only disciplinary but also affirmative, listening to MPs and their concerns. Ian Brodie confirms this, saying that "the chief government whip is probably the most misunderstood office on Parliament Hill."[21] In the end, discipline is sustained not by fear but by collective feeling. Marland writes:

> The real control emanates from the caucus itself. MPs want to know the party's position on each bill or motion, so the whip's office circulates vote sheets to follow. Party loyalists are prone to urge a united front, particularly those who have experienced the bedlam of a caucus that does not move in lockstep. They call upon the whip to do something about a colleague who votes differently than the group, publicly contravenes the leader or is the source of public embarrassment. Social shunning from peers is an especially potent rebuke to get parliamentarians to fall in line.[22]

This raises an important distinction between hierarchical party discipline dictated by the leader and collective party discipline enforced by peers. While the former is often decried as a problem, the latter is also at work. In fact, peer pressure is arguably more powerful and the true foundation of the entire system (and closer to what the international literature understands as *cohesion*).

Some MPs who complain about party discipline are arguably malcontents difficult to satisfy under any circumstances. One colourful example is Garth Turner, a Conservative MP elected in 2006 (after serving a previous term from 1988 to 1993 as a Progressive Conservative). A former journalist, Turner used technological tools of the time such as blogging to disseminate his unvarnished views, including ones critical of his own party. This was disliked by many of his party peers, and Turner was expelled from the party caucus after ten months. He sat briefly as an independent and then joined the Liberal caucus, running unsuccessfully for re-election as a Liberal in 2008. Turner later published a book, *Sheeple*, arguing MPs were docile and domesticated.[23] However, it is unlikely Turner would have been content in any party caucus, nor did he demonstrate the skills to build consensus with other dissenting MPs.

There is also often more to party discipline than what appears in public. In 2012, a BC Conservative backbencher, David Wilks, met a small group of constituents in a Revelstoke restaurant, and agreed that the meeting could be recorded on video. Wilks discussed the upcoming federal budget and explained the nature of party discipline in Ottawa. He mentioned aspects of the budget that he did not agree with, but also that the budget would be passed in the majority Parliament, and that "[i]f Canadians want it [the budget] changed, then enough Canadians have to stand (up) to their MPs and say 'no.'"[24] His videoed remarks were posted on social media and quickly became national news, suggesting Wilks would vote against the budget. But that was not his intended message.[25] Nevertheless, party leaders quickly took control and ordered an immediate statement of support from Wilks for the budget, which he issued. This was then widely interpreted as a crackdown and disciplining of Wilks. But the reality is more complicated. Wilks was not planning a rebellion, but did let his guard down in an intimate setting as he explained to his constituents how Ottawa worked.

The Wilks incident and other examples show that party discipline is increasingly driven by the perceived need for "message discipline," when idle or muddled remarks anywhere can quickly become national news through social media. This then becomes a self-reinforcing phenomenon that parliamentarians have long lamented about the mainstream media as well – that the expectations and culture of party discipline are so entrenched in Canada that the most minor cracks are blown out of proportion as indicators of full-blown rebellion. This consequently discourages even modest dissent, which in a cyclical fashion then perpetuates the original image of entrenched party discipline as the norm.

"Excessive" Discipline

Again, whether or not Canadian party discipline is actually unusual by objective international standards, it is clear that there is considerable dissatisfaction with party discipline in Canada. Yet pinpointing exactly why, or coming up with solutions, is elusive. In their 2011 book *Democratizing the Constitution*, Aucoin, Jarvis, and Turnbull argue that party discipline in Canada is "excessive" and suggest various reforms to reduce prime ministerial power in particular.[26] But it can be difficult to determine what qualifies as *excessive*, as opposed to acceptable, party discipline. It is not always a simple dichotomy or obvious line.

The experience of Carolyn Bennett mentioned above is almost certainly an example of excessive party discipline, when a MP was forced to vote against their professional judgment, background, and conscience, on a matter that was peripheral to the overall government agenda. But where should the line be drawn? How can party discipline be loosened, to serve the logic of representation, without undermining the basic accountability of governments and the logic of governance? This question is central to the long-standing tension between the two logics and not easily answered.

In the 1990s, the newly arrived Reform Party caucus experimented with allowing dissenting votes anchored on a "delegate" model of representation that prioritized constituency opinion. Leader Preston Manning had long championed the importance of MPs representing their constituencies over their parties if necessary, especially if a clear consensus could be derived from the riding. This was put to the test in a 1995 vote establishing a national long-gun registry. Manning and the party opposed the registry but three Reform MPs from urban ridings voted in favour, having determined the registry was supported in their constituencies. In a reverse situation, several rural Liberal MPs opposed the bill, also citing constituency opinion. The Liberal MPs were all punished, such as by removing them from committees. In contrast, the Reform dissenters were not punished and their dissent was even praised, as a symbol of Reform's flexible approach to party discipline.

However, as David Docherty argues, these were exceptions, and Reform and leader Manning were overall as controlling as other parties.[27] While occasional dissents like the gun registry were celebrated as central to the party image, the everyday reality was not always as flexible. In any event, this approach lost favour as the party evolved into the Canadian Alliance and the revitalized Conservative Party. We see the change in the experience of Scott Reid above when he voted against the party position on cannabis in 2017, in direct accordance with his soundings of constituency opinion, and was punished for it.

As noted above, discipline is more flexible in the British House of Commons. This includes voting as well as other freedoms such as the ability of government MPs to pose difficult questions to government ministers in the British House, and the greater cross-party cooperation in committees. (These are both discussed in more detail in chapter 5.) Canadian MP Michael Chong is thus likely correct in asserting that "[c]ompared to the British Parliament, it is clear that the Canadian system gives party leaders, particularly the prime minister, much more power over MPs."[28]

The interest in British practices has led to various Canadian reforms and proposals, including the enhancement of standing committee powers in the 1980s (following UK reforms in 1979), the secret ballot election of committee chairs in 2002, Paul Martin's promise to introduce the three-line whip in 2004, Chong's own proposals for Question Period reform in 2010, and much more. Yet most of these reforms have not endured and/or failed to significantly shift the state of party discipline in Canada.

Possible reasons why party discipline seems milder in the British House include the larger number of MPs (650 compared to 338 in Canada) and lower turnover. Since there are so many of them, British MPs have less hope for promotion to cabinet and more incentives to build their own separate careers. The larger pool also ensures more individual talent; even though many UK backbenchers are perfectly happy to toe the line, their sheer number means there will always be some exceptional ones who are willing to act more independently. Furthermore, turnover of MPs is relatively high in Canada. This may produce more "amateur" MPs with limited institutional memory and experience to act as a counterweight against the power of parties. All this may explain why practices transplanted from Britain do not seem to take root in Canada. In fact, in some areas Canadian MPs already enjoy greater support and tools than their UK counterparts, such as better office and staff resources.

The most important attempt to dilute the power of party leaders and "excessive" discipline was Michael Chong's *Reform Act* of 2014. A private member's bill passed by Parliament after much effort by Chong, the *Reform Act* sought to reduce the power of party leaders by allowing party caucuses to vote by secret ballot on up to four possible measures: "(1) Whether membership in the caucus should be controlled through votes by caucus members themselves (i.e., either expelling MPs or admitting MPs from other parties and independents); (2) Whether caucus members should choose who serves as caucus chair; (3) Whether caucus members should have the right to trigger a review of the party leader; and (4) Whether caucus members should have the right to choose the interim party leader, should the position become vacant."[29] The bill required each caucus to vote at the beginning of each Parliament on whether it would adopt any of the four provisions.

Despite considerable fanfare when it was passed, the Act initially fizzled, with a lack of transparency over the required post-election votes. After the 2015 election, some parties did not hold a vote or did not report it publicly. After the 2019 election, all parties held votes, but none voted for all four provisions. In 2021, the Liberals and NDP voted against all four measures, as they had in 2019; the Bloc Québécois also voted against all of them, a change from its 2019 position.[30] Only the Conservatives voted for all four measures in 2021, which then allowed the caucus to depose its leader Erin O'Toole and elect Candice Bergen as interim leader four months later.[31] The removal of O'Toole was a significant boost for the *Reform Act* after its initial tepid years. The only previous significant use of its provisions was a Conservative caucus vote in February 2021, ironically initiated by O'Toole, to expel Derek Sloan, a socially conservative MP who had made a series of provocative statements. O'Toole clearly wanted Sloan out of the caucus, but under the Act, it was the caucus that ultimately made the decision.

Yet the Act's future remains unknown, and it is significant that the Liberals and New Democrats have consistently rejected its provisions, nor has the Bloc shown consistent enthusiasm. To the extent that we know why, it is because their MPs see leadership removal and selection as properly the job of the party as a whole, and undemocratic for the caucus alone.

The inconsistent impact of the *Reform Act* shows that adjustments to the formal rules are not necessarily enough to change established culture, echoing Franks's dictum that "reform of Parliament is not simply a technical matter."[32] Party discipline is not simply imposed top-down; it is collective. While rules and practices can maintain discipline, it is ultimately based on norms and expectations.

Some defenders of the status quo point out that it is simple for MPs to challenge party discipline if they really want to; they simply need to start doing it, by voting and behaving differently than told by the party. This poses a collective action problem, in which the overall benefits are clear, but the costs for any one individual to take the first step are high. But regardless, most MPs seem reluctant to take on the system even when given the opportunity, such as the rejection by most parties of the *Reform Act*. MPs can be led to the water of reduced party discipline, but can't be compelled to drink.

Party discipline reconciles the logics of representation and governance, though not perfectly. It is ultimately supported collectively, rather than solely through hierarchy and fear. Yet there is clearly a mismatch between expectations and the reality of party discipline in Canada, and closing the gap is not simple.

PARTY DISCIPLINE AND THE PARTY SYSTEM

One possible reason for why Canadian party discipline seems excessive is because of the previously mentioned gap between it and party *cohesion*. Canadian parties, especially the two major parties of the Liberals and Conservatives, demonstrate a weak relationship between the two, and this is particularly relevant for international comparisons. In many parliamentary democracies, there are more smaller parties than in Canada, each typically more homogeneous than the sprawling Canadian parties. The parliamentary caucuses of such parties are more likely to be composed of the like-minded and may find it easier and more natural to stick together, and to stay in tune with the broader party as a whole. The logic of governance then flows more naturally with these highly cohesive actors.

In contrast, the two major Canadian parties have long been described as "brokerage" parties that bring together disparate elements with little in common except a desire to win power. Lacking sufficient natural cohesion to work as a singular unit, Canadian parties face perpetual internal tensions over how to represent different constituencies, regions, and other perspectives. The lower the natural cohesion, the more discipline must be wielded within the caucus and party to keep everyone in line and to play by the logic of governance. And indeed, party discipline struggles are much more muted in the (federal) New Democratic Party and the Bloc Québécois, where publicly dissenting MPs are rare. As smaller, more cohesive parties sitting only in opposition, it is easier for them to maintain ranks and cohesion.

Jean-François Godbout puts forward a complementary argument about how party discipline is bred in the bone of Canadian political parties.[33] Using his comprehensive database of all parliamentary voting since Confederation, Godbout argues that parliamentary practices shaped the evolution of parties themselves, rather than the other way around. He notes how the "loose fish" of the nineteenth century – MPs who voted regularly for both sides – existed at a time when the bulk of parliamentary time was devoted to private members' rather than government business. MPs had more license to pursue their own agendas, and pressure to support or oppose the government was far less relentless than today. Patronage was also widespread, allowing MPs to negotiate spoils in return for their support.

However, as the state grew more complex, governments sought greater control over the legislative agenda, while patronage dwindled as a major instrument. Party supporters also began to divide up into regional and linguistic clusters, but party leaders tried to downplay these cleavages within the caucus by curbing outspoken members. MPs in turn chafed under this discipline.

Godbout argues that rather than seeing dissent and change within the established parties, this new discipline channelled energy and discontent into new regional and ideological parties such as the Progressives and the CCF in the 1920s and 1930s. By starting entirely new parties, Canadian dissenters relieved pressure on the two existing brokerage parties and allowed them to maintain highly disciplined ranks, despite their continuing ideological heterogeneity and lack of underlying cohesion.

This then continues in more modern times. The Western-based Reform Party was formed in 1987 by activists disillusioned with the

Mulroney Progressive Conservative government of the day, and the Bloc Québécois was created in 1990 by dissenting Quebec MPs from both the Progressive Conservative and Liberal parties. Both represented a choice to act through an entirely new party, rather than working within the established ones. Both breakaway parties were also regionally based, meaning they had greater prospects under Canada's single-member plurality electoral system, as discussed below.

The process is cyclical. Dissenters feel limited opportunity to pursue their views through party channels, and so they create new parties that relieve pressure on the existing ones, perpetuating the lack of opportunities for dissent. The new parties can then harden themselves into disciplined operations of their own.

One of the most dramatic examples of *collective* party rebellion in Parliament, though now largely forgotten, was in 2001, stemming from deep internal turmoil in the Canadian Alliance party under leader Stockwell Day. Under Day's shaky leadership, twelve MPs had left or been expelled from the party caucus. Eventually, seven of them formed a new group called the Democratic Representative Caucus (DRC), and formed a working alliance with the small Progressive Conservative caucus in the House of Commons. This lasted until Day's replacement as leader by Stephen Harper, at which point the majority of DRC MPs rejoined the party.

The DRC arose in a time of disruption for the party system generally, especially on the political right, and has to be viewed in this larger context of broad system-level changes. Still, it is an example of the power of group dissent if MPs choose to work together. More recently in 2018, seven Bloc Québécois MPs left the party caucus for several months in protest against leader Martine Ouellet, forming a "Quebec Parliamentary Group" later titled "Québec Debout," after which they rejoined the party.

Voters must also take some responsibility for perpetuating the dominance of parties. David Smith writes that "the ideal of the independent member of Parliament persists and has even grown in appeal."[34] Yet voters have generally failed to support MPs that do not campaign with a party label. Very few MPs have been elected to the House of Commons *for the first time* as independents in Canadian history, and only three since 1974, each for unusual and eclectic reasons.[35]

Chances are slightly better for sitting MPs who have broken from their parties over policy disagreements and then tried to run for re-election as independents. Jody Wilson-Raybould was re-elected as an independent in the 2019 election after one of the most high-profile breaks in Canadian political history when she left the Trudeau cabinet and was then expelled from the party caucus. However, her colleague Jane Philpott, who quit cabinet in solidarity with Wilson-Raybould, was defeated in her own re-election bid as an independent. Another example is Brent Rathgeber, who broke from the Harper Conservatives in 2013 over policy disagreements and wrote a book, *Irresponsible Government*, that decried the excesses of party discipline.[36] Rathgeber ran for re-election as an independent in 2015 but was defeated by the new Conservative candidate.

Bloc Québécois MP Louise Thibeault also broke from her party in 2007 to run unsuccessfully as an independent, as did New Democrat Bev Desjarlais in 2005. In both cases, they opposed their party's policy supporting same-sex marriage. On the other hand, Conservative MP Bill Casey was expelled from the party after voting against the government budget in 2007, but was successfully re-elected as an independent in 2008. And former Liberal MP John Nunziata managed to be re-elected in 1997 as an independent after leaving the party caucus. Overall, while some MPs are rewarded for standing on principles and discarding their party label, others are not, and there is little predictability.

MPs may be more successful if they "cross the floor" to a different party, thus swapping party discipline rather than discarding it. Examples include Leona Alleslev, who left the Liberals for the Conservatives in 2018 and was re-elected as a Conservative in 2019; Belinda Stronach, who dramatically crossed the floor as a Conservative to join the Liberals in 2005 and was re-elected in 2006, and Scott Brison and Keith Martin, MPs from the Progressive Conservatives and Canadian Alliance parties who joined the Liberals in 2004 and were re-elected five and two times respectively before each retired from politics. Other floor-crossers such as Garth Turner have failed to be re-elected, though this may reflect the fortunes of the overall party rather than their personal candidacies. In any event, this does not change the overall state and culture of party discipline – it merely exchanges it.

Regardless of its causes or its relationship to party cohesion, party discipline is strong in Canada and rooted in the larger system of political parties. While there is grumbling about it, not much seems to change. The line between acceptable and excessive party discipline is blurry and often visible only in retrospect. Ultimately it is up to MPs themselves to challenge the culture and norms of discipline. But discipline is not only hierarchical; it is collective. And historically, where we most see change is not within the parties, but in the party system itself, as new parties arise to challenge existing ones.

PARTIES IN MINORITY GOVERNMENTS

Another aspect of parties in Parliament is the distinction between majority and minority governments. While less common in Britain and Australia (but not New Zealand in recent years), minority government is a regular phenomenon in Canada. Canada has seen fifteen minority governments since 1921, including three from 2004 to 2011 and the Liberal minorities elected in 2019 and 2021.

In a minority, the governing party does not have a majority of seats in the House of Commons and thus is less assured of winning votes in the House. But much remains the same. Governments still control the legislative agenda and party discipline remains paramount. While some governments face a rough ride, such as the Paul Martin Liberal minority of 2004–5 that lost a number of votes, many minority governments are able to enact a surprisingly high percentage of their agendas. The key is their ability to bargain and bluff with other parties – sometimes very publicly, sometimes more in private. This may involve an ongoing agreement with one party, such as the NDP support of the 1972–4 Liberal minority, a lesser deal in 2005, and a formal agreement between the two parties in 2022, or playing the different opposition parties off against each other, which Stephen Harper did skilfully in his two minorities of 2006–11.

Some, notably Peter Russell, argue that minority government is preferable because it dilutes the unilateral power of prime ministers.[37] This is partly true; prime ministers must now bargain with other party leaders. But it does not dilute the power of *parties*; rather it entrenches it. Party discipline becomes even more paramount in minority situations. The constant inter-party bargaining and counting of parliamentary numbers leaves no margin for dissent. MPs must fall into line and typically have little bargaining power, especially since the greatest pressure is often from their peers to stick with the team.

Minority government carries a constant sense of brinkmanship and tension. Most last about two years, meaning their focus is typically short-term. Minorities can be exciting to watch, with constant uncertainty and sometimes very dramatic votes. But this sucks up energy and leads to heightened tension and partisan aggression. Parliamentary votes are regularly approached as showdowns that could precipitate an election.

Minorities have strengths and weaknesses from the logics of both governance and representation. The heightened risk of failure means that governments must be focused and deliberate in their policies, building sufficient support to pass legislation and to survive votes of confidence. This is ideal for the governance principle of making decisions and then being accountable for those decisions.

On the other hand, the bargaining nature of minorities means that accountability can be blurred. Small parties and the rare independent MPs may be able to extort disproportionate demands in return for keeping the government alive. Governments can also blame any shortcomings and failures on the resistance and uncooperativeness of opposition parties. Thus Stephen Harper said in the 2011 election, after previously winning two minorities, that he was asking voters for "a strong, stable, Conservative majority government" to properly enact his agenda, which the voters then granted to him.[38]

From the logic of representation, minority governments have some inherent appeal because they distribute power more widely and at least nominally incorporate a broader array of voices. Prime ministers and governing parties must spend more time listening, both within their own ranks and to other parties and voices.

But the flip side is a tense and often hyperpartisan atmosphere. In a minority parliament, MPs have even less agency to act independently, lest they bring down the entire fragile house of cards. Party discipline is heightened; leaders hoard bargaining power behind closed doors;

thinking is inevitably more short-term, and motives are constantly questioned. Overall, while minority government has clear merits and does curb *government* power, it has little to offer to address the internal deficiencies of Canadian parties and their possibly excessive discipline.

ELECTORAL AND PARTY SYSTEMS

Discussions about the merits of minority government are often connected to debates about the Canadian electoral system. Canada has a single-member plurality (SMP) electoral system (sometimes called "first-past-the-post") in which parties run candidates in each electoral district across the country, and the candidate receiving the most votes in the district wins. This is the system used in Britain and most legislative elections in the United States. However, other Westminster-style systems use other methods.

In 1996 New Zealand adopted a mixed-member proportional (MMP) system in which electors cast two votes – one for the local race as in SMP, and a second for parties as a whole, with additional seats rewarded based on the second vote. Australia uses several methods. Elections to the House of Representatives (equivalent to the Canadian House of Commons) are held using the Alternative Vote (AV), which requires electors to rank each candidate in order of preference. Ballots are then counted using the preferences until one candidate receives a majority of support. Australian Senate elections are held using Single Transferable Vote (STV), a variation of the above AV in which multiple candidates from all parties run state-wide and preferences are transferred until a sufficient number of candidates have been elected. Australian state elections have further variations.

There are perpetual calls for electoral reform in Canada to address the deficiencies of SMP. Among these deficiencies are its distorting effects, so that governments tend to win a majority of Commons seats with only a minority of the national vote, or even less than another party. For example in both the 2019 and 2021 elections the Conservatives won more votes than the Liberals, but the Liberals won more seats and formed minority governments. SMP also has regional effects, favouring regionally concentrated parties like the Bloc Québécois, while national parties like the Greens struggle to win seats with their votes spread thinly across the nation.

In the 2015 election, Liberal leader Justin Trudeau pledged it would be the last election fought under SMP, and in 2016 his government created a special parliamentary committee on electoral reform. But the committee failed to come to a unanimous agreement and Trudeau declared that the country itself had not come to a consensus on a new system. Several provinces have also made serious attempts in the twenty-first century at electoral reform, including multiple referendums in British Columbia and Prince Edward Island, and once in Ontario. British Columbia and Ontario further held elaborate "citizens assemblies" to deliberate on options before their referendums. Yet all attempts have failed, sometimes because of high threshold requirements needing more than a simple majority to trigger a change. Indeed, based on provincial experience, Trudeau should have known beforehand that it is extraordinarily difficult to come to a consensus on a new electoral system.

Why has electoral reform repeatedly failed in Canada? One simple reason is that the system serves the major parties well. It allows them to alternate in power with majority governments while smaller parties are kept at bay, and so they have little interest in changing a system that works for them. Indeed, the likely reason why Trudeau did not aggressively follow through on his promise of electoral reform was that his preferred alternative, AV, was not supported by other parties. Thus many electoral reform proponents argue that referendums have failed because the major parties have been indifferent or outright obstacles, while voters did not receive sufficient education about the available options.

However, voters may also see advantages in the SMP system. SMP produces distortions, but it is simple and easy to understand. The focus on a single member representing a single constituency has an inherent appeal for many Canadians. One of the largely unanticipated objections in the 2007 Ontario referendum, which recommended New Zealand-style MMP, was an argument that the party lists of additional candidates for top-up seats was undemocratic and would lead to substandard appointments of unqualified individuals not capable of winning a regular constituency race, even though the opposite is generally true in New Zealand and other MMP systems. But the greater complexity of MMP and its two categories of MPs does make it harder to understand than the simple SMP.

Electoral reform arguments, at least the most fervent, tend to be deeply rooted in the logic of representation. They focus primarily on producing a legislature that represents the proportionate array of voters' choices as accurately as possible. Yet some advocates (though certainly not all) spend limited time reflecting on how this affects decision-making in Parliament – the purview of the logic of governance.

How would a different electoral system affect party discipline and legislative proceedings, especially if it creates a more fractured House difficult to manage or pilot legislation through? Would it create more instability, especially through more minority or even coalition governments, as New Zealand has seen under MMP? Could it lead to an influx of small parties and independents, as seen under STV in the Australian Senate, who can extort demands from governing parties? Some thoughtful proponents like Peter Russell have argued instability is a reasonable tradeoff for electoral reform.[39] But most alternative systems would likely further entrench party discipline in Canada, because of the increased instability and preponderance of minority governments. This would further diminish the logic of representation through individual MPs, the opposite of what many reformers might have in mind.

CONCLUSION

Disciplined political parties are an essential component of legislatures in all large parliamentary systems. Yet there is a strong ambivalence in Canada about their role. Party discipline is high in Canada, though not as exceptional as many think. The real issue may be the gap between cohesion and discipline. The large Canadian brokerage parties lack sufficient natural cohesion, and must turn to artificial, imposed discipline to keep everyone in line. And while some favour minority government and/or electoral reform as solutions to excessively concentrated power, they would likely entrench party control of MPs further.

Ideally, parties are the mechanisms that allow the paradox of the logic of governance and the logic of representation to be reconciled. Yet this does not always work in practice. In the next two chapters I will look further at the power of parties, first at how it is fundamental to the role of MPs, and then how it dominates the business of the House of Commons.

CHAPTER FOUR
MPs

A study in 2014 noted that there was no job description for a Member of Parliament.[1] But it is hard to envision exactly what that would be. While we can make a list of the general duties typically expected of them, the role of a Member of the House of Commons is ultimately decided by each individual MP and the voters that send them to – or take them away from – Parliament. The previous chapter explored how the paradox of Parliament plays out in political parties, and how parties imperfectly reconcile the two logics. In this chapter I focus on how MPs themselves struggle with the two logics.

An MP has multiple and conflicting expectations placed on them, with many interests and stakeholders. They are accountable to their party, their constituency, their electoral district association, their own conscience, and more. Their re-election or defeat is only loosely related to their own job performance, and depends far more on their party affiliation than their personal qualities.

The lifestyle of an MP is hard, with constant travel and usually an expectation of seven days availability, either in Ottawa or their own constituency. There is no day off unless they consciously make the effort, often at cost and possible risk to re-election. Family life is strained, and women in particular find the challenge of being an MP amid family responsibilities to be very difficult.

Some MPs lament their powerlessness and disillusion in the job. Many say it is not what they expected. Commonly this is because they came to Parliament under a logic of representation; they were elected to represent their constituents, to speak their minds, and to pursue good policies, but they feel crushed under the weight of party discipline and the slow complex processes of government. Others may be more able to accept party discipline, but are worn down by the cacophony of voices and the kaleidoscope of seeming disorder that characterizes the House of Commons. In either case, they have seen the paradox of Parliament and don't like it.

And yet others flourish in the position. Long-standing parliamentarians can exhibit an almost effortlessness in the job, fielding travel, constituent queries, parliamentary questions, and a myriad of other demands with a cool equanimity. There can be a certain world-weary resignation to such characters, but also sophistication and wisdom, for they have recognized the paradox of Parliament and found ways to reconcile the two logics to be effective and strong parliamentarians.

In studying the role of Members of Parliament, it is essential to approach and understand MPs as *individuals*, with aspirations, dreams, skills, failings, frustrations, and disappointments, in a system that emphasizes their *collective* identities: as government or opposition; cabinet or backbench; members of party caucuses and committees; and more. The House of Commons "incorporates the people as a nation."[2] Yet it is composed of 338 very human members. Understanding their behaviour and motivations as individuals is essential for understanding the institution as a whole and the ongoing tension between the two logics.

WHY DO MPS RUN?

In exit interviews asking MPs why they first ran for office, the Samara organization found "few discernable patterns."[3] Most MPs said "they had not planned to enter politics, and that they chose a political career quite by accident" and "only a handful sought the nomination on their own."[4] There is some reason to be skeptical of these claims, since there can be a suspicion of aspiring politicians who seem too eager for the job. So even the most determined may be prone to modesty. But some are more candid about their ambitions, such as this post-office reflection by Barry Campbell, elected as a Liberal MP in 1993:

> It doesn't usually just happen to you out of the blue, however. You are seldom plucked out of obscurity to serve; you do it to yourself. I had dropped more than a few hints over the years that I might be interested in running, had paid my dues working on the executive of the local riding association, and had attended the requisite number of brain-numbing policy conventions where earnest young women and men (like me) bashed heads over resolutions adopted at plenary sessions, printed in glossy summaries, and promptly forgotten. Still, I had done things to get myself noticed, and I asked people close to the newly elected party leader how my candidacy might be received.[5]

Undoubtedly many MPs had experiences similar to Campbell's – intrigued by politics, "interested in running," and steadily working their way ("paid my dues") through the system to get the chance to run for Parliament.

Less clear is whether this has significantly changed since Campbell's time, especially for women and racialized people. Well-established literature demonstrates differences in expressions of ambition between women and men, with men more likely to forcefully seek opportunities while equally or even more qualified women may not. There is no single path to Parliament, and there are gendered and racial patterns, explored further in chapter 6. Some MPs do end up in political careers somewhat "by accident," while others seek it. And most are likely in between: potentially interested in a political career, but needing support or invitation to pursue it.

Whether they are specifically encouraged or not, why do potential MPs run for office? Again, research on this must take into account that MPs might be selective in memory, or inclined to spin things a certain way. Loat and McMillan identify a number of motivations, such as duty to serve a particular community – whether geographic or otherwise – and to learn and grow as professionals and citizens. But most, they say, "had taken a look at politics and found it wanting" and were motivated by what they saw as deficiencies in public policies, systems, or leaders.[6] A large 2001 survey by the Association of Former Parliamentarians similarly found community service to be the prime motivation.[7] Again, there is reason to view these responses with moderate skepticism; more probable is that individuals have multiple, overlapping motivations, including personal ambition. But David Docherty suggests that individuals who make it to Parliament are indeed not in it solely for themselves: "While it is true that ambition drives many individuals in political life (as it does in the worlds of business, academia, journalism and others) most members who make it to Ottawa are driven by far more altruistic goals."[8]

As discussed in chapter 3, Canadian local nomination contests are typically driven by signing up individual members to support one's candidacy. In some cases nomination meetings are massive affairs with thousands of participants, though most are smaller. If the party is very popular in the constituency, getting the nomination may be more challenging than winning the general election; if the party prospects are low, candidates may be acclaimed with no competition at all.

Parties have become much more directly involved in constituency nominations over time. Candidates are vetted and approved by the central party, which looks carefully at their backgrounds, including social media history, financial and professional background, and personal character and reputation. As noted in chapter 1, since 1972 party leaders have had to give written approval of a local candidate's nomination under the party label; this is a potent but rarely used weapon against particularly problematic candidates, including sitting MPs. Parties have also set increasing requirements of diversity in the nomination pool. While ensuring better quality and diversity of candidates, this involvement shows that the controlling hand of the party begins well before election day.

Occasionally MPs are appointed without having to contest a nomination.[9] There are usually two reasons for this. One is to ensure greater diversity in the party's candidates, such as by appointing women or racialized individuals directly as candidates. The second, which can overlap with the first, is to attract "star candidates" – accomplished individuals with limited political experience. While some appointed candidates may have already been seeking the party's nomination, others might not have run at all without the promise of an uncontested spot. Appointed candidates, particularly star candidates, are thus often described as "parachuted" into their ridings.

Parachuted candidates are also likely to have been promised, at least implicitly, a cabinet position to lure them into public life. One of the most striking is David Emerson, a prominent businessman who was appointed as the Liberal candidate in a Vancouver riding in 2004. Emerson was elected, served as a cabinet minister in the Martin Liberal government, and was re-elected in the 2006 election, even though the government was defeated. But shockingly, he then changed his affiliation to the Conservative Party, accepting a post in the newly elected Harper government. He did not run in 2008.

While no other appointees have displayed disloyalty as blatant as Emerson's to the party that appointed him, there is natural suspicion about the loyalty and attachment of parachuted candidates, and probably further resentment when they are fast-tracked for cabinet positions. Appointment of candidates has thus declined in recent years, likely out of conviction that aspiring MPs should display a reasonable level of political skills and pay their dues by winning a contested nomination.

This is different from *protecting* sitting MPs from nominations; occasionally party leaders may re-nominate MPs without requiring a local contest. This is a powerful instrument to reward loyalty. It may be used for unusual situations when a well-regarded MP faces a divisive challenge that the central party wants to squelch; at times it may be used as an incentive to reward MPs who have kept up a minimum base of local constituency members and fundraising. It is also sometimes used across-the-board in minority parliaments when the party anticipates an imminent election and wishes to get its team immediately in place.

The truly "accidental MP" – an individual who did not harbour at least some political ambition before getting elected – is rare, though not unheard of. One of the most notable is Ruth Ellen Brosseau, elected in 2011 as a New Democrat in the Quebec riding of Berthier-Maskinongé. While numerous New Democrat candidates found themselves unexpectedly elected in the "Orange Wave" of that year, Brosseau stood out as she had no history of political activism, had no ties to the riding, and had been named the NDP candidate by others active in the party, for a constituency the party had no expectations of winning. Brosseau's improbable win led to considerable and often negative and sexist media attention, but she was by any standard a truly accidental parliamentarian. She became highly respected and was re-elected in 2015, while many of her other NDP colleagues were defeated.[10]

Regardless of their ambitions and the route they took to get to Parliament, many MPs say the same thing: they had no idea what they were getting into. The full complexity of Parliament, the constraints of party discipline, and the myriad demands of public life come as a shock. Prospective MPs naturally focus primarily on the first and daunting step of getting elected, and much less on what happens after election day. Unless they have been well exposed to the system, such as by being a parliamentary staffer, most newly elected MPs have only a vague idea of what the job entails.

WHO GETS ELECTED AS AN MP?

This section reviews some key demographic characteristics. More difficult to track are previous occupations and previous political experience.

Gender and Race

The first woman MP, Agnes MacPhail, was elected in 1921; the next was Martha Black in 1935. Four women were elected in 1953, but representation remained tiny, with only one woman elected to the entire House of Commons as recently as 1968.

Representation slowly increased, with momentum beginning in 1984, with 10 per cent of those elected being women, rising to 21 per cent in 1997. However, the representation of women in the House then plateaued remarkably for the next four elections, which saw almost no movement up from the 21 per cent figure. Only in 2011 did the proportion of women MPs begin to rise, moving to 25 per cent, followed by 26 per cent in 2015, 29 per cent in 2019, and just over 30 per cent in 2021. These trends and the role of women MPs will be addressed more in chapter 6. Note that as of the time of writing, no MP has self-identified their gender as other than a man or woman.

A second category of interest is ethnicity and race. Again, we will examine this more fully in chapter 6. However, parliamentary history shows the evolution of "race" as a social construct. The House of Commons in 1867 was overwhelmingly British, but MPs might be sorted by their backgrounds as "Irish," "Scottish," and so on. The importance of these categories diminished in the twentieth century as other European ethnicities gradually gained "first" representatives. The first Ukrainian-Canadian MP was Michael Luchkovich, with the United Farmers, from Vegreville, Alberta. The first Italian-Canadian MP was Hubert Badanai, elected as a Liberal from Fort William (Thunder Bay) in 1958, and the first Portuguese-Canadian MP was John Rodriguez, a New Democrat elected in 1972 from Nickel Belt near Sudbury. A Jewish-Canadian MP, Henry Nathan, was briefly elected in 1871 from Victoria; the second was Samuel Jacobs, elected in Montreal in 1917.

Nowadays, the importance of "ethnic" European representation has been eclipsed by the focus on representation of non-European racialized backgrounds. As we will see in chapter 6, the percentage of racialized MPs has steadily grown from 4.4 per cent in 1993 to 15.7 per cent in 2021. However, the racialized Canadian population has also grown, so underrepresentation continues.

The first individual of non-European and non-Indigenous background elected to the House of Commons was Douglas Jung, of Chinese-Canadian background, elected in 1957 from Vancouver as a Progressive Conservative. 1968 saw several "firsts": Lincoln Alexander, a Progressive Conservative from Hamilton, was the first Black Canadian elected to Parliament, while Pierre deBane, a Liberal of Palestinian background, was the first Arab-Canadian MP. This was also the year in which Len Marchand was elected as the first First Nations MP, as discussed in chapter 2.

Non-European representation, especially racialized women, continued to be extremely low for more than two decades. The first MP of Filipino background, Rey Pagtakhan, was elected in 1988 from Winnipeg. 1993 saw the first four South Asian MPs elected (Gurbax Singh Malhi, Jag Bhaduria, Herb Dhaliwal, and Hedy Fry), and the first Black woman MP (Jean Augustine). The first Muslim MP, Rahim Jaffer of the Reform Party, was elected from Edmonton in 1997. More "firsts" continue, such as the first Vietnamese-Canadian MP, Ève-Mary Thaï Thi Lac, a Bloc Québécois MP elected in a 2007 by-election, and Nelly Shin, the first Korean-Canadian MP, elected in 2019. We return to this subject in greater detail in chapter 6.

Socio-economic and Occupational Backgrounds

MPs are clearly drawn from higher-status socio-economic and occupational backgrounds than the general Canadian population; they are wealthier and more educated, with higher status jobs and backgrounds. However, exactly *how much* higher can be difficult to determine, along with what conclusions can be drawn from this.

Early research on MPs' backgrounds in the 1950s and 1960s conclusively found that MPs came from higher socio-economic backgrounds, though as Franks noted in 1987, "there is no real agreement on the significance."[11] The connection between socio-economic background and representation is fuzzy. For example, a wealthy MP may have been raised in humbler circumstances; such "self-made" individuals may identify with their original backgrounds, at least publicly, more than their current status. Parliamentarians are naturally sensitive about accusations that they are out of touch with the lives and circumstances of most Canadians, and most strive to demonstrate their credentials as "ordinary" people. Still, it is clear that the majority of MPs do come from reasonably comfortable circumstances.

Various studies have been made of parliamentarians' occupations. The job most commonly associated with parliamentarians is lawyer – a flexible profession with an analytical and detail-oriented nature relevant to parliamentary business. But the percentage of lawyer MPs, steady for much of the twentieth century, has declined in the twenty-first century.[12] Increasingly, a MP's occupational background may be unclear or mixed, reflecting the diversity and variety of jobs and multiple careers in Canada today. Like socio-economic status, job/occupational background can be a flexible and evolving characteristic, whose exact significance is difficult to determine.

It is probably more useful to recognize the *generic* nature of most MPs. As early as 1987 Guppy et al. noted a growth in all parties of "employed professional or middle management positions," eroding more historic distinctions and categories.[13] For the Liberals, this was a change from more "top executive or self-employed professional ranks"; for the New Democrats, it was a decrease in more "blue collar or lower white collar backgrounds"; and the main change in the Conservative Party was a decline in the number of farmers. It is reasonable to assume these converging trends have continued, including with newer parties like the Bloc Québécois and the Greens. The typical member of the House of Commons, while increasingly diverse in race and gender, is a university-educated, middle-class individual with a professional or managerial background, regardless of party.

Age

MPs are an overwhelmingly middle-aged group, and always have been; the average age of MPs has continually been in the early fifties for many years. This should not be surprising, given the general emphasis on qualifications and experience for candidates. It is also reasonable to hypothesize that slightly younger individuals in their thirties and early forties, especially women, are less likely to run at their stage in life while they are building their careers and raising families. A few MPs are elected in their twenties, and a handful in their thirties, before the main group in their forties and fifties surges. A number are first elected in their sixties, and very few in their seventies.

2011 saw possibly the youngest ever Parliament, tied to the unexpected NDP surge in Quebec.[14] A large number of young candidates were elected, including the youngest ever MP elected, Pierre-Luc Dusseault, who was nineteen. Dusseault was one of several university students elected in the NDP surge, three of them women aged twenty to twenty-two. But normally the election of MPs younger than twenty-five is very exceptional.

Does age make a difference for parliamentarians? In particular, would the election of more younger MPs, especially in their twenties have a significant effect? This is difficult to say. The typical young MP is an outlier from their generational peers: highly ambitious and focused on a political career, with arguably more in common with their middle-aged counterparts than individuals their own age. Examples include Andrew Scheer and Pierre Poilievre, both elected in 2004 as twenty-five-year-olds after previously working for Conservative MPs, and each eventually rising to lead their party.

The crop of young New Democrats elected in 2011 was more distinctive – an unexpected collective wave rather than a single individual victory, and including both women and men. Again, most had politically active backgrounds that led to them running as NDP candidates, even if they did not expect to be elected.[15] And it is hard to see a major effect from this wave, perhaps because the entire NDP was grappling with its unexpected surge, and most lost their seats in 2015. In chapter 9 we return to this question of whether a radical change in the type of MP elected would make a substantive difference to Parliament.

LEARNING TO BE AN MP

MPs often do not really know what the job entails and what they are getting into. For most MPs, this is their first taste of elected life. Unlike some other countries, there is no obvious career ladder in Canadian politics in which politicians normally serve at the provincial or municipal level before ascending to the national stage; only a minority come to the House of Commons with prior sub-national elected experience. For some MPs it is also their first time in Ottawa. While they may have substantive credentials and accomplishments, are well-regarded in their home communities, and have fought hard to be elected, most MPs are starting the job from scratch.

A common complaint among Members of Parliament, at least in the past, is that they received very little orientation, guidance, or mentoring after being elected. Political parties may be partly to blame here, as they cultivate candidates for their own interest but give limited guidance. Alison Loat and Michael McMillan write that "MPs were startled to find how little help there was for them after they arrived. It felt a little duplicitous, this aspect of the political career. The party that, in many cases, had pleaded with the candidates to run in the election, approved their nominations and whose logos adorned their lawn signs, now was proving itself anything but supportive.... During the first few days in Ottawa, MPs experience their first inkling that the party doesn't value them as much as they'd thought."[16]

However, the House of Commons and other entities have steadily increased the amount and scope of orientation activities and information for MPs. Prior to the 1980s, MPs seem to have received little or no orientation at all. Since then, investment in orientation has steadily increased. Following the 2015 election when more than two hundred MPs were newly elected, the entire cohort was invited together to a "boot camp" in Ottawa; in 2019 and 2021, the smaller waves of new MPs were broken into groups for initial orientation.[17] Significantly, spouses and partners are also invited to orientations, reflecting attention to the personal side of parliamentary life. Yet this is only the formal orientation. Over time, MPs must develop their practical understanding of the job, adapt to a new lifestyle and responsibilities, and reconcile their aspirations with the realities of parliamentary life.

MPS IN THE HOUSE

MPs have long lamented that parliamentary life is not what they expected. Gordon Aiken, an MP first elected in 1957, wrote in 1974 in the gender-exclusive language of the time and when the House of Commons had 264 seats:

> Every Member arrives in Ottawa with a mission. He had probably got into politics on that account. He has talked about it during his campaign. He has pictured himself getting up in parliament within a couple of weeks at least, and really blowing the roof off. But everything runs along as if he were not there. The people on the front benches seem to get the floor, and by the time they are finished the day is over. He is catching on to another truth. His dearly loved party isn't really interested in his private projects. They have enough on their hands with general public business.... Not only is the Member on his own, there are 263 others fighting for equal time.[18]

Aiken's observations hold true a half-century later. Jody Wilson-Raybould, elected in 2015, writes: "It is ... a reality that MP disillusionment sets in for many, and often pretty quickly. The reality is not what you imagined it would be and that is a hard pill to swallow, especially when one sacrifices much and works so hard to get into politics and to actually get elected."[19]

Parliament is a crowded place. Ambitious MPs discover everyone else, or nearly everyone, is equally ambitious, and competing for the same opportunities for attention and influence. Parliamentary time is limited and precious. Committee work is often obscure and struggles to have impact. And the more high-profile and important the matter, the more parties take interest and control, limiting the MP's individual autonomy. Thus C.E.S. Franks wrote in 1987 that "[m]any MPs, once they reach Ottawa, discover they do not like the job."[20]

Each individual MP embodies the logic of representation – they naturally feel they are there to represent their constituency and perhaps other communities and identities, and to render their best judgment. But Parliament runs primarily on the logic of governance. If MPs do not understand this before they are elected, they soon learn the reality of the paradox of Parliament.

The learning curve of MPs varies. MPs who have previously served as political staff on Parliament Hill typically have a leg up, since they have a grasp of the institution and its realities, though there can still be much to learn. Aptitude is not always predictable. A newly elected lawyer may have good skills for parsing legislation and an accountant may be good at analysing government financial statements, but they must learn to fit that knowledge into the overall vortex of clashing values and interests.

Occupational background is less important for determining an MP's effectiveness than the specific skills and competencies they bring to the job. For example, some MPs who have been entrepreneurs and business owners find it difficult to cope with the hierarchical and complex world of Parliament, where they are no longer their own boss. But others with the same background are able to adapt nimbly because they are comfortable with change and managing diverse demands on their time. Successful adaptation often depends on personality as much as anything else; MPs need a combination of resilience, optimism, and an overall groundedness that allows them to withstand the ebbs and flows of elected life, including the fraught personal dimension as we explore below.

Various studies have been made of parliamentary careers in Canada. David Docherty distinguishes between "amateurs" in their first term, "seasoned" MPs in their second, and "careerists" who have run for a third term or more, thus clearly making a decision for a long parliamentary career.[21] However, longevity itself is an imperfect indicator of mastery of the job. Some rookie MPs quickly find their feet and are highly effective; some long-term careerists never really flourish, at least not visibly.

The *formal* opportunity structure of Parliament is limited. Docherty also noted in 1997 that "the structure of opportunities of the House of

Commons does not appear to match the desires of its members," and this remains true today.[22] Most, though not all, government MPs aspire to be cabinet ministers, but the ratio of ministers to MPs is typically about 1 to 6; for example, in 2015 the Liberals elected 184 MPs, of which 30 were named to cabinet. Even with future shuffles and changes, most MPs will never make it to cabinet.

A variety of lesser positions are also available to MPs, especially on the government side. Many of these positions come with (modest) additional pay, which sometimes causes a conundrum – do MPs aspire to these jobs primarily for the influence and opportunities, or mostly for the incentive of additional pay? The answer is often mixed. Most MPs certainly want to do the best job they can. But financial incentives mean that a formal position can also be a reward for loyalty and support of the party.

The main such job is parliamentary secretary, an often ill-defined role that usually involves carrying out ministerial-style duties. While it is a stepping stone to cabinet and a chance for MPs to prove themselves, a parliamentary secretaryship can also be used simply to reward general loyalty, especially given the extra salary (in 2022 this was $18,400 on top of the normal MP salary of $189,500). Because of its value, some governments rotate all parliamentary secretaries on a fixed cycle, spreading the spoils around, regardless of performance.

The office of whip also often serves as an apprenticeship to cabinet, though care is taken to appoint a skilled individual. In opposition parties, there are fewer offices to distribute, especially ones with extra pay. However, leaders appoint critics for each portfolio (lately known as "shadow ministers" in the Conservative Party) and these follow an important, if not always fully agreed, hierarchy; for example, finance critic is typically among the most prized assignments.

Standing committee chairs and vice-chairs were once very much under the control of parties, who designated their preferred choices. In recent years, this grip has loosened somewhat as committees can now elect these positions by secret ballot, theoretically allowing for more independence, though parties still exert indirect control. As I will discuss in the next chapter, chairships have always been a difficult issue. Committees represent a possible vehicle for greater MP independence. Yet a committee chairship can also be seen as a prize for good behaviour, since it is also a paid position and a possible apprenticeship for further promotion. This is not necessarily good for committee independence. Furthermore, committee assignments themselves (which are unpaid) are still made by parties.

The one other formal career opportunity for MPs is in the House itself, as Deputy Speakers and perhaps ultimately the Speaker. I discuss the speakership in more detail in chapter 5. Since 1986 Speakers have been elected by the House, increasing the position's appeal as an independent career track rather than a consolation appointment by government. Being Speaker has traditionally been seen as a terminal role lasting until political retirement or electoral defeat. But Andrew Scheer's ability to move from being Speaker in 2011–15 to leader of the Conservative Party in 2017 and Geoff Regan's defeat for re-election as Speaker in 2019, showed it is no longer so, and so its place in the parliamentary career structure may be shifting.

These are the *formal* opportunities available for MPs. They are limited, are in most cases determined by the party hierarchy, and sometimes are clouded by the incentive of extra pay that may or may not reflect actual performance.

More widespread but elusive are *informal* opportunities. What constitutes an "opportunity" can be different for each MP, reflecting their interests, circumstances, personality, ambitions, and other factors. But MPs inevitably seek to "make a difference" in some way, and to find personal satisfaction in doing so. Sometimes this can be done via formal roles, especially opposition critic positions where MPs can build a profile and hone their expertise and skills in a policy area. But often, especially for government backbenchers, MPs turn toward what Loat and McMillan call "freelancing" – developing a profile and expertise in an area that is not a high-profile priority and is less likely to trigger partisan reactions.[23]

MPs' frustration with their jobs often pivots on their ability to find opportunities *that they find personally satisfying*. "Freelancing" is rewarding to some, but frustrating for others because the chance of direct impact remains small. MPs can raise the profile of an issue, assist in building networks, and perhaps facilitate direct contact with those who do have power, such as cabinet ministers. But it is sometimes hard to identify a specific instance where they clearly made a critical difference relative to the effort involved. MPs may also decide to focus on constituency needs, pushing for specific demands. This can be a very tangible achievement back home, even if no one in Ottawa notices. But many MPs grow tired of constituency work, with its relatively small scope, and yearn for a larger national impact.

Some MPs turn their focus internationally. Parliament has a large and complex array of international associations, including interparliamentary groups that specifically connect legislators from different countries, and others such as "friendship" groups that connect MPs and senators with a country more broadly. These may or may not include travel itself, but may include contact with diplomatic representatives in Ottawa and discussion of mutual interests. Many MPs enjoy these chances to learn and to feel that they are taken seriously, something they do not always feel within the House itself.

Personal satisfaction also varies in relation to parties and party discipline. Some MPs clearly chafe early on with the demands of partisan teamplay, and never feel entirely comfortable with being told what to do. But most MPs generally adapt to party discipline and can see its advantages, while lamenting its excesses. And a few seem to wear it exceptionally naturally, staying remarkably on-message, comfortable in attacking the other side, and always in tune with the party, at least publicly. Such individuals can be derided as overly ambitious and too eager to please party leaders. Yet it may also be natural, befitting their skills and personality.

MPS IN THE CONSTITUENCY

While the parliamentary precinct in Ottawa provides a uniform setting, no two constituencies in Canada are exactly alike. They range in size, composition, and priorities. Northern and remote ridings tend to have sizable Indigenous populations and often a strong sense of alienation and dependency on government and faraway corporations. Rural ridings will vary in their economic mix and levels of prosperity, but typically with agriculture as a top concern and recurring issues of attracting new economic investment and maintaining services. Suburban ridings are typically most preoccupied with managing growth, framing public policy in terms of taxes and services, especially for families and the middle class. Finally, urban ridings often have a profound mix of the rich and poor alike, and have the most unpredictable array of issues. Some constituencies have a strong natural identity, because their boundaries follow natural physical and population patterns, or fit neatly with municipal and provincial boundaries. But most are more artificially drawn, and many Canadians, especially in cities, do not even know what riding they are in, nor the name of their MP.

I have already touched on how MPs' personalities, skills, and aptitude for different parts of their job will vary. Similarly, MPs will have diverse approaches to their constituencies, based both on their own personality and ambitions, and the context of the constituency.

Koop, Blidook, and Bastedo identify different "styles of representation" by MPs in their constituencies, which can emphasize policy connections, service connections, symbolic connections, or party connections.[24] These constituency styles develop according to the MP's personal goals and background; the constituency context; and their own experiential learning over time. For example, in their study Koop et al. found MP Leon Benoit held structured town hall meetings and other gatherings to discuss public issues, while MP Niki Ashton preferred to visit "public events and venues to ask constituents if they had any problems she could assist them with."[25]

Since the 1970s Canadian MPs have had constituency offices to assist constituents in their interaction with government services. Immigration issues are the largest area of activity, especially for urban MPs, but casework spans all areas of government, sometimes even including provincial and municipal areas. In the early 2000s, researcher Peter McLeod visited one hundred constituency offices across Canada and reported:

> Every imaginable grievance passed through their doors: nasty child custody fights; accusations of workplace discrimination; decades-long battles to reunite distant families; shocking miscarriages of justice; and stories of intractable tax collectors run amok. Any new staffer would immediately find himself or herself swamped by the endless stream of employment insurance claims, missing passports, and neglected veterans.[26]

Constituency casework is an important aspect of parliamentarians' responsibilities, far from the intrigues of Parliament Hill. The personal involvement of MPs here varies. Some delegate nearly all of it to staff;

others prefer to be somewhat involved; a few seem to relish getting into the details. Again much depends on the characteristics of the riding and the level and types of inquiries. Precedent may also be a factor; if the previous MP was known for a high level of personal attention to case work, that expectation may be placed on their successor.

MPs also engage in extensive "retail" constituency activity, especially showing up to events. Newfoundland MP Scott Simms told researchers he received invitations to forty firefighters' balls every year and had to carefully decide which ones to attend,[27] while Ontario MP Ted Hsu found himself asked to be a judge at a chili-tasting contest. In his memoirs, Lincoln Alexander writes, "After I became an MP I didn't go to my church much anymore, but instead started going to everyone else's churches."[28] MPs can easily find themselves attending six or more events in a single day, and still turning down others.[29] Newly elected MPs are often particularly stressed and bewildered by the many invitations and expectations; over time, veterans may develop discernment in deciding which to accept. However, many MPs genuinely prefer interacting with constituents through these gatherings, as they meet and hear from a broad cross-section of people who might never request a formal appointment or attend a town hall meeting.

All MPs inevitably claim to enjoy constituency work, given the danger of admitting otherwise. But some are clearly frustrated by its parochialism and endless demands. Much constituency casework could be ably handled by regular government channels. But MPs are reluctant to turn anyone away lest it damage their reputation. Former Prince Albert MP Brian Fitzpatrick decries the "chamber of commerce" mentality that a MP's top priority should be hustling for economic development for the riding, rather than contributing to national lawmaking.[30] Introverted MPs struggle with the expectation that they should always be available to converse with anyone at any time. Most must fight to preserve private and family time in the constituency. Many MPs may even enjoy their relative anonymity on the streets of Ottawa, compared to the challenge of shopping for groceries at home without being accosted by constituents. Constituency offices also attract disgruntled and abusive individuals, with the main brunt typically shouldered by the staff.[31]

It is unclear whether there is much electoral reward for constituency efforts. Attempts to track the "personal vote" for Canadian MPs – the extent to which electors vote based on the specific individual, rather than their party label – are limited, but suggest it is small, perhaps 5 per cent of all voters.[32] How much of this incorporates appreciation for constituency work, as opposed to the MP's efforts in Ottawa, their personal qualities, or simply their campaign efforts and spending, is unclear. MPs thus cannot be confident whether any of their constituency activity will pay off. But they are inevitably mindful that *failure* to be seen as responsive could be electorally disastrous, especially in closely fought ridings. For this reason, parties and party leaders generally encourage MPs to pay close attention to their constituencies and engage in as much constituency activity as possible.

Some have argued for a transformation of constituency offices and roles, away from services to policy. Loat and McMillan write dismissively that "[i]f [MPs] are interested in processing immigration or veterans' claims, they should join the civil service."[33] In their 2018 "Beyond the Barbecue" report, Ghebretecle et al. argue that "constituency offices should be reconfigured so that they become the shopfront not for public service delivery, but for innovative consultation and democratic deliberation,"[34] and "[i]f MPs and staff are relieved of some of their casework responsibilities, the resulting new capacity must be committed to more meaningful engagement with constituents on issues of local and national importance."[35] Peter McLeod argued in 2014 that "tomorrow's MPs may be more inclined to think of their offices and local budgets as open platforms for community building and learning. The humble MP's office remains Parliament's most malleable and low-risk site for civic innovation."[36]

These suggestions are squarely in the logic of representation, prioritizing the role of MPs as representatives of their constituencies, either as delegate or trustee. MPs do engage in extensive local policy work, through meetings, town halls, surveys, and so on. But while most MPs probably would prefer to focus on structured policy activities rather than the random "retail" activities, it is not clear this would assist them in their Ottawa roles and navigating the realities of the logic of governance. MPs are not short of policy ideas and input from constituents; they are short of opportunities in Ottawa to make them happen.

Nor do these suggestions take parties into account. While most casework and "retail" appearances are relatively non-partisan, policy discussions often are not. MPs from the governing party inevitably spend much of their time at home defending government policies, while opposition MPs are more free to agree with criticisms. As in Ottawa, the more high-profile and pressing the issue, the more there will be partisan stakes and disagreements. While it is admirable to think of MPs facilitating deeper citizen deliberations and engagement, MPs may be wary of raising expectations if this work does not lead to tangible results. Overall, as in the House back in Ottawa, MPs approach constituencies in different ways. Some genuinely enjoy the work; for others, it is a necessary part of the job.

LIFE AS AN MP: THE PERSONAL DIMENSION

Being a Member of Parliament is an all-encompassing lifestyle. As a public official, MPs exist primarily in the public sphere, with a high level of transparency and availability. The personal demands and costs of this unusual job are substantial, and yet can be overlooked or treated as a secondary matter.

In this section I look at the personal dimension of being an MP in two ways. First is how MPs manage different aspects of their *public* roles; the different faces they must wear for different situations. Second is the truly personal and *private* spheres of MPs, especially family relationships and personal health and well-being.

Managing Their Public Roles

A small proportion of MPs seem to lead extraordinarily open lives, seemingly available to attend any event, take any phone call, and generally give freely of their time and energy in service of their public roles. This type of individual is rare and possibly diminishing. They may have been more common in an earlier era, when communication was not as ubiquitous and intrusive, and cultural norms meant men MPs in particular spent limited time home with their families. This level of availability may also be more expected in rural constituencies, where MPs are usually more visible and well-known. Peter McCreath, a Nova Scotia MP in the 1990s, writes: "You would be amazed how many people phone their MP on Christmas [Day]."[37]

The vast majority of MPs struggle with finding time and setting priorities for their *public* roles. Rushing between obligations, they lament the lack of time to "think," to properly prepare for meetings and discussions, and generally to take a more reflective and deliberate approach to their duties. This complaint is common among other professional roles, where work seems endless, technology allows for constant availability, and the "urgent" always seems to outweigh the "important." But there are several things that make the dilemma especially acute for MPs.

First, as already described, is the lack of a job description or standards of evaluation and accountability. MPs struggle to focus their time and efforts because they are accountable nowhere and everywhere at the same time: to a hundred thousand or more constituents; to their party leader and colleagues; to their electoral district association; and others. The one unmistakable form of accountability for MPs – re-election or defeat – is only loosely tied to the MP's individual performance. Many hard-working and talented MPs go down to defeat because their party is no longer in favour, while less exemplary individuals can be returned to office because their riding is loyally partisan. Performance rewards can be perverse; promotion within the party ranks is based at least partly on loyalty and deference, rather than initiative and effort. MPs thus struggle to know what is expected of them, and it is not always related to conventional standards of job performance.

Second is the vastness of MPs' briefs. MPs struggle to prioritize their time and efforts when any issue or problem under federal jurisdiction is within their scope of responsibility. They also represent a constituency and constituents whose priorities will inevitably not be perfectly aligned with the MP's. And no individual can possibly be an expert in all areas of public policy. While some MPs are able to "freelance" as above and build recognized profiles in specific issue areas, most struggle to truly specialize. If they do become noted for expertise in a particular issue, they may risk being seen as narrow and out of touch with the constituency's concerns as a whole. Related is the imbalance between interest and opportunity structures. For example, a MP may be particularly interested in environmental policy, yet this is not a critical concern for their constituents relative to other local priorities, and they are not assigned to the Standing Committee on the

Environment and Sustainable Development because of limited spots for their party. They may find other ways or routes to work on environmental policy, yet they must balance this with the more pressing priorities of their constituency and/or party.

Third is the wide number of skills and competencies needed for MPs. These include public speaking, both formally and extemporaneously; a strong ability to grasp detail while balanced with good general knowledge and common sense; the ability to interact with all kinds of people, from top officials to the disadvantaged and powerless; and many other skills. Very few MPs have all of these, and while good staffing can fill in some gaps, MPs understandably sometimes fumble through activities they are not very good at or find less than energizing. This is commonly one of the biggest shocks for new MPs: discovering how many things they have to do that they find tedious or unnecessary – or at least they are told they have to do, by their staff, party, or others. Experienced MPs may develop a filter to decide which are truly worth their time and energy. But doing things that they don't enjoy is another dimension of the balancing act faced by MPs.

A fourth aspect of managing MPs' public roles is their lack of place. To be a member of the House of Commons is to experience permanent geographic dissonance, since both Ottawa and the constituency serve as "home." We explore the private side of this below, but can also note here that even the concept of a physical workplace is complicated for MPs. While all MPs have an office suite in Ottawa, these are scattered in different buildings around the parliamentary precinct, often quite separate from the House chamber, committee and caucus rooms, and other locations where MPs are most visibly seen "at work." All this travel – whether to, from, and around the constituency, or riding the small bus that ferries MPs between buildings in Ottawa – chips away at MPs' sense of a single, focused workplace where they can concentrate their minds and efforts, rather than moving to the next location and shifting into the correct mindset for that context. The pivot to online meetings and parliamentary sittings in the COVID-19 pandemic partly mitigated this by keeping MPs more in one place, but at a time of unprecedented stress and challenges that did not give a sense of normality. A permanent move to hybrid sittings and the regularizing of remote work for MPs could give them somewhat more control over their daily movements.[38] But it will not address the larger sense that their focus is never in a consistent place.

All these build into a burden for MPs as they try to manage their time, efforts, and energy toward the things that they feel most matter. Of course, this is the job that they asked for and fought to get. And over time, most MPs seem able to cope with this ambiguity, accepting it and developing tricks and tools to cope and find time to focus. Yet it is a constant dilemma to balance the public demands of the job.

Managing Their Personal Lives

Managing public demands is only part of the challenge. Balancing public life with personal lives is an even greater challenge for MPs. As with other workplaces and society in general, relatively little attention was paid to the dimension of private lives for MPs until the late twentieth century, and almost certainly due to the changing role of women in society – not just their increasing numbers in the House of Commons but also evolution in societal attitudes and family relationships, for both women and men.

The job of being an MP places strain on marriages and intimate partnerships, with its constant travel and long and often unpredictable hours. When MPs return "home" to their constituencies, they may have even higher expectations to be out and about, rather than spending time with their families. And while MPs themselves may enjoy their jobs and even be invigorated by the demands and stress, their partners may feel quite differently, and can feel neglected and a secondary priority. The good but not lucrative salary of MPs and the lack of job security beyond the next election can further contribute to domestic strain and stress. One alarming but unconfirmed study in 2013 suggested that divorce rates were twice as high for MPs compared to Canadians in general.[39] A 2001 survey of former parliamentarians, mainly men, found 16 per cent blamed their parliamentary career for the break-up of their marriage.[40]

Family life and children pose even greater strains. In previous eras when most MPs were men, the widespread practice was to commute to Ottawa alone, living in rental accommodation while their spouse and children remained in the family home in the constituency. This was not a happy arrangement for most families, leading to stress and loneliness, but was widespread. The 2001 survey also found, again drawing mainly from male respondents, that "[m]ore than one commented regretfully that they have seen more of their grandchildren growing up than they did of their own children, and blame themselves and the long and thankless working hours and travels of their political job for this misfortune."[41]

This "family back in the constituency" model is increasingly problematic for women MPs with children or planning to have children, and also for men who do not want to be disconnected from their families like their predecessors. Yet there is no easy solution that can accommodate a partner's career, children's schooling, child care, and other important considerations. And an MP who locates their primary home in Ottawa for family reasons is ripe for criticism that they have lost touch with their constituency.

Single MPs and those without family in Ottawa often find parliamentary life very lonely. Lacking permanent community, with families and friends back home, lifestyles can become corroded by the highly competitive pressures of parliamentary life. Receptions and events on Parliament Hill provide social interaction, but often at the cost of too much unhealthy food and/or alcohol. The MP's perpetually unbalanced lifestyle is ripe for destructive habits such as excessive alcohol consumption or extramarital affairs. Remarked one MP: "You leave the office at 7 pm to go home; what the hell do you do? That's where guys get in trouble, if they don't go home. That's when they get in trouble."[42]

The lifestyle can feel unfulfilling. Kim Campbell, Canada's first woman prime minister, remarked candidly in 1992 when she was Minister of National Defence and a Vancouver MP that "in the course of my life in Ottawa my marriage has ended and I'm very far from home. I find life here often unspeakably lonely and very difficult."[43] More recently, a veteran political observer wrote in 2016:

> In Ottawa, MPs once again live like students who have just moved out of residence and into their first apartments. In middle age, they often live with roommates, eat off mismatched dinnerware, leave pictures unhung. Their commitments, understandably, are to their own communities, not to Ottawa. And so with no families to come home to, every day becomes the same. After

work, receptions and dinners fuel the makings of a toxic brew of power, exhaustion and a feeling that "no one else understands our world." The grim, but too often unspoken, reality is that many politicians end up struggling. Marriages end. Relationships fray. Families suffer. Substance abuse issues emerge. Some MPs' struggles make it to the front page but dozens more struggle in the loneliness of the shadows.[44]

Some MPs bond together in support of their unique vocation. Some share rental accommodation or form informal sports groups. A "prayer breakfast" group of Christian MPs has met continually for decades, acting as a mutual support entity. But while there are other quiet and private gatherings, many MPs are lonely and struggle to stay grounded.

Some lament an earlier era when MPs may have socialized more, especially across party lines, and suggest this contributed to a more collegial and less nasty parliamentary atmosphere. In its report on partisanship in the House, Samara Canada quotes MPs who complained they were unable to socialize with members from other parties, lest they be chastised for "fraternizing with the enemy."[45] Former Speaker Peter Milliken said in 2011:

> The change in the hours of sitting has had a significant effect. Members used to go up to the parliamentary restaurant to eat between six and eight when we had night sittings. Needless to say, they sat there with members not of their own party and chatted and maybe had a drink. It helped people get to know one another and be respectful to one another. So getting rid of the night sittings really altered the way the place operated. Plus, the lunch hour is gone. They took away the night sittings and added two hours [of sitting] at lunchtime. So lunch is served in the lobbies [the private spaces behind each side of the House of Commons chamber, one for the government party and one for the opposition parties]. Well, you don't mix in the lobbies.[46]

Milliken is likely correct in describing a more genteel and less abrasive era. But it is impossible to envision returning to what was surely a highly gendered and largely homogeneous world. The rise of women

MPs, greater emphasis on family life – for both women and men MPs – and the ever-increasing racial and cultural diversity of MPs makes for a more diverse community of parliamentarians less likely to spend long hours socializing together. And some MPs are simply not comfortable with this clubby atmosphere where partisanship switches on and off. Samara quotes another MP as saying:

> What I didn't like is one minute you're attacking one another during committee and then the cameras are off and it's, "Hey, let's go for a beer." And I'm not built like that. I'm not built like that. So, I had a very hard time when I first got there, because I'd be like, "What do you mean go for a beer? You just called me a liar. You just called me a liar during committee. I don't want to go for a beer with you." … And they don't take any of those things personally. It's a completely different world from what I'm used to. … My opposition members would say, "Hey, let's go for a drink." I would be like: "I don't like you."[47]

Unsurprisingly then, when MPs do seek community, they are likely to stick within their own party ranks, and probably increasingly so. This both feeds off and reinforces the sense of team solidarity within parties. MPs naturally feel more comfortable and safer among members of their own party, but this can breed even greater suspicion and wariness toward members from other parties, and this influences parliamentary behaviour. There is no easy solution here.

MP PAY

The salary and other benefits for MPs have long drawn attention. In 2022, MPs received an annual salary of $189,500. As noted earlier, MPs receive additional salary for serving as whips, parliamentary secretaries, chairs of committees, caucus chairs, Deputy Speakers, and so on. MPs also receive funds to cover travel and housing expenses in Ottawa, and are eligible for a pension if they serve at least six years in the House. MP pay and expenses are perpetually controversial, sometimes phrased as "perks of the job" or similar language.[48] Yet others argue that MPs are underpaid, or receive at most fair compensation.

For the first century or so of Parliament's existence, the job of MP was widely considered to be part-time, and was compensated as such. Lawyers maintained their practices; businessmen (and they were all men) might continue their enterprises; and so on. In the 1960s and 1970s, some MPs continued to maintain occupations outside the House. But more and more, MPs approached the job as full time; similarly, they began to be funded for staff assistance and constituency offices.

This led to increases in pay and controversies over pay. Beginning in 1976, commissions were struck after each election to review parliamentarians' compensation. Each commission recommended increasing MPs' pay, yet most of the recommendations were not accepted, primarily because this required the concurrence of the House itself, and MPs were reluctant to vote themselves a pay increase. As Atkinson and Rogers document, this meant that by the 1990s Canadian MPs were underpaid relative to comparator jobs as well as legislators in other countries.[49] This led to increasingly acrimonious debates about whether inadequate pay deterred the best people from running for office, while others argued salary should not be the primary motivation for parliamentarians. In 2001, the Chrétien government pushed through a major change that abolished the commission model, simplified MP compensation (removing a tax-free expense allowance), and increased overall pay by about 20 per cent. Since then, salary increases have been tied to automatic external drivers – since 2005, the average of wage settlements in federally regulated industries. While the 2001 changes were enormously controversial at the time, they successfully doused the perennial problem of setting legislator salaries.

Whether MPs are overpaid, underpaid, or fairly paid remains in the eye of the beholder. As we have seen, being a member of the House of Commons is an unusual job. The hours are long, MPs must maintain two households (in Ottawa and the constituency), and the pressures of travel and maintaining a presence in both places mean there is little downtime. As we have seen, most MPs themselves do not fully grasp the demands and character of the job until they are in it. So it is unsurprising that the general public may have little sympathy for individuals drawing salaries well above the national average.

The pension plan, first established in 1952, also attracts attention, along with severance payments for MPs. These receive considerable notice especially around election time; for example, in both 2019 and 2021 the Canadian Taxpayers Federation released a report of the individual severance and pensions to be received by retiring or defeated MPs.[50] Inevitably some amounts are considerable. However, there is a strong defence for these.

One reason is the weak relationship between MP performance and job security. An exceptional and well-performing MP in a swing riding may go down to defeat, while mediocre MPs in safe seats retain their jobs for decades. Pensions and severance pay partly compensate for the arbitrary nature of most MPs' termination.

A second is the unclear future employability of MPs. While difficult to study systematically, considerable anecdotal evidence suggests that many ex-MPs struggle to find new careers.[51] Their professional expertise and networks may have atrophied and grown outdated during their years in office; their past employers may have disappeared or no longer have a place for them; the world has moved on without them. While some parliamentarians find work as lobbyists and other positions directly connected to their political careers, the majority do not. MPs cannot easily shake their reputations as partisan actors, even if they have moved on from political life, and in some fields and positions this ex-politician image may be seen as detrimental and the wrong fit for a job. It can be a letdown; after four or more years of being constantly in demand, defeated MPs suddenly feel a dreadful silence. Former MPs can report feeling depressed and directionless. Again, severance and pensions ease the transition back to unelected life.

Staffing

For many years MPs operated on their own. Many paid for assistance out of their own pocket, used resources and staff from their other jobs, and almost certainly many male MPs relied on their wives to provide unpaid labour. MPs were first given shared secretarial assistance in the 1950s, upgraded a decade later to one assistant per member.[52] The exact origins and first adopters of constituency offices are unclear, but they emerged in the 1960s with funding instituted in 1972.[53] In modern times MPs are given an overall budget to cover all salaries and administrative expenses, and considerable discretion in how to allocate it.

Each MP's office is a substantially independent operation, to the point that the House of Commons can be seen as 338 individual small businesses, each with its own quirks and staffing practices. Paul Wilson finds that MPs have 5.2 staff on average, typically two in Ottawa and three in the constituency, but there are many variations.[54] Larger ridings receive additional funds to support extra constituency offices, but MPs may choose to stay with a single office, or will open satellite offices even without additional funding. The New Democratic Party has long had unionized staff with set pay rates, fixed job descriptions, and other standards, making its practices somewhat more consistent. The other parties typically give more leeway in hiring and paying staff, though rules are formally set by the Board of Internal Economy, the internal body that administers the House (see chapter 5.)

There are gender patterns in staffing. While parliamentary staff are relatively equally men and women, Snagovsky and Kerby find that men are more likely to hold higher-prestige legislative roles, while women hold more administrative positions; Cloutier and Thomas further finds that women comprise the majority of constituency staff.[55] While some staff are young, eager, and ambitious partisans, a substantial number are older and experienced, and may move around to different offices over the years. Offices may also include paid or unpaid interns and other volunteers. It is thus unclear whether there is a "typical MP staffer."

Staffing and running an office is challenging for many MPs. Some have never supervised other people before, while experienced managers may be used to a very different environment. There is almost always a steep learning curve. MPs who have previously served as political staff themselves will typically have it somewhat easier. But even they can face challenges as they shift from employee to manager.

Problems typically arise in two areas – poor hiring and poor management. In poor hiring, MPs will hire individuals unsuited for the demands of the job; for example, an effective election campaign manager is not always ideal for managing policy and legislative issues. Increased oversight by both parties and the House of Commons administration means MPs are less likely to – or are prohibited by law – hire relatives and clearly unqualified individuals. But the unique nature of an MP's office means it can be difficult to identify successful prospects. And inevitably, as in any job, it takes time for a fit to develop and for people to find their stride or realize the job is not for them.

Poor management is when the MP struggles to run their offices effectively. Again, both lack of management experience or the wrong kind of experience may apply here. MPs may struggle to understand their oversight role, especially as a travelling manager with two separate offices in Ottawa and the constituency.

A typical impulse for inexperienced managers is to try to oversee everything directly, rather than delegating and setting up an appropriate reporting structure. This may lead to confusion and/or paralysis. MPs may also struggle with managing employee performance appropriately and setting the right professional tone – in some cases earning a reputation across the institution as poor employers. But another problem is when experienced managers from other sectors may import structures and practices that do not work well in the parliamentary environment. The experience of Majid Jowhari, a Liberal MP elected in 2015, is instructive:

> As a former consultant, I defaulted to lifelong practices and sought to import the norms I had learned and internalized over decades of private sector experience to systematize my duties. In this mission to create clarity, I turned a task-oriented mind to establishing metrics, measuring data at the minute level, and setting performance qualifiers on everything from community barbecues to the correspondence I received to my staff's every move.
>
> It took me much longer than it should have to realize that rather than bring order to my office, all too often this process ground it to a halt. For MPs like me who use order and systems as a salve for the anxieties of a high-stress job, this only compounds their concerns…. What became clear was that it was not only unreasonable to transpose the metrics of a private sector executive onto my staff, but also that those metrics often simply didn't translate to the unique work environment of Parliament.[56]

Over time, most MPs do get better at managing their unique environments. Veteran MPs' offices can be remarkably smooth in their functioning, with longtime loyal employees. Yet even a well-run office will have a surprisingly complex set of roles, because MPs *have* complex roles. For example, a staffer in one office will typically have overall responsibility for maintaining the MP's schedule both at home and in Ottawa, but another staffer decides or consults with the MP about what events to attend. Each office has its own distinct processes, reflecting the diverse styles and approaches of MPs themselves.

AN MP'S DAY

What do MPs do all day? Given the competing demands and expectations of their roles, their existence in both Ottawa and the constituency, and the diversity of 338 individuals, it is hard to pinpoint "a typical day" for MPs or a set of standard activities.

However, there are two common characteristics to MPs' daily routines: much of it is *transactional* (meetings and other communication) and *in multiple places*. MPs may not spend a lot of time working alone at their desk. Rather, MPs spend much of their time interacting with different people – fellow MPs, political staff, parliamentary staff, the media, lobbyists and interest groups, constituents, and more. Relatedly, MPs in Ottawa may spend relatively little time in their actual office suites, as they roam the parliamentary precinct for different duties and events. In the constituency, they may hold meetings in their constituency office but spend much time out and about at more events and more meetings. The pivot to remote sittings and meetings in the COVID-19 pandemic slowed some of this moving around, but not the pace of transactions as meetings shifted to computer screens.

One place where MPs definitely minimize their time is the House of Commons chamber itself. MPs typically only enter the chamber for one of several specific reasons: to speak; in assigned "house duty" to ensure a sufficient party presence at all times; or because they are expected to be at Question Period and major events. This is not to say that MPs do not value being in the central symbol of Canadian democracy – rather, they correctly calculate that most of their time is better invested elsewhere.

We do not know how much the introduction of television affected the amount of time MPs spend in the House. Today, it is typical in any parliamentary office when the House is in session to have a monitor playing the proceedings at low volume – an almost ubiquitous background that allows MPs and others to know what is happening and perhaps to feel a connection. But what was the case before 1977? Anecdotally, it seems that MPs spent more time in the chamber, perhaps to hear what was going on, and possibly just as a general social area and workspace. But in the modern era, television not only allows them to keep tabs on things remotely, but also increases the stakes when they do enter the chamber, lest they suddenly be on view. No one wants to be captured on screen in an unflattering moment or looking inattentive. The chamber is not entered into lightly, as MPs are highly self-conscious that they may be instantly visible across the country. So most stay away unless specifically required to be there.

When MPs are in their constituency, the routine varies but the principles of transaction and multiple places remain. While they do not always feel very powerful in Ottawa, MPs are commonly the centre of attention in their constituencies. While perhaps gratifying at one level, this can contribute further to stress and a sense of always needing to be "on," lest an unintentional slip or misjudgment take place – and even worse, be recorded and posted online. And as we saw earlier, balancing the time and service demands of constituency work with personal and family life is especially daunting. In the words of one observer, "It's all glamorous, until the MP finds themselves attending their seventh church strawberry social instead of watching their child's T-ball game."[57]

Travel itself is a significant aspect of any MP's time – both to and from the constituency and around the constituency. For the first century or so of Parliament's existence, until the advent of mass air travel, parliamentarians travelled by train, which could take days to get to and from Ottawa. MPs stayed in Ottawa for weeks or even months at a time, unless they lived nearby in Ontario or Quebec.

Those days are gone and MPs often go back to their constituencies every weekend, usually travelling on Thursday night or Friday and returning on Sunday night or Monday morning. Patterns vary depending on the distance to the constituency, family life, and also – particularly for senior and "star" MPs – requests to appear elsewhere in the country for policy and partisan events. MPs may need to take multiple flights from Ottawa along with additional driving to finally get home; Ontario and Quebec MPs from outside major cities may also drive for many hours in the absence of convenient flight options.

Travel *within* the constituency is also significant, varying according to constituency size and population distribution. Urban MPs may have very concentrated dense ridings, where travel is limited (though perhaps constrained by traffic and transit or parking issues). The larger the riding, the more MPs spend time simply getting around it. In the largest ridings, typically in northern areas, it may not even be possible to drive across the constituency in a single day, and some communities can only be reached by air. MPs may use this time in different ways – for example, making phone calls while driving, or bringing a staff member (or perhaps unpaid family member) to drive so that they can attend to other work and rest and sleep.

The bottom line, regardless, is that travel, and its attendant hassles, stress, and boredom, is a major part of any MP's life, even if not often explicitly recognized. And arguably, Parliament was constructed and developed in an earlier era of lengthy train travel when MPs were not constantly dipping in and absorbing themselves in two different worlds, only a few hours' flight apart. Now they are, and this is an important aspect of the demands on members of the House of Commons.

DEPARTURE, TURNOVER, AND "AMATEURISM"

MPs' careers in the House of Commons end for one of four reasons: they are defeated; they choose not to run again; they die in office; or they leave early for other opportunities. And the Canadian House of Commons has long had more turnover than its counterparts. A study of twenty-five democracies from 1979 to 1994 found Canada had the highest turnover of MPs, with an average of only 53 per cent of incumbents returned per election; the comparative figures for Australia were 80 per cent and the United Kingdom 75.7 per cent.[58] A more expansive study from 1953 to 2006 found somewhat greater stability, with an overall average of two-thirds of MPs re-elected – but still below the comparative Australian or UK figures.[59]

This has produced a unique situation in Canada. Matland and Studlar wrote in 2004 that Canada and the United States were the only countries "in which turnover of legislators has been a major topic of scholarly concern,"[60] but for opposite reasons; while Canadian turnover was seen as too high, turnover in the United States was considered too low. Kerby and Blidook concur: "the study of Canadian turnover differs from any other industrialized country in so far as the debate tends to focus on how to reduce turnover rather than increase it."[61]

In the 1980s and 1990s, the Canadian pattern of high turnover and the resultant "amateurism" of the typical MP was seen as a critical problem for the House of Commons, and a primary reason why it struggled to reconcile the opposing logics. Critics argued that MPs did not arrive in the House of Commons well prepared for their roles, and a high level of turnover meant that most did not stay long enough to master the job.

This "amateurism" was said to be a cause of weak backbenches that could not reconcile the paradox of Parliament. Inexperienced MPs were unable to fully animate the logic of representation, and were too easily cowed by the logic of governance, lacking the weight and experience to defy their parties or perform more than superficial scrutiny of government. C.E.S. Franks argued in 1987 that party discipline was not the "root cause" of MPs' problems; rather it was that Canada had "a House of Commons composed of amateur and short-term members who are asked to perform a very difficult and underappreciated job."[62] Atkinson and Docherty wrote in 1992 that "among Canadian academics there is virtually no dissent from the view that amateurism – defined as short careers undertaken by political novices – has contributed to deficiencies in both political discourse and public policy in Canada,"[63] and in 1997 Docherty affirmed that "it is clear that amateurism is a defining feature of the House of Commons. The lack of long-serving members is problematic and viewed as detrimental for a number of reasons."[64]

A relative lack of "safe seats" in Canada and a competitive multi-party system does mean that many MPs' careers are cut short because of changes in the electoral winds, rather than their own performance. But a second reason for amateurism is more internal: MPs choose to not seek re-election because they cannot find meaningful roles. This then becomes self-reinforcing; if amateur MPs make for a less effective House of Commons, then a less effective House of Commons in turn leaves less incentives for MPs to stick with the job and grow into it. Indeed, Kerby and Blidook find that rates of "voluntary turnover" – MPs choosing not to seek re-election – have grown over time.[65] This suggests that amateurism and turnover, rather than only a *cause* of Parliament's problems, is also the *result* of the institution's existing deficiencies, in a self-reinforcing cycle.

When rookie MPs decide not to run again, travel and family pressures are typically given as the key reasons. But a few openly express frustration with the job and the demands placed on them. In her 2019 farewell speech in the House, as the chamber sat late to push through legislative business before the election, BC MP Pamela Goldsmith-Jones said, "I am deeply disturbed by the stultifying and soul-destroying House of Commons rules that stipulate that the House sit on Fridays every week, or until midnight, or all night long. This is not democratic. This is not even humane. We should all be here in the House of Commons as our best selves, energized, not sleep-deprived; optimistic, not frustrated."[66] Kerby and Blidook note, "The Canadian case is that of a legislature which does a poor job in allowing members to achieve policy goals specifically, and where those members who prioritize making a personal difference will be least satisfied.... We believe that Canada's particularly high turnover rate – both overall and among comparable legislatures – is therefore partly due to those who find life less satisfying in the legislature for specifically this reason."[67]

Frustration with the system combines with other factors, especially strains on personal life. While Kerby and Blidook did not find gender to be a significant factor in decisions to not seek re-election in their 1953–2006 study, anecdotal evidence strongly suggests that in more recent times, it is family and personal dimensions that primarily influence many women, and at least some men, not to continue their parliamentary careers.

For the logic of representation, there is a certain purity to short-term amateur MPs, such as the Reform caucus of 1993 or the New Democrats of 2011; individuals drawn from the citizenry not unduly corrupted by the pursuit of power, with turnover allowing newcomers and, especially in the case of the 2011 NDP surge, greater diversity. But inexperience and turnover is also perilous for representation, as experience and knowledge are often necessary to be effective. And the amateur MP is ultimately a liability for the logic of governance as well. Amateurs can be steady soldiers, likely to remain disciplined in the ranks rather than going off on their own quixotic projects. Yet inexperienced MPs may be weak at playing effective roles, especially at scrutiny and holding government to account.

CONCLUSION

There is no real job description for MPs, and there is unlikely to ever be one. Instead, there are multiple dimensions to being an MP, some more public than others. Most Members do not fully understand the job until they are in it, and while many thrive and find their niche, others never feel entirely comfortable and tend to exit after one or two terms. The personal cost of being an MP can be high, though it can also be extremely rewarding. For most parliamentarians it is the height of their professional life, and winning elected office is a proud accomplishment they can carry forever.

But it is an ambiguous role in an already ambiguous institution, and a critical part of the overall paradox of Parliament. The individual MP is central to the logic of representation. But in the next chapter I will examine the business of the House of Commons, which is dominated by the logic of governance.

CHAPTER FIVE

House of Commons Business

Members of Parliament are primarily driven by the logic of representation. But the business of the House of Commons is dominated by the logic of governance. MPs can and do play independent roles in the House, more than is sometimes assumed, and in fact much of the language of procedure emphasizes MPs as *individuals*. Yet the overall business of the House is deeply shaped and determined by political *parties*, playing their roles as government and opposition according to the logic of governance.

This chapter looks at the rules and processes of the House of Commons. Some of these processes are also found in the Senate. However, the rules of each chamber are distinct, as are the dynamics, especially as the post-2016 Senate evolves into a chamber with fewer and fewer openly partisan appointees. Accordingly, while aspects of this chapter apply to the overall business of Parliament, I focus explicitly on the House of Commons.

I will not attempt to explain in detail the highly technical field of parliamentary procedure. Parliamentary procedural rules can be intricate and complex, and they evolve over time. This chapter, and indeed this book, only scratches the surface, and other resources are available to give considerably more background on individual elements of House procedure and processes than space allows here.[1] Instead, I will look primarily at how the House serves as a terrain of struggle between different actors, and at the motivations behind their actions.

Parliamentary proceedings may seem predictable and dominated by government. But as Ian Brodie, former chief of staff to Prime Minister Stephen Harper, observes: "The government's scarcest resource is time in Parliament."[2] From the outside, government may look like a steamroller, able to roll through Parliament and do whatever it wants. Yet from a government perspective, Parliament is a bottleneck.

There are many steps in the legislative process and only so many sitting days, so that even a majority government with disciplined MPs can only squeeze a finite amount of business through Parliament. Consequently, governments must choose how to manage parliamentary time and what to prioritize. In turn, the opposition does what it can to keep the bottleneck narrow, eating up time and forcing governments to abandon lower priorities and to pay a price for their top ones, while holding them to account on a daily basis through Question Period and other means.

Parliamentary procedure and House business is thus best seen as a terrain of struggle, an escalating game, and an arms race. Every reaction produces an opposite reaction. Government and opposition continually try to outwit each other, as the logic of governance pushes each to pursue their self-interest. Governments will try to get their programs through the chamber, and the opposition will do its best to get in their way. The opposition constantly tries to disrupt and embarrass the government through scrutiny, while the government defends itself and launches countermeasures to keep the opposition off balance. The opposition parties are also competing against each other. The constant impetus by all sides to outplay each other means that procedure and the parliamentary process get more intricate and complex, despite regular resets and reforms to the rules.

Parliamentary procedure is ultimately a tool to achieve political goals. It is less a universal truth than a means to an end. We see this most clearly when, with remarkable regularity, parties switch their views on procedure as they move in and out of government. A governing party may accuse the opposition of constant obstruction and frivolous delays. But when it loses power and lands in opposition itself, that party will inevitably start using similar tactics, while lamenting that the new government is showing contempt for Parliament by ramming legislation through too fast. Similarly, opposition parties will criticize government dominance and control of committees, but switch their tune once they hold power. And while there is no consensus in Canada on what exactly constitutes a confidence vote that could bring down the government, both government and the different opposition parties are sure to argue the perspective that happens to favour their current circumstances.

Typically this is a transparent and self-aware game, at least at the top. Each side understands the role it has been assigned and plays it to the hilt. We saw earlier the theoretical justification for much of this through the logic of governance. The system works when everyone plays their roles; the government proposes, the opposition opposes, and the former typically prevails while the latter extracts a cost.

But for many individual MPs and the general public, it is discouraging precisely because much of the business of the House of Commons is a "game" – one that plays heavily with people's emotions and hopes and dreams.

From the logic of representation, parliamentary proceedings often feel like a tease: pretending to give MPs autonomy and independence, but delivering far less than promised. Lisa Young wrote in 1999 that "parties are the crucial unit within the political system, yet ... the formal workings of Parliament are all predicated upon the fiction that individual Members of Parliament enjoy sufficient autonomy to represent the interests and opinions of their constituents in a meaningful way."[3] As far back as 1962, W.F. Dawson referred to "the parliamentary fiction that all members are alike in the House and that it is the duty of every member to bring his [sic] suggestions for legislation before Parliament."[4] Longtime parliamentary expert Jack Stillborn concurs, arguing in 2017 that parliamentary procedural language "conceive(s) the House as a deliberative assembly of local representatives and therefore need(s) comprehensive updating"[5] to reflect the reality of party dominance.

Many procedural reforms have attempted to expand the agency and role of individual MPs, in line with the logic of representation. This is best seen in private members' business and in committees, both of which are far more robust than in the past. But overall, House business is rooted in the logic of governance, while the logic of representation plays a secondary role

In this chapter I look at key persons in the House of Commons; the chamber and its setting; the place of debates, Question Period, private members' business, and opposition days; the dynamics of procedure in minority parliaments; and House of Commons committees. For each, I examine how House of Commons business is ultimately a game that runs on the logic of governance.

THE ROLES

To understand House of Commons business, one has to understand the players. I have already discussed MPs and political parties in earlier chapters. But House business involves additional specialized roles – some partisan, some non-partisan, and sometimes again with ambiguity woven into the role.

The Speaker

The Speaker of the House of Commons is possibly the most familiar figure in images of Parliament; clad in black robes and sitting at the head of the chamber. The Speaker has two main responsibilities. The first and most familiar is to oversee parliamentary proceedings (assisted by Deputy and Assistant Deputy Speakers): calling on members, keeping them to time, ruling on procedural business and, on very rare occasions, casting the deciding vote in a tie. The second, less familiar, is responsibility for the overall House organization. The Speaker chairs the Board of Internal Economy, a body of party representatives that controls the operations of the House, and oversees the Clerk of the House, who is chief administrator of the permanent parliamentary bureaucracy.

The Speaker is one of the House's elected MPs and thus walks a fine line and embodies a parliamentary paradox of their own. Typically a member of the governing party, they do not sit in the party caucus and generally avoid partisan activities. And yet they run under the party banner at election time, against candidates from other parties. In contrast, British Speakers usually run unopposed, at least by the major parties. This practice has never taken off in Canada, although one Speaker, Lucien Lamoureux, ran as an independent in 1968 and 1972. Still, despite their partisan ties, Canadian Speakers have generally acted with neutrality and fairness.

Most House Speakers have been senior veterans in the governing party. Only one has been a woman, Jeanne Sauvé. Their valuing of the job varies. Some Speakers appear to have been passed over for cabinet appointment and viewed the Speakership as a consolation prize, not entirely to their liking. Some may have sought the job for its salary and prestige more than specific interest in the role itself. Others, notably Peter Milliken, Speaker from 2004 to 2011, who famously subscribed to records of parliamentary debates as a high school student, brought a long-standing interest in procedural affairs and clearly revelled in the job. For most Speakers, the job has been the final stop of their political career. But Andrew Scheer used his single term as Speaker from 2011 to 2015 to raise his national profile and run successfully for the Conservative leadership in 2017, a very unusual career trajectory.

Until 1986, the Speaker was designated by the government and elected perfunctorily by the House. However, in 1986, a secret ballot system was introduced, making it more challenging for prime ministers to install their preferred choice. This has led to some unexpected results, such as Scheer's 2011 election when he was generally not considered to be the government's preferred candidate. A further precedent was set in 2019 when Geoff Regan became the first Speaker defeated in their bid for re-election.

Like Parliament as a whole, the exact power of Speakers can be difficult to establish. The Speaker makes day-to-day decisions to facilitate Commons proceedings. But much of this is reasonably routine, and the Speaker's true power is limited. While a Speaker calling the House to order is a familiar image to parliamentary watchers, they have limited authority to back up their verbal pleas. Real power to determine the course of parliamentary business, and to reward or punish members, resides not in the Speaker but in the parties.

One of the most curious and murky developments in Canadian parliamentary history is the evolution of the role of the Speaker in determining opportunities to ask questions in Question Period. Until the early 1980s, the Speaker appears to have had primary discretion in who to call on for questions. However, a practice arose in which party whips began to supply the Speaker with daily lists of which of their MPs would ask questions. The precise origins of this are unclear. Partial lists appear to have been in use since the 1970s. However, Michael Chong writes that Jeanne Sauvé, Speaker from 1980 to 1984, "found it difficult to choose from among the several MPs who would spontaneously rise to be recognized for a question" and so arrangements were made among the parties to submit lists of their designated speakers beforehand for convenience.[6] In another account, Elizabeth May writes that the practice "started innocently enough under Speaker Jeanne Sauvé. Sauvé said she could not see well enough to identify MPs from a distance. She asked the party whips if they would be so kind as to give her a list in advance of which MPs were to ask questions – and in what order."[7] Regardless of its origins, this practice has long been standard, even though Speakers are not statutorily bound to follow the lists.[8] The practice also expanded to include other parliamentary business such as members' statements under S.O. 31, described later in the chapter.

This is quite different from Britain, where the Speaker still primarily determines who will speak, and it is often identified as one of the significant differences between the British and Canadian Houses. Control over speakers gives the British Speaker, and individual MPs, considerably more power independent of parties. Yet the Canadian innovation may well have been meant as an improving reform, allowing more orderly proceedings rather than a cacophony of MPs all attempting to get the Speaker's attention. It also relieves the Speaker of the responsibility for distributing opportunities on the spot fairly, including being mindful of gender or regional balance or other considerations. But as May remarks, "Unintentionally, more power was conferred to political parties."[9] As discussed in chapter 2, this is an example of how seemingly simple changes to "improve" Parliament can have unanticipated results.

In 2010, Conservative backbencher Michael Chong attempted to introduce new guidelines returning primary discretion to the Speaker.[10] While attracting considerable attention for a short while, the reforms never took hold. Why? One simple interpretation is that the parties resisted giving up their power. But another is that most MPs felt the current system worked, and preferred to have parties, rather than the Speaker, distribute and determine questions. As in other areas, technical adjustments cannot necessarily resolve broader structural issues and cultural norms in Parliament.

Occasionally the Speaker is called on to make dramatic decisions, including voting in the case of a tie. The most notable recent period was the minority government period of 2004–11, overseen by Peter Milliken. Up until Milliken's time, Canadian Speakers had cast four deciding votes in Canadian history; Milliken cast five of his own, four of them during the 2004–5 Paul Martin Liberal minority, including on a vote of non-confidence in the government.[11] But even this tie-breaking is less powerful than it seems. Principles have long developed in Westminster systems that a Speaker should always vote "to continue debate" or, if debate cannot be continued, to maintain the status quo[12] – thus in the case of the non-confidence vote, Milliken's appropriate vote was to support the government and keep it alive, which he did. However, Milliken did make other dramatic decisions, such as his 2010 ruling that the Harper government needed to produce documents related to Afghan war detainees, discussed further in chapter 8.

Speakers also hold considerable authority over the administration of the House of Commons. The Clerk (described below) and parliamentary bureaucracy report to the Speaker, and the Speaker oversees a considerable budget. Yet even here their power is diluted, as major decisions are made by the Board of Internal Economy as a whole. Still, the Speaker is the dominant figure and can exercise considerable influence over the House as an organization.

In short, as with other aspects of Parliament, a Speaker's power can be elusive and is not always what it seems. Some reform attempts, such as election by secret ballot, have worked; others, like party speaking lists, have had unintended consequences. Ultimately the Speaker is one aspect of the overall system, and reflects the norms and processes of the institution as a whole.

The Clerk, Sergeant-at-Arms, and Procedural Staff

The Clerk of the House of Commons is another office largely inherited from Britain and the Westminster model. The Clerk is visible but silent in televised proceedings sitting in front of the Speaker, and their role and power are almost entirely out of public view. The Clerk is the top administrative officer and senior non-partisan official in the House. While reporting to the Speaker of the day, clerks have considerable staying power (the House has only had thirteen clerks since 1867) and oversee a considerable bureaucracy covering all aspects of House administration. This includes the Hansard service that produces written transcripts of all parliamentary proceedings, established in Canada in 1880; prior to that, debates were recorded and reported in newspapers, often with a partisan tinge. (The term "Hansard" comes from an early parliamentary reporter in Britain, Thomas Hansard, and is generally used in various Westminster parliaments to refer to their official records of proceedings.)

Another historic and highly visible position is the Sergeant-at-Arms. Also dating back to medieval times, the Sergeant-at-Arms plays both ceremonial roles (such as carrying the parliamentary mace into the House each day) and more substantive administrative roles, which have varied over the years. Typically only the ceremonial side of the role is on public display, but a dramatic exception was in 2014, when an armed terrorist broke into the parliamentary precinct and then-Sergeant-at-Arms Kevin Vickers became a national hero for his part in the response.

House of Commons employees cover a wide range of jobs but most notable is the large class of procedural "clerks." Clerks are the officers of the parliamentary bureaucracy, holding the key professional positions relating to House business alongside more standard administrative and management employees. The profession is well-organized and connected, both across Canada, with provincial and territorial legislatures, and internationally, especially with Commonwealth countries sharing the Westminster model. Most clerks and many other professional parliamentary staff have spent their entire careers in the parliamentary precinct, sometimes moving between the House, Senate, and Library of Parliament, but rarely beyond.

Clerks and other professional staff are permanent employees, expected to act on a strictly non-partisan basis. While the same is expected for public servants throughout the Government of Canada, the rules are stricter for parliamentary employees, and the hothouse atmosphere of Parliament makes this even more essential. As a result, clerks typically display an extremely high level of discretion while keeping very low public profiles. But they possess considerable perception and wisdom, and hold deep procedural and institutional knowledge. They are thus essential to the business of the House and are critical players behind the scenes.

Parliamentary staff are valued for their discreet professionalism and service to all sides. But are they too discreet and timid at times? A provocative question is whether there is too much of a divide between the professional, institutional aspect of Parliament and the partisan side. As with the Speaker, sometimes there is a strong assumption that partisan neutrality means one must be silent and unable to stand up for the integrity of the institution itself. This means there is arguably no one to speak openly about the institution and its interests, except through a partisan lens.

House Leaders and Whips

The main partisan players in House of Commons business are the House Leaders of each party. The Government House Leader is normally a member of cabinet, with primary responsibility for managing the government's legislative program. Each opposition party also appoints its own House Leader, and together they meet regularly to negotiate legislative business. These negotiations typically determine the parliamentary timetable, such as what bills will go for debate and how much time will be allocated for each, though impasses and disagreement are also common.

The private House Leader meetings are mutual bargaining sessions in which each party trades and attempts to reach its goals: for the government, to get its business through the House, and for the opposition parties, to scrutinize and highlight their opposition without appearing excessively obstructive, as well as positioning themselves against each other. Ideally, a certain mutual respect develops between the leaders, along with their staff, and agreement on schedules and other matters can be reached. But this is not always the case.

As mentioned in chapter 3, each party also has a whip, and they are also important players in House business. While House Leaders oversee the business and timetable of the House, the whips oversee the House's members. As its name implies, the whip has a coercive function, to "whip" MPs into line – thus the whip's office's most important function is to ensure MPs are present to vote and in the correct way. Whips' offices are clearinghouses of information about MP whereabouts, and monitor any doubts or concerns about their ability to support party positions. The whip is the instrument of the party leader, and wields authority as the assigner of office space and other incentives and punishments for MPs. Less known is that whips' offices may also serve a more supportive role, for example identifying MPs under strain and informing leaders of looming problems that must be addressed.

THE SETTING

The Chamber and Decorum

Two differences between the layouts of the Canadian and the British House of Commons chambers often draw attention. Despite having almost twice as many MPs as Canada (650 compared to 338), the British chamber is smaller. Furthermore, every Canadian MP (except the Speaker) has a designated seat and desk. The British House consists entirely of benches, with no assigned seating for MPs.

The assigned seating of the Canadian House implicitly symbolizes the logic of representation – giving each MP a clearly designated space in the chamber that represents the voice of an individual constituency. (Canadian MPs are also addressed by constituency, as "the member for xxx," while British MPs are addressed by name.) In contrast, the British House does not have sufficient seating for all MPs, so that at busy times it looks chaotic, with MPs standing or even sitting on the floor. Yet the irony is that the British House gives somewhat more autonomy to individual MPs, even if they cannot find a place to sit down. And even when lightly attended, the British House can still look reasonably populated. In contrast, the cavernous Canadian House never looks crowded, even when nearly all MPs are there, and can appear very sparse when only a few MPs are present.

The behaviour of MPs also regularly draws concern. MPs are prohibited from referring to each other by name along with other restrictions, most notably accusing each other of lying. This has led to a long and sometimes entertaining list of rulings on language and insults deemed unparliamentary, such as "political sewer pipe," "ignoramus," and "inspired by forty-rod whisky."[13]

Less easy to control is heckling and other informal behaviour. It is a long-standing tradition in Westminster legislatures for MPs to freely interject when others are speaking, a practice not found, for example, in the US Congress and many other legislatures.

To be interrupted is a normal experience when speaking in the Canadian House of Commons, and it is a particularly defining feature of Question Period. Members will yell out criticisms of speakers from the other side, who will then often be defended by their own party colleagues. This is so institutionalized that many, though not all, interjections are included in the Hansard record, noted by staff specifically tasked with catching them.

This behaviour has long drawn criticism, including the perennial joke that school tours should not include Question Period lest students begin to copy MPs' behaviour. There are potentially important gender implications, as women generally appear less comfortable with this aggressive behaviour. Cultural and personality differences also make some MPs very uncomfortable with interrupting another person, while others do it very naturally. Heckling can also get very personal, as well as sexist, homophobic, racist, and otherwise offensive. In extreme cases, tempers flare and MPs can also get physical. For example, in 2016, Prime Minister Justin Trudeau grew exasperated at a delay in voting and tried to grab the Conservative whip to get the vote started, accidentally shoving a New Democrat MP, Ruth Ellen Brousseau, in the chest.[14] Trudeau apologized for his behaviour, and fortunately such incidents are rare.

While the 1977 introduction of television is sometimes blamed for MPs' behaviour, decorum possibly improved, or at least shifted, with the arrival of cameras. Most notably MPs moved to applause, rather than their past practice of thumping their desks, to signify approval, and they appear to have generally acted with heightened professionalism. On the other hand, the higher stakes of being on camera, especially in Question Period, may have encouraged more aggressive and distracting behaviour to throw speakers off, especially ministers. Conservative MP Michael Cooper argues that an apparent growth in applause, especially in Question Period in recent years, is "excessive" and "disruptive" in its own right, even if more positive than heckling.[15]

A 2015 survey by Samara Canada found a contradiction: 69 per cent of MPs felt that heckling was a problem, and yet 72 per cent also said they did it themselves.[16] A 2011 survey by Mackenzie Grisdale found even higher levels: 90 per cent of MPs agreed or strongly agreed that "I see heckling as a problem in the House of Commons," yet 83.3 per cent said they had heckled in the House. As in other aspects of

Parliament, there is a cyclical, escalating pattern at work – if one side is heckled, the other will heckle back. Indeed, much heckling is defensive; if an opposition MP heckles a minister in Question Period, government backbenchers will then yell to drown them out. The intense atmosphere heightens tempers and reduces inhibitions, leading more MPs to blurt interjections and for attacks to become personalized. This makes it difficult for MPs to see a way out; Grisdale's survey also found that 68.4 per cent of MPs agreed or strongly agreed that "Heckling is a fact of life in the House of Commons" – suggesting they saw no way to break the pattern.[17]

When it arrived in force in 1994, the Reform Party eschewed heckling and other practices it found detrimental to Parliament. But, in this and other well-meaning ways, the party eventually joined the game everyone else was playing. Conservative Michael Cooper suggests that in the early days of the Justin Trudeau government the Liberals toned down excessive applause, though not heckling, but suggests this was not a "virtuous effort" so much as "a self-interested strategy to calm Question Period criticism of their government."[18] Again, party self-interest lurks behind so much of House business.

The Speaker is sometimes identified as the one figure that can make the House behave better. But this is difficult to accept, given the Speaker's modest overall power. The Speaker has the power to caution and cut off members, and even expel members from the House for the day. But expulsions are an extreme response and rare. Interestingly, the Australian House of Representatives has a more moderate provision to expel rowdy MPs for an hour (a practice known as the "sin bin," like a penalty box in hockey) and it is regularly used, sometimes on a daily basis.[19] But behaviour and heckling in the Australian House are generally no better and possibly more raucous than in Canada, showing the limits of that provision. The Speaker cannot compel a change in the overall House culture by themselves, and so the cycle of heckling back and forth continues.

The Parliamentary Day

The number of days Parliament is in session varies from year to year, especially if there is an election, and the House and Senate operate on separate schedules, as do committees. However, data clearly shows that since the 1990s the House of Commons has had fewer sitting days than in previous decades.[20] This trend is also evident at the provincial level.[21] But the significance of this is debatable.

For some, the decline in sitting days is further evidence of the decline of Parliament. But this argument is not cut and dried. While fewer sittings means fewer Question Periods and other opportunities to hold the government to account, it also means less time for the government to get its legislation passed. This is especially noticeable in June, when Parliament typically breaks for the summer months. Governments push to finalize legislation, often leading to extended sittings into the evening and bargaining as the opposition extracts concessions, all with a view to rising by the end of the month. On the other hand, less legislative time may mean governments enact more policies by other means. Still, MPs may appreciate less formal time in Ottawa, giving them more opportunity to spend time in their constituencies and enjoy better family and life balance. As with many aspects of Parliament, there are several interpretations of the evidence.

More concerning is the completely unsystematic and opportunistic approach in Canada to prorogation and parliamentary sessions.

A "parliament" is technically the group of MPs elected in the most recent election along with all sitting senators. Thus the parliament that began in 2021 is formally called "the 44th Parliament," as it was the 44th since 1867. "Parliaments" are then divided into sessions. Importantly, all parliamentary business, such as bills and committees, is organized by session rather than the parliament as a whole. A new session begins with a Speech from the Throne, the message of government priorities written by the government and read out by the Governor General. When a session ends, business not only stops but is actually cancelled entirely, almost as if an election had been called. This leads to phrases like "the bill died on the order paper," meaning a bill working its way through Parliament had not been passed prior to the end of the session and now has to be reintroduced entirely (though there are provisions to return it to its previous stage). Similarly, committees are dissolved and must be reconstituted and start entirely anew.

When a session ends, it is known as "prorogation." Prior to the 1980s, prorogation in Canada approximated an annual cycle. Historically, this made sense when being an MP was a part-time job and travel to Ottawa was difficult. Parliaments would sit in sessions for months at a time, dealing with legislative business. MPs would then go home for an extended period until the next session and a new Speech from the Throne. While not fully regularized, the general pattern was clear.

This changed in the 1980s. The House of Commons adopted an annual calendar that spread its business out more, and MPs had become full-time and were able to fly back and forth from home more easily. Sessions began to go longer, typically two years. This served governments well, as they now had less pressure to push bills through before the session ended. It also assisted committee continuity, as committees were no longer dissolved every time a session ended. Prorogation moved from a more or less annual event to a mid-term reset for majority governments halfway through the typical four years of a parliament.

But in the 2000s, governments began to use the prorogation power more opportunistically. In 2003, Jean Chrétien prorogued Parliament in the midst of the "sponsorship scandal" that was consuming the Liberals just as Paul Martin was beginning to take power – shutting down Question Period and other opposition vehicles to pursue the scandal. In 2008, Stephen Harper prorogued Parliament to escape a looming vote on non-confidence, as discussed in chapter 2, and in 2009 he did so again and thus ended a committee inquiry that was damaging to the government. In the 2015 election, Justin Trudeau pledged to not use prorogation "to escape difficult political circumstances" and the 2015–19 Parliament did not prorogue at all. However, in 2020 Trudeau suddenly prorogued Parliament without notice. He said it was time for a reset amid the COVID-19 pandemic, but it also ended parliamentary committees looking into the WE Charity affair that was damaging to the government and Trudeau personally.

As briefly discussed in chapter 2, prorogation has thus moved from a nominally neutral practice in Canada to an active tool to be used for political ends, and part of the escalating game and see-saw battle between government and opposition. Notably, Australia and New Zealand have long abandoned regular prorogation and "sessions" at all, while Britain more or less continues on an annual cycle. Canada thus sticks out in its continuing random use of prorogation, and not in a good way. It is clearly a sign of the larger weakness of Parliament as an independent institution.[22]

The House of Commons has always had a daily and weekly schedule of its activities, though this has evolved considerably over time. Originally, vast amounts of time were available for private members' business, reflecting a time when government legislation was modest and many private matters, such as business incorporations or sometimes even divorces, required legislation. Over time, the balance has shifted. Private business was relegated to a small block while government business has become dominant. However, some of this reflects Parliament delegating its power on minor responsibilities. (See the discussion on private bills below.)

Many changes reflect the institutionalization and regularization of proceedings. Most notably, Question Period ("Oral Questions") gradually evolved from an informal practice to become a scheduled activity in 1964 and the familiar institution of today. Other less high-profile activities have similarly evolved from occasional practices into being built into the formal schedule. Relatively few aspects have simply been introduced into the House schedule without a previous informal history of the practice – reflecting the evolutionary nature of parliamentary procedure, as opposed to planned design.

As with all aspects of procedure, the parliamentary calendar has also lurched and evolved in reaction to issues and events. As we will see below, creative and unexpected tactics by the opposition or the government often reveal loopholes or vulnerabilities in the proceedings, which are then subsequently tightened up. Some changes have an underlying motive, such as the introduction in 1995 of singing "O Canada" every Wednesday morning, advocated by the Reform Party at the height of national unity tensions and maintained ever since. Overall, then, the parliamentary calendar, both throughout the year and day to day, is simultaneously fixed and yet flexible, like many other aspects of Parliament. It serves and adapts to the complex relationships between political parties as they each pursue their goals.

THE PARLIAMENTARY PROCESS: FOUR ASPECTS

While the House of Commons agenda has numerous aspects, its business can be broken down into four major areas: debate on government bills, Question Period, private members' business, and opposition days and motions of non-confidence. We cannot possibly cover the full intricate detail of any of these, nor the many other aspects of parliamentary business. But I will look at these four primary areas of activity, evaluating each through the competing logics of governance and representation.

Government Bills and Debate

Parliamentary business comprises "bills" that propose laws, and also "motions" that authorize action or express a view. (For simplicity, this discussion will refer simply to "bills.") Bills are further divided into those proposed by government and by individual MPs. While any MP can introduce a bill, the government has the overwhelming power to decide what bills will actually proceed to debate. Ordinary MPs must wait for opportunities through private members' business, as described below.

We saw above that parliamentary time is a government's most precious resource, that is, time to get legislation through the bottleneck of the House. Under parliamentary procedure, a bill goes through three "readings" or stages in the main House. The first reading is simply the introduction of the bill, its public debut (and the stage where any MP can introduce a bill). Second reading involves debate, followed by a vote. Assuming it passes, the bill is then sent to committee for further examination, and later reported back to the House for another vote. It then goes to debate and a final vote at third reading, after which it proceeds to the Senate for a similar process, and ultimately Royal Assent.

Some bills move fairly swiftly through this multi-step process; most do not. There is no set amount of time for debating a bill. Instead, this is typically one of the main items of business negotiated by party House Leaders, along with the order of what business will be debated. Opposition parties will typically bargain, demanding as much time as possible for controversial legislation. Rob Walsh writes: "As a rule, the Government wants its bills to go through the House as quickly as possible, while the opposition parties want them to go through as slowly as possible."[23] This is why time is a precious resource. A government with a majority may be assured of winning parliamentary votes, but it first must get to the vote.

The quality of "debate" itself varies considerably. C.E.S. Franks writes that MPs speak to "a vast wasteland of empty desks."[24] Former MP Nathan Cullen writes that he was bored by his own first speech in the House.[25] Debates are minimally attended, to the point that each party must specifically assign members to be in or near the chamber – known as performing "house duty" – primarily to guard against any surprise procedural moves from the other side, rather than to hear the actual debate.

The advent of television in the 1970s is sometimes blamed for diminishing attendance and quality of debates. But it is more likely that television enabled MPs to escape an often tedious duty, with limited evidence that debates were of better quality in the past. Speaking times have been tightened since then, and MPs have an opportunity to respond to speeches with short questions, almost certainly an improvement from the vast majority of long-winded and uninterrupted speeches of the past.

While often unexciting, debate and the time devoted to it are essential to the logic of governance and what Samuel Beer has called the "mobilization of consent."[26] Writing about the British Parliament in the 1960s, Beer observed that public policy was increasingly shaped by government working directly with organized interests – that is, without much input from the legislature. However, Parliament still had an essential role – to legitimize decisions by mobilizing public "consent" – and political parties composed of MPs were a fundamental aspect of this. In this framing, the "mobilization of consent" takes place through the furious arguing back and forth between government and opposition. This provides a test of fire and a running of the gauntlet that forces governments to plan and prepare; to be confident in their proposals; and to be prepared to discard, modify, or simply abandon items.

The function of parliamentary debate is thus to *debate* rather than persuade or change participants' minds. It gives government and opposition the chance to make their case, to get it on the record. The government must defend; the opposition searches for holes and advantage. Each side's interest is clear and acknowledged.

In the course of this struggle, flaws may be revealed and bills amended, slowed, or even abandoned. The great secret of parliamentary debate is not so much the bills that make it through, but the ones that are quietly set aside and abandoned. A recent study of Parliaments from 1993 to 2021 by Charlie Feldman finds that in majority parliaments 31 per cent of government bills never make it to Royal Assent, and 49 per cent in minority parliaments.[27] There are many possible reasons for this. Governments may simply run out of available parliamentary time; they may also abandon their own legislation if it receives a rough ride, typically without announcement and often simply by letting the bill sit without proceeding further. Legislation that is passed has thus successfully been tested by fire. Both its supporters and opponents have been mobilized, and the process ascribes consent and democratic legitimacy.

Debate is also part of the overall Canadian political system beyond Parliament, even if it does not change the course of legislation. The struggles are not confined to Parliament Hill, and this is a variation of Beer's "mobilization of consent." As Ian Brodie writes, "When the opposition parties drag out debate, they slow down the government's progress and give themselves time to mobilize public opinion on the issue. Mobilizing parts of the voting public against parts of the executive's legislative agenda can, if done properly, build an opposition party's electoral support in the next election."[28] In short, debate and votes are part of the larger picture and political struggle. But all or most is determined by the parties. Individual MPs may be crucial players in the overall game, but they often consider their own individual contribution to be unfulfilling.

The rules and procedures of debate have evolved considerably over time. Some are designed to make debate more lively and engaging with greater interaction among MPs. But most are ultimately explained by the perennial interests of government and opposition, respectively, to advance and to slow the government agenda. And as noted above, parties' attitudes to debate and procedure are almost always reliably determined by whether they sit in government or opposition. This is best illustrated in controversies over omnibus bills.

OMNIBUS BILLS

While there is no fully agreed definition, omnibus bills are inevitably described as combining a large number of disparate proposals into a single bill, rather than proceeding with smaller bills for greater individual attention.[29] Theoretically, omnibus bills allow for comprehensive legislation on a common theme. Among the most famous omnibus bills in Canadian history was the *Criminal Law Amendment Act*, first introduced in 1967 by then-Minister of Justice Pierre Trudeau, which abolished laws against homosexuality, granted limited access to abortion, and updated a wide range of other laws. However, most omnibus bills are far less coherent.

Debates over omnibus bills illustrate several aspects of Parliament and the competing logics of governance and representation. From the logic of governance, omnibus bills are efficient, allowing Parliament to process large numbers of related matters effectively. Indeed, at least some omnibus bills are probably necessary and normal, given the complexity of public policy-making.

But from the logic of representation, omnibus bills are clearly troubling, as they can allow governments to push large decisions through with minimal opportunity for opposing voices to be heard. They can reduce the amount of parliamentary time devoted to important topics, and allow controversial items to slip through with little notice. Indeed, this can even be a concern from the governance logic, as some omnibus bills are such convoluted monstrosities that it is impossible for parliamentarians to engage substantively with them. Some may be so complex and technical that governments themselves may not even fully know what is in their own legislation, odd as that may seem. An example was in 2007 when a Conservative government bill, largely consisting of measures originally proposed under the previous Liberal government, was found late in the process – at the Senate stage – to include a measure allowing governments to deny film tax credits based on objectionable material. This attracted national attention as evidence of a possible social conservative agenda by the Conservative government. Yet the government denied this agenda, and emphasized it was not even proposed by the government.[30]

Controversy over omnibus bills is not a recent phenomenon. Andre Barnes and Michel Bédard state that the first controversy in the Senate over an omnibus bill was in 1923, and in the House of Commons in 1953.[31] However, they appear to have accelerated in the twenty-first century, particularly the ballooning of bills to implement budgetary decisions (which may or may not be considered omnibus bills, there being no universally accepted definition). C.E.S. Franks noted in 2010 that "[b]etween 1995 and 2000, budget implementation acts averaged 12 pages in length. From 2001 to 2008, they averaged 139 pages. In 2009, the two acts added up to 580 pages – 32 per cent of Parliament's legislative output that year. The 2010 Budget Implementation Act, Bill C-9, contains 883 pages of varied and unrelated legislative provisions."[32] The Trudeau government continued this tradition of large budget implementation bills.[33]

Ultimately, views on omnibus bills are an excellent illustration of the overarching principle that views on procedure are malleable and depend on where one sits. Omnibus bills serve the government interest by allowing more expeditious and efficient progress on a wide range of government business. Opposition parties generally oppose them, for the same reason.

Most opposition parties solemnly pledge to not use omnibus bills, and then abandon this promise in government. In 2004, the then leader of the Official Opposition, Stephen Harper, protested against a Liberal budget implementation bill, stating, "We have a chance to right some of the wrongs and some of the questionable practices we have fallen into, in particular the practice in recent years of presenting omnibus legislation with respect to budgetary matters."[34] Yet, as noted above, his government followed the same practice.[35] Similarly, in 2015, Justin Trudeau and the Liberal Party pledged to end "inappropriate omnibus bills to reduce scrutiny of legislative measures,"[36] yet the Trudeau government also turned to omnibus legislation to implement its agenda. Donald Savoie says, "When a political party is in opposition, omnibus bills never make sense, but somehow they do when the party sits on the government side of the House."[37]

Omnibus bills are thus a perennial issue, unlikely to be resolved. Even defining them is unclear. Technically, any bill that amends or repeals more than one past parliamentary act can be considered an omnibus bill, and many bills do this. In 2017, the Standing Orders were revised to define omnibus bills as "a government bill [that] seeks to repeal, amend or enact more than one act, and where there is not a common element connecting the various provisions or where unrelated matters are linked."[38] However, this still leaves much open to interpretation. Debates on "omnibus bills" thus centre on bills of unusual size and complexity, on contentious issues, and bills that clearly address unrelated and disparate issues rather than being bound by a common theme.

But there is no exact measure to determine what that is, and naturally governments avoid using the term entirely. In 1971 the Speaker of the House of Commons suggested that a time might come when bills might need to be ruled inadmissible and divided because they addressed too many distinct areas, and in 1981 the Speaker did split such a bill. In 2017, the Standing Orders were amended to allow the Speaker to divide up a bill and hold separate votes on each part. But Speakers have not used these tools aggressively, given their modest power, the ambiguity around omnibus bills generally, and the reality that opinions on them are driven almost entirely by parties' self-interest.

CLOSURE, TIME ALLOCATION, AND OBSTRUCTION

Another example of cyclical concerns is closure and time allocation. Closure, first introduced in 1913, allows governments to terminate debate on a bill and force a vote on it. Time allocation is a different but similar tool, allowing governments to schedule and limit debate on a bill before calling a vote.[39] Both allow governments to push legislation through even when the opposition is firm in its delay and refuses to reach agreement through the House Leaders.

Closure was once seen as a drastic measure, most notably when it was used in 1956 for a pipeline bill, leading to a furious controversy and the defeat of the St. Laurent Liberal government. But it has become an accepted aspect of Parliament along with time allocation, which was introduced in the 1960s and has become a very common tool. And like their response to omnibus bills, opposition parties tend to decry the use of closure and time allocation, yet turn to them once in government, though the level of usage does vary.

In turn, opposition parties (and governments) seek constantly to find new tools and creative options to delay and obstruct progress. Often these loopholes are simple and obvious in retrospect. A famous example in 1982 was the "bell-ringing" incident in response to the Pierre Trudeau government's bill enacting the controversial National Energy Program (NEP), deeply unpopular in Western Canada.

At the time, rules stated that House voting could not proceed until both the government and Official Opposition whips were present. To indicate the party's strong opposition to the bill, the opposition Progressive Conservative whip simply stayed out of the chamber. It was routine (and still is today) for bells to ring throughout the building, summoning MPs to vote. Because of the Conservative absence, the bells rang continually for eighteen days, until the Conservatives finally allowed the vote to proceed. It was clever of the Conservatives to recognize and use this simple tactic, and the Standing Orders were soon amended to allow votes to proceed in the absence of whips, eliminating this loophole from future use. And while the bell-ringing marathon did not stop the NEP bill, it called enormous national attention to the issue, making the party (and regional) positions clear and helping set up the Conservatives for a landslide victory two years later.

The constant quest to delay government legislation or at least extract a high political price means the House of Commons sees regular disruptions, delays, and obstruction as rules are bent or creatively interpreted, similar to the bell-ringing incident. These include introducing hundreds or thousands of amendments for bills and demanding votes on each, denying assent on routine matters, and any other activity that is technically permissible even if clearly frivolous and against the spirit of the rules. Commonly, as in 1982, the Standing Orders are then revised to prevent that particular trick from happening again.

The constant give-and-take, and the creativity in finding loopholes before the other side plugs them, again gives the impression that parliamentary debate is just an elaborate game. But there is logic and significance to it. Major delays and obstructions are particularly important as they gain national attention, increasing public scrutiny and knowledge of the issues and forcing government and opposition to justify their positions. More routinely, but often out of the public eye, legislation is slowed or abandoned because the government knows it faces difficulties, and thinks twice about the benefits versus the costs. And the time and elaborate ceremonies devoted to debates and voting enhance the legitimacy of the final product, giving bills the stamp of democratic legitimacy and the rule of law.

While it may work on a collective level, debate remains unsatisfying for most MPs, who are largely pawns in the overall game between government and opposition. As noted, reforms over the years have tried to make debate more focused and lively, with shorter speaking times, opportunities for short questions and exchanges, special evening sessions known as "take-note" debates that focus on a general issue rather than specific legislation, and other adjustments. MPs can use their debate remarks to highlight particular issues and concerns and transmit these to constituents and stakeholders. Speaking in the House, even to an empty audience, is still important; as Ian Brodie notes, "something said in the House has a status that a local speech or media interview does not have."[40] But these individual roles are, in the end, marginal, while the logic of governance is particularly dominant here in the great clash between government and opposition.

Question Period

Question Period is probably the most familiar activity of Parliament for Canadians. While asking "oral questions" is a longtime tradition, the institution of a fixed daily period to pose questions to ministers was first codified in 1964, and soon became the highlight of the parliamentary day. While some suggest the introduction of television in 1977 is the primary reason for the ascent of Question Period to superstar status, a 1975 study found even then that newspaper coverage massively favoured Question Period over debates by a ratio of 35–1.[41] Similarly, a 2015 retrospective found that the ratio of opposition leaders to MPs asking questions – tracking whether Question Period had made leaders more prominent – had not changed before and after the introduction of television and had remained surprisingly steady for decades.[42]

Question Period brings out both the best and worst of democracy. Like debate, the players are clearly divided into government and opposition, though it is now the opposition driving the agenda. Question Period is a critical aspect of scrutiny and accountability, as government ministers are expected to attend and to be prepared to field questions on any aspect of their portfolios.

As many point out, Question Period is not "Answer Period." Each side has a role to play, and the importance of actual information can be low. Opposition questions are designed to embarrass and throw off ministers, while extolling the opposition's own virtues and positions. Ministers in turn are there to counterattack, giving information selectively and sometimes briefed with counterintelligence to use against their opponents. Andrea Ulrich writes: "In a setting where every detail is anticipated and planned for on both sides, it is unlikely that meaningful dialogue will result, since the MPs come armed with questions, and the ministers come armed with answers, and whether the two correlate is purely a matter of chance."[43]

Question Period's greatest value is often behind the scenes. Ministers and both their personal political staff and departmental public servants spend considerable effort preparing for it, anticipating possible issues and preparing responses. In pre-electronic days, it was a familiar sight to see ministers arriving for Question Period carrying thick binders crammed with possible issues and responses; today the materials may be more discreetly carried on electronic devices. The Harper government further instituted a daily mock session in private just before Question Period in which ministers were quizzed and tested in preparation for the actual event. All this preparation, though behind the scenes, is part of the overall value of Question Period. It ensures ministers of the Crown are well-informed and ready to account for their portfolios. Problems are anticipated with responses, if not necessarily full solutions. And after Question Period is done, any issues that unexpectedly arose and surprised the minister are quickly tracked down and addressed.

In turn, Question Period preparation is a top priority for opposition parties, as they search for vulnerabilities and issues on which to quiz the government. The opposition can prepare as assiduously as the government, including their own rehearsals. Many political careers have been made, and lost, in Question Period. Weak ministers struggle to explain themselves while strong ones articulate and defend their actions. Determined and well-briefed opposition MPs are able to wear down the government, while lesser ones go through the motions, observed and judged by all.

Unlike many other aspects of Parliament, there is little mystery to Question Period. It is not only the highlight of the parliamentary day, but also the most straightforward. Nothing is blurred; the dynamics are simple – offence and defence – and everyone's actions and motivations are logical and clear. While Question Period has flaws and a corrosive element, it clearly fulfils its overall purpose of scrutiny.

Question Period in Canada differs from its counterpart in Britain in two significant ways that have often attracted reformers' attention. First is the daily appearance of ministers. For many years, Question Period in Canada was a whole-of-government affair in which the prime minister and all members of the cabinet customarily attended every day, prepared at any time to take a question. The prime minister typically fielded the first few questions from the opposition party leaders, after which questions were posed by other opposition MPs to different ministers. In 2016 newly elected Justin Trudeau adopted the long-standing British practice in which the prime minister only attends once a week, but takes *all* the questions. While allowing the prime minister to spend less time in Parliament, this is generally considered an improvement as it places a more intensive accountability on the prime minister. It also allows a wider range of MPs to quiz the head of government, not just opposition leaders or their top lieutenants, and they can pose questions directly to the prime minister about matters specifically affecting their constituency. However, Canada has never adopted the other British practice of assigning all other ministers to specific days as well. Canadian ministers generally attend Question Period every day, always alert for a query but often receiving no questions at all. While keeping them on their toes, this sucks up much time and energy for limited benefit. In contrast, UK ministers appear on a rotating basis every few weeks, and like the PM they then field all questions.

The second is the assignment of question opportunities. As discussed above in the section on the Speaker, the parties tightly control who gets to ask a question, unlike in Britain where the Speaker exercises independent judgment. This is most sharply evident in questions from government backbenchers. In Britain it is not unusual for a government backbencher to pose a somewhat difficult question to a minister or even the prime minister. In contrast, tight party control in Canada means that Canadian government MP questions are pre-arranged and never confrontational. Instead they are limp and affirmatory, often setting up a planned answer by the minister. ("Can the minister please tell the House if this new program will benefit my province?"; "I'm happy to tell the member that their province will indeed receive considerable funding under this new program, and here are the details….") The enfeeblement of government MPs in Question Period is among the most embarrassing aspects of the Canadian Parliament. And yet it has become long-institutionalized and easy for incoming governments to continue, since they and not the Speaker control the opportunities for backbenchers to speak.

Opposition members are less constrained but their opportunities are still controlled by the parties. Front-bench critics/shadow ministers ask most questions; lower-ranking MPs have fewer chances. Effective questioners may be able to add some local and personal colour to their questions. But this means nothing if they cannot be approved for a slot in the party's daily lineup, and typically their exact text must be pre-approved. Overall, while it may seem the perfect venue for the logic of representation through the voices of individual MPs representing the concerns of the nation, there is actually little evidence of that logic in Question Period. MPs serve their parties in team roles, through the overall logic of governance.

Private Members' Business

A third area of parliamentary activity is private members' business. Government bills and Question Period are dominated by the logic of governance. But private members' business is, at least in principle, the premier showcase of the logic of representation. Here MPs can pursue their own bills and motions, away from the relentless game between government and opposition, and there is opportunity for MPs to be entrepreneurial. But it is a crowded field, in which MPs must compete with each other for limited space, and the power of the party still looms. In this section we will look at private members' business and three related activities: private bills, members' statements, and petitions.

In the nineteenth century much of the parliamentary day was open for MPs to introduce and pursue their own legislation. Government was vastly smaller than today, meaning not only that governments had less legislation to pass, but a great deal of petty business flowed through the chamber in the form of *private bills* (distinct from "private members' bills"). Private bills covered matters that at the time were only in the power of Parliament to address, such as the incorporation of certain types of companies and, amazingly, the dissolution of marriages. (Divorce bills continued to be a parliamentary matter, mainly handled by the Senate, as late as 1968 for provinces that did not have divorce courts.)

Over time, Parliament devolved these responsibilities so that today private bills are very rare and obscure, often less than one a year, and largely forgotten. But Bosc and Gagnon confirm that "while they are now relatively rare, private bills once constituted a large part of the legislative business of the House."[44] The one-time prevalence of private bills must be recalled in any reflections of "a golden age" or time when MPs were less shackled by party discipline and able to pursue their own legislative goals. The nineteenth-century House of Commons was a lively and more freewheeling place where MPs did have more freedom and introduced more legislation than today. But many of these were private bills, generally not worthy of significant debate.

Private members' bills were also more prevalent and prominent in the nineteenth century than today. But their low point is not today, as some may assume, but rather the mid-twentieth century.

The chief characteristics of private members' business is that (1) it can be either bills introducing or changing a law, or motions declaring Parliament's view on a subject; (2) they are introduced by non-ministers; (3) they address a matter of public interest as opposed to the purely private benefits of private bills; and (4) they do not involve public expenditure, a power limited to the government, though the interpretation of this is often fraught. A fifth characteristic, but by no means a fixed rule, is that they are less subject to party discipline and MPs are more free to vote as they wish.

In the nineteenth century a majority of the parliamentary day was consumed by private members' business (which included private bills). This proportion steadily declined as governments decided it was necessary to take up more and more time for their own legislative agenda. By 1955 government business "had appropriated virtually all the time remaining for private Members."[45] Private members' business was close to extinct. Eventually specific times began to be set aside for private members' business again, with a major overhaul in 1986 and continuing regular changes since then. At present, one hour each sitting day is devoted to private members' business, which compares reasonably well with much of the twentieth century.

Private members' business naturally covers a very wide range. At one end are uncontroversial and sometimes mocked symbolic initiatives, such as establishing the official national horse of Canada in 2002. At the other are rare bills that advance public and social change in some specific and sometimes previously inconceivable way. A 1988 bill by NDP backbencher Lyn Macdonald advancing non-smokers' rights is perhaps the most famous, and was quite significant in its time. A more recent example is Conservative MP Rona Ambrose's bill establishing mandatory training on sexual assault for all judges, though its passage was very slow, as discussed below.

There are two major challenges for private members' business. The first is the perennial issue of parliamentary time. Most MPs have at least one bill or motion they would like to pursue, and often many. While most receive little public attention, there is modest glory in even introducing a private member's bill or motion, especially if it has strong constituency implications, and outright triumph in getting it passed. For many MPs, it can be the pinnacle of their career.

Yet there are too many MPs competing for too few opportunities. A ballot system has long been used to set a random but fair order of precedence for private members' business, meaning luck is a considerable element in success. In a typical four-year parliamentary term, most MPs will get one opportunity for a private member's bill or motion; some get none.

A powerful example of the slow path of private members' legislation is the bill introduced by Conservative MP Rona Ambrose to mandate mandatory training for judges on sexual assault.[46] Introduced in February 2017, Bill C-337 passed unanimously through all stages in the House, and then proceeded to the next step, the Senate. But it languished there for two years, as other legislation took priority, and various technical concerns were raised including whether this approach infringed on judicial independence. Not until May 2019 did the bill proceed to committee, and it was not yet passed when Parliament was dissolved for the fall 2019 general election. The re-elected Liberals introduced the proposal in February 2020, this time as a government bill. Minister of Justice David Lametti said, "One of the arguments that was raised last time was that it was a private member's bill and so certain senators thought that because it was a private member's bill that it could go to the bottom of the pile.... Now it's a government bill, and senators have an abiding obligation to treat government legislation expeditiously."[47] But the government's own August 2020 prorogation of Parliament meant the new government version of Ambrose's bill also expired. It was reintroduced in September 2020, passed by the House of Commons in November, and finally by the Senate in May 2021. Meanwhile, Ambrose herself had left Parliament in 2017.

The slow passage of this proposal is remarkable considering its widespread public appeal and support from all parties. But it illustrates the great underlying issue of Parliament and the challenge of the logic of representation – whether a mass of more than four hundred MPs and senators can get anything done unless they have the driving and disciplining force of the logic of governance. Ambrose could not control her bill's fate. Even though no one particularly opposed it and any technical concerns were resolvable, no one could, or would, sufficiently champion it either. The result was a four-year odyssey before it finally became law.

The second issue for private members' business is the ever-present role of parties. While parties wisely see private members' business mostly as a useful outlet for their backbenchers, private members' bills and motions can trigger ideological battles or otherwise fall along tricky faultlines. Consequently some private members' votes are still unmistakably whipped or parties otherwise attempt to control them.

One of the most interesting and unexpected episodes of party control was under the Harper Conservative government, when several Conservative backbenchers introduced bills and motions touching on abortion. While anti-abortion views were common in the party, Conservative prime minister Stephen Harper had generally avoided the subject. The private members' business threatened to reopen the issue in a manner that Harper did not want. Consequently, the Conservative leadership increasingly cracked down on this activity, leading to unusual sights. In 2012 the Conservative Party whip spoke against an anti-abortion motion by one of the party's backbenchers, giving an unexpectedly blistering pro-choice speech.[48] Prime Minister Harper himself voted against the motion along with most of the Opposition, while most of his own caucus supported it, a very unusual and perhaps unprecedented vote for a prime minister in the Canadian House of Commons.[49] The party establishment fought against further attempts by social conservative MPs to introduce abortion-related bills and motions.

This convoluted episode gives us a glimpse into the separation between *political parties* and the parliamentary party leadership. In this case, it was arguably the backbench MPs who were more in tune with their party and its core ideological leanings, both in caucus and the broader membership. Yet their independent activity clashed with the *government*, its agenda and self-image. The government prevailed, although this issue continued to dog Harper's successors.

Overall, private members' business offers a chance for MPs to be independently effective, following the logic of representation. But demand far exceeds supply of opportunities. Progress is not easy, and parties will still assert their self-interest as they see fit.

Another area of backbench activity, though not technically falling under "private members' business," is members' statements, widely known as "S.O. 31 Statements" for their place as Section 31 in the House of Commons Standing Orders. Regularized since 1982 as a fifteen-minute period just prior to Question Period, this is an opportunity for any MP to give a statement for no more than one minute on any topic. The time limit is strictly enforced. As with Question Period, the Speaker operates with speaking lists set by the parties.

Members' statements serves as a frantic warm-up act to Question Period, as MPs wait to be called on and then must barrel through their remarks in sixty seconds, after which their microphones are cut off. The subject of members' statements vary widely. Historically, MPs primarily spoke on issues of interest to their constituency, thus allowing them to proudly report that they had brought locally important matters to the attention of Parliament. Statements also addressed policy issues of personal interest to the MP.

In the twenty-first century, statements started to become more partisan, with less personal touch. More MPs presented statements attacking other parties. Blidook documents this in a 2013 study, noting Conservative and NDP MPs were the most likely to include partisan references.[50] Yet even at their highest levels in Blidook's study, only a minority of members' statements mentioned another party, and more recently the partisanship of members' statements appears to have diminished again.

It is unclear how much MPs value members' statements. While still competitive, opportunities are far easier than introducing a private member's bill or motion. But most statements are obscure with only marginal public policy relevance at all, and no direct impact. For many, the trivial nature of members' statements symbolizes the larger impotence of backbench MPs, reducing them to making obscure community announcements in Parliament rather than engaging on matters of national importance.

However, as with other aspects of Parliament, the primary function of members' statements is *symbolic*. The typical member's statement is instantly forgettable to most observers, but so is the average debate on a government bill, no matter the weightiness of the subject. Members' statements allow MPs to strengthen links and visibility of their constituency in a way that is meaningful to at least some constituents.

More than any other aspect of Parliament, members' statements highlight specific individuals and communities, and the daily fifteen-minute package of members' statements is a colourful whirlwind tour across Canada. MPs can then post videos of their statements on social media, showing constituents proof of their representative activities in the House. They thus help, modestly, to strengthen the connections between Parliament and Canadians. They also allow MPs to nudge items a little further onto the public agenda, even if their individual impact is negligible. While modest, this is the logic of representation at work.

A final activity in which MPs play individual roles is the presentation of petitions. This is a long-standing tradition in which MPs can present and briefly introduce any written petitions on matters within parliamentary jurisdiction. The government must then respond, however perfunctorily, within a certain period of time. In 2015, electronic petitions were introduced, allowing the public to initiate and sign them via the House website; these can then be presented to the House if they are supported by at least five MPs.

Sponsorship of a petition by a MP does not necessarily mean agreement. This allows MPs to freely present petitions from constituents whether or not they agree with them, thus acting as pure delegates of constituency opinion. But this can lead to obvious confusion over MPs' own views. In November 2020, then-Conservative MP Derek Sloan sponsored a petition with 41,000 signatures questioning COVID-19 vaccines, yet did not say whether he agreed with the petition himself. This among other actions led to Sloan's eventual expulsion from the Conservative caucus.

Petitions are an obscure corner of parliamentary activity, exciting and empowering to their organizers but with likely negligible policy effect, though they can serve as barometers and indicators of public opinion and concern. They constitute an extreme example of the logic of representation, giving power to citizens, with MPs acting more as messengers than active agents.

Opposition Days and Confidence/ Non-confidence Motions

A final major aspect of the parliamentary calendar are the days when legislative initiative falls to the opposition rather than government. These are called "opposition days" or "supply days" (both terms are common) and may include motions of non-confidence.

Modern opposition/supply days were introduced in 1968 by giving up the ancient parliamentary right to supply. Prior to 1968, Parliament had to specifically approve government spending for the year, known generally as "supply" (i.e., the supply of funds). This power to deny supply was at the heart of the development of the British parliamentary system in medieval times, to moderate the power of the monarch. As Parliament developed, including in Canada, it could be used as a weapon by the opposition against the government. Without money, governments could not govern. However, in practice the denial of supply was merely another procedural weapon in the parliamentary arsenal. Unlike other jurisdictions, notably Australia in 1975 (discussed in chapter 7), Canada never faced a complete deadlock over supply.

As part of the general overhaul of parliamentary business in 1968 supported by all parties, new rules were adopted deeming that spending estimates were automatically approved on June 30 every year, even if no supply vote was held. The right to deny supply was thus extinguished. But in return, the Standing Orders granted a fixed number of days for opposition parties to devote to subjects of their choosing. There are currently twenty-two "opposition days" a year, distributed proportionately to recognized parties. This trade-off (still marked in the reference to opposition days as "supply days") remains a prime example of the give-and-take evolution of parliamentary procedure. Opposition and government maintain a certain balance of power, conscious that, at least for the two major parties, their perspective and interests will inevitably shift someday to the other side of the chamber.

Opposition days include the opportunity to introduce "opposition motions" and put them to a vote. As Kady O'Malley writes, "opposition supply motions tend to either propose that the House call on the government to take a particular action or, alternately, condemn that same government for taking action – or implementing policy, or, really, doing anything ... with which the party putting forward the motion disagrees."[51]

Opposition motions can put governments in a tight corner. An example was in February 2021 when the opposition Conservatives introduced a motion condemning China for human rights abuses. The Liberal cabinet abstained, sensitive to the diplomatic impact, but was embarrassed when even most Liberal backbenchers joined the opposition to support the motion. (See further discussion of this in chapter 8.) But most opposition motions are annoying yet not perilous to governments, and sometimes governments will even concur in the motion. And they are *motions*, not bills, and cannot institute new laws or spend funds. They often compel no direct action, though they may direct a parliamentary committee to inquire into an issue or require the government to report on a matter.

The peril is when a motion in a minority parliament expresses a lack of confidence in the government. Such "non-confidence motions" triggered the fall of minority governments in 2005 and 2011. A planned opposition non-confidence motion also nearly brought down the government in the 2008 parliamentary crisis, when the Liberals, NDP, and Bloc Québécois made a pact to introduce it on an upcoming opposition day. However, the government used its scheduling power to postpone the opposition day by a week, and then prorogued Parliament entirely.

While the 2005 and 2011 non-confidence votes were opposition day motions, there are other types of votes testing whether the government has the confidence of the House. Non-confidence motions can show up in a variety of ways, typically as proposed opposition amendments to money-related government motions, which brought down governments in 1963, 1974, and 1979.

Votes that are precipitated by governments themselves are typically known as *confidence* rather than *non-confidence* votes, the difference being that an affirmative vote is good for the government. There is no consensus on exactly what qualifies as a confidence vote, and in the intricate world of parliamentary procedure, this issue is among the most esoteric of all.[52] Votes on the Speech from the Throne and budget are widely agreed to be confidence votes – if the government is defeated, it is assumed to have lost the confidence of the House and must call an election. But even this can be fuzzy; the Liberals lost a budget-related vote in 1968 but refused to resign and called and won a new vote. Governments may also declare any upcoming vote to be one of confidence. In majority governments, this is typically to get their own dissenting backbenchers in line on an unpopular issue. In a minority, this is a high-risk move to split the opposition parties, on the assumption that one or more parties does not want to trigger an election and will not vote against the government. (In some cases, the government wants an election, but does not want to pull the plug themselves.) In contrast, a *non-confidence motion* by the opposition is usually specific and unambiguous.

PROCESS IN MINORITY PARLIAMENTS

As seen above, while the rules remain the same, the dynamics of the parliamentary process shift in minority parliaments, when the government has the largest number of seats but falls short of a majority of the House. Mastery of parliamentary process and creative use of its tools and loopholes becomes even more important in minority parliaments. The government can no longer swamp the institution with sheer numbers and must bargain and calculate risk. In turn, opposition parties must also be shrewd and calculating, against not only the government but each other, especially as the government will attempt to split and play them against each other.

Minority situations pose obvious problems for governments. But minority parliaments also force opposition parties to lay their true cards on the table. In a majority parliament each opposition party can happily flail away at the government, knowing it can only do limited damage while posturing for the next, possibly distant, election. But in a minority parliament the opposition can actually destroy the government and trigger an election. An opposition party may not be ready to fight an election and/or be pessimistic about its prospects, and this will influence its parliamentary strategy.

The Conservative minority governments under Stephen Harper from 2006 to 2011 were particularly skilled at playing opposition parties against each other. Time and again, the Conservatives either made deals with individual parties or simply forced votes that at least one party did not want to win, lest it trigger an election in which the party might not do well. Most notably, after escaping near-death in the 2008 crisis mentioned above, the Conservatives were able to avoid losing a confidence vote on their budget only seven weeks later, because the Liberal Party no longer wanted an election. When the Conservatives did fall on a non-confidence motion in 2011, they welcomed it and went on to decisively beat their opponents and win a majority in the subsequent election.

Justin Trudeau's minority governments also played on the reluctance of opposition parties. For example, in October 2020, the opposition Conservatives introduced a motion to establish a special parliamentary committee to investigate the WE Charity scandal that had engulfed the Liberals and Trudeau personally. The Liberals fought back by declaring the motion a matter of confidence, signalling that if it passed, the government would resign and call an election. The NDP, not confident of its election chances and further unwilling to force an election during the COVID-19 pandemic, voted against the motion (as did the Green Party), even though it played into Liberal hands and saved the government from an embarrassing committee inquiry.[53] But sometimes the government loses this parliamentary game of chicken. The 1979 Conservative minority government of Joe Clark famously miscalculated that it could bluff its way through the House because it assumed both that the Liberals feared an election and that the Conservatives could win one. This was a fatal error. The government lost a budget-related vote and the Liberals won the subsequent general election.

As discussed in earlier chapters, the minority era of 2004 to 2011 was a double-edged sword for many parliamentary reformers. The instability and unpredictability of voting meant that Parliament was the centre of attention. It was no longer criticized as a mere rubber stamp that ratified the will of majority governments – rather, it was a place of relevance and power.

Yet this power was overwhelmingly concentrated in parties and in the service of the logic of governance. In a situation of constant battle and vigilance, individual MPs had to toe the line more than ever, and their influence as individual agents of representation was further diminished. Only with spectacular and one-time acts of defiance – such as Conservative MP Belinda Stronach's crossing the floor to the governing Liberals in 2005, giving them a crucial vote to escape defeat – could individual MPs make a difference. And minority parliaments are likely more bitter and tense. The constant brinkmanship, bargaining, and fear of error or miscalculation do not create a conducive atmosphere for trust.

Minority parliaments have certain advantages. They constrain government power, and force parties to cooperate and pursue policies that reflect a greater swath of opinion. Yet they are often unstable, and at times lurching and incoherent as they are driven by constant bargaining, opportunism, and short-term tactics rather than a coherent governing plan. As well, while not seen much in Canada, they can leave governments vulnerable to excessive demands from individuals or minor parties that hold the balance of power. This is seen most clearly in Australian upper houses, where "crossbench" independents and small parties elected through proportional representation can extract concessions from governments desperate to pass legislation and retain power.

In short, while parliamentary process and its quirks becomes more important in minority parliaments, so does overall party power. Activity is best understood through the overall motivations of each party. The logic of governance rules supreme, while MPs have even less individual power and the logic of representation struggles for prominence.

Committees

Committees are important aspects of most legislatures. Committees can mitigate some of the disadvantages of legislatures as a whole, especially their size and complexity. Committees allow legislators to work in smaller, more intimate groups, and to focus in more depth on specific bills and issues. However, committees remain very much creatures of their legislative context, and so Canadian House of Commons committees follow the overall patterns of the House.

The Canadian House of Commons has always had committees. But the modern system dates only from 1968. Previously, committees were irregular, found in some policy areas but not others, and with no standardization of their size or mandate. Befitting an earlier age, the Railway Committee was the most popular, with 147 members in 1887.[54]

In 1968 this ad hoc system was replaced with a system of fixed "standing committees," covering all major areas and in most cases linked to specific departments, such as Finance or Health. Membership was fixed at twenty MPs, distributed by party standings. And these new committees were given a specific job – examining all legislation and estimates in their area. Previously, most bills moving to "committee stage" after second reading were still considered in the House chamber, which sat as the Committee of the Whole with more relaxed procedures. Now a small group of MPs, ideally developing expertise in the subject, would do the job.

The 1968 change was innovative (the British House did not set up an equivalent system until 1979) and seemingly a triumph for the logic of representation. Committees could allow individual MPs to shine, to contribute meaningfully, and to work in an intimate environment across party lines and separated from the power of overall discipline in the House as a whole.

Yet as with many other parliamentary reforms, the bloom was soon off the rose. In 1971, C.E.S. Franks identified the dilemma of House of Commons committees that remains today: a struggle between *autonomy* and *relevance*.[55] Commons committees can work quite successfully across party lines and by consensus the more that the issue is unimportant and a low priority for the government and other parties. The likely impact and relevance of the committee's efforts is thus low, and its reports are likely to end up largely ignored and forgotten. In contrast, when the issue is important with potentially high impact, parties take a strong interest in the outcome and pressure committee members accordingly.

The dilemma reflects the duel between the logics of representation and governance. Committee MPs can work autonomously in certain areas, representing views and stakeholders, but issuing reports and resolutions of potentially little impact. To have impact and relevance, they must give themselves over to the logic of governance, going with the flow of government and opposition dynamics.

In addition to the regular standing committees, the House also has special committees, struck for a single purpose. Special committees are typically used for very prominent matters, such as the constitutional debates of the 1980s and 1990s, the Special Committee on Electoral Reform in 2016, and a Special Committee on Canada-China Relations in 2019. Special committees can be well-resourced and extensively followed in the media. Yet by definition they focus on *relevant* high-profile matters, meaning their autonomy from parties is typically low.

The standing committee system has been extensively adjusted since 1968. The configuration and names of standing committees have evolved over time, as has the number of members on committees. In 1982, committees were given the power to investigate issues of their choosing, without first needing a resolution from the House. In 1984, the system was split to produce a separate system of "legislative committees" to consider individual bills. This is the practice in the British House, allowing the regular permanent committees to focus on issues and investigations of their own choosing. But the system in Canada turned out to be excessively complex and was consolidated in 1994. In 1991, committees began to be televised. In 1994, the Standing Committee on Finance began a tradition of "pre-budget hearings" that has become institutionalized on the political calendar. A Government Operations and Estimates Committee was created in 2002 to specifically review government workings. In the 2000s, a practice began of distributing some committee chairships to opposition MPs, in addition to the Public Accounts Committee, the chair of which has always been an opposition MP since 1957. Committees are modestly resourced with Library of Parliament researchers and sometimes have the opportunity to travel. But the core dilemma – autonomy or relevance – remains.

A chief vulnerability of committees is their membership, which is not fixed. Committee assignments are determined by party whips. While MPs are asked for their preferences, the sheer number means that many MPs are not assigned to their preferred committee – sometimes because there is no space, but sometimes because the party does not want them there. Assignments are typically shuffled between parliamentary sessions and completely overhauled after an election. Combined with the general phenomenon of MP turnover, this means that only a small number of MPs are likely to spend multiple years developing expertise on a single committee.

Furthermore, substitutions are allowed – meaning that parties can temporarily remove MPs from a committee hearing and replace them with others. While sometimes benign, this is blatantly used in high-profile hearings where parties substitute effective and highly loyal MPs to achieve the party's goals – sometimes known as "sending in the goon squad." For example, in March 2019 when the Standing Committee on Justice held hearings to investigate the resignation of Liberal cabinet minister Jody Wilson-Raybould, including listening to her damaging testimony, both the Conservatives and NDP used substitute MPs, as did the Liberals, all to manage a very high-profile situation embarrassing to the government. The appearance of "goon squad" substitute MPs is an excellent indicator that an issue has become relevant, at the expense of committee autonomy.

All committees have a chair, drawn from their membership. Chairs remain very much party MPs, but, like the Speaker of the House, do not normally vote, and their role requires a certain neutrality as they conduct proceedings and oversee committee administration and business, along with a steering committee of representatives of the other parties. As discussed in chapter 4, one challenge of chairships is where they fit on an MP's career ladder. Ambitious MPs may desire to be committee chairs as one step toward further office as a parliamentary secretary and minister. There is thus a powerful incentive to stay on the good side of party leaders and demonstrate one's loyalty, in hope of promotion.

Improving the appeal and quality of chairships is a common focus of parliamentary reformers. For reformers, the ideal committee chair is one who values the position as a career in itself, and is prepared to steer the committee in independent directions even if it means sacrificing further advancement. But such individuals are rare, and in any event the power of parties to appoint and remove committee members further curbs their growth. Having said this, many MPs turn out to be excellent chairs, carefully threading the needle between their partisan identities and the collective mission of the committee.

Despite their limitations and the dilemma between autonomy and relevance, committees are not ineffective. As with Parliament as a whole, their value and contribution can be subtle and nuanced, sometimes in frustratingly intangible ways. We can assess this through three committee functions: *policy-making, scrutiny,* and their role as a *public forum.*

Committees typically have a limited impact on *policy-making.* Yet their impact and added value is still more than in the House itself, as committees have the power to call witnesses and amend bills, and not simply debate them. In minority parliaments this is a potent power, as the government committee members cannot vote down proposed amendments or avoid unwanted witnesses and activities without help from other parties. Even in majority parliaments, committees are typically able to make some adjustments, though normally in uncontroversial areas. It is also common for governments themselves to introduce amendments at the committee stage, reacting to new thinking and new developments.

But any dreams that MPs may have about making committees a pivotal place for policy decisions are soon curtailed. Unfortunately this abrupt realization is sometimes also experienced by witnesses, particularly those less knowledgeable in the ways of Ottawa, who appear before committee hearings to plead their case on specific bills. By the time legislation reaches the committee stage, it has been almost wholly baked, with a long backstory within government. It is typically far too late in the process to make significant changes, unless the government is rethinking its own plan. Sadly this is not always recognized by witnesses and observers that approach committees and their members as autonomous decision-makers. Again, committees do have some agency and influence here, and outcomes are not as starkly predictable as regular debate in the House. But impact remains limited.

Committees can have a more substantive effect on the second function of *scrutiny*. While scrutiny in the House, especially Question Period, is inevitably short-term and sensational, committee scrutiny is more nuanced and typically less combative. The primary public business of committees is the hearing of witnesses, with individual questioning by each member. Ministers and public servants are regularly called as witnesses, allowing MPs to quiz them. The objective is not necessarily to change minds, but to hold individuals to account and make them explain and justify policies and actions. Furthermore, as with Question Period, one of the greatest impacts is behind the scenes – the *preparation* for scrutiny. Government officials scheduled for committee appearances spend considerable effort anticipating MP questions and ensuring they can respond effectively.

Some standing committees are primarily devoted to scrutiny rather than policy. The most prominent is the long-standing Public Accounts Committee (PAC or PACP), which has been chaired by a member of the opposition since 1957 to signal its special importance. The PAC is closely linked to the Auditor-General of Canada, with responsibility for reviewing Auditor-General reports and following up on identified issues. While the Government Operations and Estimates Committee now also has a strong scrutiny function, the PAC retains a long-standing pre-eminence, and is mirrored by counterparts in provincial legislatures. Canadian PACs even have their own association – the Canadian Council of Public Accounts Committees – which has no equivalent for any other standing committee portfolio.

But despite its unique status, the Public Accounts Committee is not always a desired spot for MPs. Like all committees, the PAC struggles with the dilemma between autonomy and relevance. Many of its inquiries and reports can be technical and of limited public interest, while more explosive issues naturally attract strong partisan lines and sometimes invite "goon squad" substitutions of other, more combative members. And as noted, scrutiny is often more about reviewing actions rather than changing minds, and is retroactive rather than future-focused. (We discuss scrutiny practices, the Auditor-General, and the financial cycle further in chapter 8.)

Most MPs prefer "policy" rather than "scrutiny" committees, where they feel they can have a more relevant impact on future events, and can point to specific and tangible accomplishments of interest to constituents and Canadians. But some MPs clearly do value the scrutiny role. For example, John Williams, a Reform/Conservative MP from 1993 to 2008 and a chartered accountant by profession, sat on the PAC continuously throughout his fifteen years as an MP and served three terms as chair from 1997 to 2006. Williams was a politically attuned chair who was highly effective, especially during the Liberal "sponsorship scandal" of the early 2000s, and continued to be active in public accountancy matters after leaving elected office. But MPs like Williams are exceptional in both their interest in the PAC and their effectiveness on it.

The third and most abstract function performed by committees is as a *public forum*. Committees provide a formal link between Parliament and the outside world. Unlike the House chamber, committees feature non-parliamentarians as witnesses, providing variety and a wider set of voices that link them to Canadians as a whole; committees can also travel, taking them outside the Parliament Hill bubble. Their inquiry function allows committees the ability to dig into and investigate issues in a way that the House cannot. Every MP on a committee receives regular opportunities to speak, far more than in the House, and opportunities are rotated fairly and equally. Finally, as instruments of Parliament, committees are automatically places of public attention. Their proceedings are broadcast and officially chronicled. They are supported, modestly, by the power and resources of the House of Commons bureaucracy and Library of Parliament. Even if peripheral to the grand operations of Parliament, anything a parliamentary committee and its members do is taken seriously and still automatically matters.

We saw above that committees have only limited impact in policy-making or scrutiny. Much of their influence is through this third function – the power to provide a forum for public attention and discussion. This can bridge the dilemma of autonomy versus relevance for committees. Even if wracked by partisanship with a predictable outcome, a committee hearing matters, because it has collective power to focus attention and discussion on a public issue.

While still partisan, committees allow backbench MPs to work on their own without being directly overshadowed by party leaders and ministers in the same room. They have more freedom in the choice of witnesses and the choice of questions. Similarly, if a committee chooses to investigate a matter of limited relevance or importance to government, the choice itself makes the matter slightly more relevant, because a House of Commons committee is now studying the matter. There are very few examples – perhaps none – of a committee report single-handedly changing public opinion or government policy on an issue. But there are many cases where committee reports have been part of a larger and broader influx of public discussion that ultimately led to change.

Still, the public forum function is abstract, indirect, and a collective rather than individual phenomenon. Unsurprisingly, individual MPs thirst for more direct and tangible committee impacts that satisfy their ambitions and can be shown off to voters. But like all aspects of Parliament, these are often elusive. Yet this is still the logic of representation at work. As publicly linked instruments run by backbenchers, committees can be powerful instruments of representation, providing a diversity of voices. But this is divorced from actual decision-making, which remains the purview of the logic of governance.

CONCLUSION

Parliamentary procedure and processes are very intricate. But the overall themes are clear and enduring. Players play their roles in the game, driven by the logics of both governance and representation. Action provokes reaction, and the system constantly adapts, evolves, and resets, as government and opposition seek to outwit each other. MPs struggle to find autonomous roles, while parties attempt to keep a rein on them. This chapter has barely scratched the surface of the full extent of parliamentary procedure and processes. But regardless of the intricacies, what really matters is the overall game, which never ends.

CHAPTER SIX

Diversity

For much of its history, the Canadian Parliament was almost exclusively a place of white men, not only in its membership but in its structure, design, and assumptions. The institution and its predecessors arose in an era of colonialism and deep racism, when women were excluded from public life, as were people with disabilities, and homosexuality was illegal. The story of the twentieth century was the slow growth of a greater diversity of parliamentarians. This continues, but the story of the twenty-first century is also about the (also slow) adaptation and change of the institution itself.

Issues of gender, race, and other dimensions of diversity have already been raised at several points in this book. However, this chapter focuses directly on the experiences of specific equity-seeking groups in Parliament – Indigenous people, persons with disabilities, LGBT people, women, and racialized Canadians.

Hannah Pitkin's categories of symbolic, descriptive, and substantive representation will guide our discussion.[1] *Symbolic* representation emphasizes representatives whose very presence carries great meaning and significance – such as the "first" person elected from a previously unrepresented group. *Descriptive* representation refers to representatives whose qualities (i.e., "description") reflect the people that they represent, ideally as closely as possible. Thus, an ideal Parliament from a descriptive representation viewpoint would have equal numbers of men and women, along with other genders, reflecting their proportions in the general population. Finally, *substantive* representation focuses on the substance and actions of representatives as they correspond to a group's needs and issues – less about numbers and more about actions.

These categories help us sort out different dimensions of representation and diversity. Discussion about diversity and representation in Parliament may focus on the *descriptive* aspect of increasing the numbers of women or other groups elected into the House of Commons and appointed to the Senate. At other times it reflects on the *substantive* aspect: what they do once they get there, in a system dominated by political parties and the competing logics. There is also powerful *symbolism* in "firsts" that allow Canadians to see "someone like me" in Parliament, separate from actual laws and policies stemming from it.

And yet, few or no MPs care to be defined solely by their gender, race, disability, or other personal characteristics, even if these are crucial to their self-identity, daily life, and their political values and activities. It can be a challenge for many parliamentarians to both have their diverse identities respected and accommodated, and yet not be framed and marginalized as "the" MP from an underrepresented group. Furthermore, individuals will differ in their priorities, values, and what they feel a group's interests actually are.

All these ideas are primarily rooted in the logic of representation. They prioritize the importance of seeing a diversity of voices in Parliament, the inclusion of previously excluded perspectives, and the power of having a seat at the table. But they must also grapple with the logic of governance in which decisions are made in a system dominated by political parties, where the overriding identities are simply "government" and "opposition."

Earlier chapters have shown how many or most MPs, including many white men, struggle with reconciling the two logics and finding their place in Parliament. This struggle is even greater for MPs not from the historically dominant group. They may ask not only what their role is as a generic MP, but also specifically as a member of an underrepresented and equity-seeking group. This dilemma can increase even further for individuals with intersectional identities, such as racialized women.

How can parliamentarians from equity-seeking groups approach the paradox of Parliament? How can they reconcile the logic of representation, especially representation of their group(s), with the reality of the logic of governance and its pressure to compromise and stick with the party? To what extent can they challenge the system and the relationship between the two logics entirely – when many other reformers from more privileged groups have already tried?

Over time, researchers have broadened their focus from electing diverse people into Parliament to analysing the institution itself and examining how Parliament itself is not neutral terrain. Its physical layout, its ways of doing business, its culture, its schedule, and the lifestyles of MPs are increasingly being questioned and interrogated.

Women MPs have spoken out against the sexist and sometimes hostile and toxic environment of Parliament and systemic issues like barriers to child care and maternity leave. Racialized MPs similarly have spoken out about racism and micro-aggressions in parliamentary life. Indigenous MPs are highly conscious of the colonial foundations and assumptions of the institution. MPs with physical disabilities are acutely aware of the physical limits and barriers of the parliamentary precinct and other spaces in public life; attention is slowly being paid to MPs with other types of disabilities. While Senate membership is changing more rapidly than the House, many of the same systemic issues remain. And all this confronts the question of whether the logic of governance is itself neutral or is too rooted in a patriarchal and colonial environment that prioritizes competition and adversity over cooperation and consensus.

In this chapter, I will focus on the experiences in Parliament of five equity-seeking groups: Indigenous people, persons with disabilities, LGBT people, women, and racialized Canadians, with attention to intersectional identities as well. (No federal parliamentarian in Canada has openly identified with a gender other than cisgendered men and women as of the time of writing, though it is likely that gender diversity will become an additional important aspect in the future.) I will look mainly at experiences in the House of Commons, but also examine the Senate.

For each, I will use Pitkin's framework of symbolic, descriptive, and substantive representation to understand the complexities and different dimensions to diversity and Parliament. As noted, work in this area is heavily rooted in the logic of representation – bringing diverse voices to Parliament. But we will also consider the implications for the logic of governance, and how legislators from equity-seeking groups attempt to reconcile the two logics.

INDIGENOUS PARLIAMENTARIANS

As discussed in chapter 2, the relationship between Indigenous peoples and Parliament is complex, especially for First Nations (individuals holding status under the *Indian Act*). For most of Canadian history the relationship was non-existent. First Nations people were denied the right to vote in Canadian elections until 1960 unless they surrendered their status under the *Indian Act* in the process known as enfranchisement. Inuit were also denied the vote until 1950. Few voluntarily chose enfranchisement, but some, especially individuals who had gained educational and professional credentials, were *involuntarily* enfranchised. This created a regrettable direct association between voting and assimilation of Indigenous people. Furthermore, most First Nations espouse a nation-to-nation relationship with the Crown, separate from Parliament and the Government of Canada. Consequently, some First Nations people will not vote in Canadian elections at all on principle, much less run for office. Many or most First Nations, along with Inuit and Métis, see Parliament as a colonial and discriminatory institution that lacks legitimacy and a positive history.

In chapter 2 I quoted Len Marchand, the first First Nations MP, elected in 1968, who wrote that his first speech in the House "was the first time, in all the centuries since the Europeans had begun arriving in what would one day become the Dominion of Canada, that any of us, the original inhabitants, had had the right to stand up in the centre of government and speak."[2] In that speech, Marchand went on to say, using terminology of the era:

> It is important to the Indian people to know that one of us can become a member. It is important for the younger Indians who are in school and at university to know that, with reasonable hope, they can aspire to become whatever they wish to become and are capable of becoming. It is important for all Canada to know that this is not a land of bigotry and prejudice.[3]

This is an example of *symbolic representation* of which Marchand and others were well aware – the symbolism to both First Nations and non-First Nations of an Indigenous member of the House of Commons; "that one of us can become a member."

Marchand was followed, very slowly, by more Indigenous MPs. Parliamentary records[4] indicate that as of 2022, forty-nine MPs have been Indigenous – nineteen First Nations MPs, eight Inuit MPs, and twenty-two Métis MPs, including Louis Riel and two other Métis MPs elected in the nineteenth century.[5] The first Inuit MP was Peter Ittinauar in 1979; the first First Nations woman MP was Ethel Blondin-Andrew, elected in 1993; and the first Inuit woman MP was Nancy Keretak-Lindell in 1999. Only one self-identifying Métis woman has been elected – Shelly Glover in 2008. While overall progress has been slow, Indigenous representation increased in the 2010s. In 2015 eleven Indigenous MPs were elected, by far the largest ever number at the time; ten were elected in the 2019 election, followed by twelve in 2021, comprising 3.5 per cent of the total House.[6] This remains below their proportion in the Canadian population (5 per cent in the 2021 census),[7] an important dimension of *descriptive representation*.

The experiences of Indigenous MPs have been mixed, and the diversity of individuals and community backgrounds limits our ability to generalize too far. But many report feeling they did not belong in Parliament.

One of the most high-profile Indigenous MPs in recent times was Jody Wilson-Raybould, elected in 2015 and immediately appointed Minister of Justice. In 2019 Wilson-Raybould resigned from the cabinet and was later expelled from the Liberal caucus over her refusal to grant the prime minister's request for a deferred prosecution agreement in the SNC-Lavalin affair. She was then elected as an independent MP in the 2019 election. Wilson-Raybould was both an Indigenous MP and an Indigenous cabinet minister, and she writes in her book *"Indian" in the Cabinet* that "[m]y 'experience' was so out of the norm for Ottawa that it needed to be exiled, pushed back to the margins – to which Indigenous peoples, people of colour, and women have long been relegated in this country."[8] Robert Falcon-Ouellette, another Liberal MP elected in 2015, writes: "It is hard to be an MP and it is particularly hard to be an Indigenous MP. There are great expectations placed on your shoulders and you are placed within a large institution which has its own worldview. It can consume you."⁹ And Mumilaaq Qaqqaq, an Inuk New Democrat MP elected in 2019, said in a poignant and disturbing farewell speech in the House:

> I have never felt safe or protected in my position, especially within the House of Commons, often having pep talks with myself in the elevator or taking a moment in the bathroom stall to maintain my composure. When I walk through these doors not only am I reminded of the clear colonial house on fire I am willingly walking into, I am already in survival mode. Since being elected, I expect to be stopped by security at my workplace. I have had security jog after me down hallways, nearly put their hands on me and racially profile me as a member of Parliament. I know what to do in these situations. My life in Canada, and especially through this experience, has taught me many things. As a brown woman, I do not move too quickly or suddenly, do not raise my voice, do not make a scene, maintain eye contact and do not hide my hands.[10]

This feeling of an institution not made for them and unaccustomed to people like them recurs for others later in this chapter.

What about *substantive representation*? Michael Morden finds that Indigenous MPs are "massively overrepresented in parliamentary advocacy on Indigenous issues," such as by asking questions during Question Period on Indigenous topics – that is, Indigenous MPs are far more likely to raise and discuss Indigenous issues than non-Indigenous MPs.[11] Morden notes, however, that "this could simply be an indication that Indigenous MPs are deployed strategically by their leaders, as the most effective advocates on these issues." In other words, given the overall power of parties to direct parliamentary proceedings including Question Period, it is not clear how much the presence of specifically Indigenous MPs leads to greater discussion of Indigenous issues. But we can assume a connection; more Indigenous MPs likely means more attention to Indigenous issues. Indigenous MPs have also attempted to influence the workings of Parliament itself. For example, in 2017 Robert Falcon-Ouellette spoke in Cree in the House of Commons despite rules that only French or English could be used; while it was not the first time an Indigenous language had been spoken in the House, Falcon-Ouellette's actions led to changes in the Standing Orders to accommodate Indigenous languages.[12]

As with any group of representatives, there can be differences between Indigenous individuals in political styles and tactics. Len Marchand, the first First Nations MP, writes in his memoirs about how as an MP he worked within the corridors of power to pursue Indigenous interests. Speaking of his role in a 1973 government decision to begin a modern treaty process, he writes: "I hadn't beaten any drums or chained myself to any public buildings. Instead, I had been a constant, quiet voice at the centre of power, and I had helped redirect that power onto a path that would at last bring my people justice."[13] Other more recent MPs may differ with Marchand's fundamental faith in the system, but this is a strong illustration of the diversity of views and opinions in how *substantive* representation is best accomplished.

Party may indeed be an important factor in how Indigenous people operate in the House of Commons. The vast majority of recent Indigenous MPs have been elected as Liberals, well above the overall proportion of Liberals in the House; the New Democrats have the second most Indigenous MPs, while only four Conservative First Nations MPs and one Conservative Inuit MP have been elected, the last in 2011. Morden's study primarily spanned the Harper Conservative years, when the Liberals and New Democrats were in opposition. But under the Justin Trudeau government, most Indigenous MPs were in the government ranks, possibly meaning less opportunity to freely raise issues in Parliament or elsewhere in public. It may be that Indigenous government MPs are able to pursue Indigenous goals more discreetly within the government caucus, like Marchand in earlier times, but as we have seen throughout this book, such influence is difficult to track.

Of the twenty-five Indigenous senators in Canadian history as of the time of writing, including three MPs who moved on to the Senate, ten were appointed since 2016 under the independent advisory board established by Justin Trudeau. Unlike MPs, these newer senators are not constrained by party and are potentially able to pursue objectives and priorities more freely, and may provide a distinctly different pattern from their predecessors. (I discuss the changing role of senators generally in the next chapter on the Senate.)

It is particularly difficult to generalize about the experience of Métis parliamentarians. While the above figures cover all self-identifying Métis in Parliament, the connection of their Métis identity to their parliamentary activities may vary. Longtime parliamentarian Gerry St. Germain is an example. Elected as a Progressive Conservative MP from 1983 to 1988, he returned as a senator from 1993 until 2012, switching his party allegiance to the Canadian Alliance (the renamed Reform Party) in 2000. Though of Métis ancestry, St. Germain was not originally known for strongly championing the rights of Indigenous nations, and in 2000 he joined the Canadian Alliance's opposition to the Nisga'a treaty, the first modern Indigenous treaty in Canada. In later years he became more involved in Indigenous-related matters and more openly discussed his own Métis identity.[14] In contrast to the variety of Métis experiences, every Inuit MP has been elected from Nunavut, the Northwest Territories (prior to the creation of Nunavut in 1999), or Labrador, inevitably meaning Inuit MPs pursue issues of strong interest to these heavily Inuit-populated areas.

In the past, consideration was given to setting aside special House of Commons seats for Indigenous peoples.[15] New Zealand has had such seats for Maori Indigenous peoples since 1867, dividing the country up into special electoral districts in which only Maori can vote. (Maori can alternatively choose to vote in New Zealand's regular electoral districts instead.) While recommended by a 1991 royal commission looking at Canadian political parties and elections, this has not been seriously pursued in recent years.[16] The unsuccessful Charlottetown Accord of 1992 included a provision for separate Indigenous members of the Senate with special voting rights over legislation affecting Indigenous peoples, and in 1996 the Royal Commission on Aboriginal Peoples recommended a "House of First Peoples" separate from the House of Commons and Senate with similar veto rights on Indigenous issues. But, notably, enthusiasm among Indigenous peoples themselves for these solutions has been mixed. This may indicate a wariness of parallel structures away from the political mainstream, and/or the larger ambivalence among Indigenous peoples toward the institutions of the Canadian state.

Overall, Indigenous peoples have a unique and complex relationship to Parliament, and for most of Canadian history there were very few Indigenous MPs and senators. Their numbers are now growing. But little research has yet been done to analyse and understand their specific experiences and impact in Parliament. And many of their experiences, in an institution that historically excluded them and was not built or designed for them, recur in the experiences of the other groups outlined below.

PEOPLE WITH DISABILITIES

There is also little research on parliamentarians with disabilities. One reason is because this is an exceptionally wide category, covering physical, mental, and intellectual disabilities. Some disabilities, especially mental and intellectual disabilities, may not be easily visible and individuals may not choose to disclose them.[17] We also know little about the history of parliamentarians with disabilities, though at least some war veterans with disabilities served in Parliament, such as Pierre Sévigny, an amputee who lost his leg in the Second World War and was elected to the House in 1958. It is likely that military service valorized certain types of disabilities, especially for men, while members of the general population with disabilities may not have received the same respect and opportunities. Some MPs may acquire disabilities while in office, such as former Bloc Québécois leader Lucien Bouchard, who lost a leg due to illness in 1994 while serving as Leader of the Official Opposition and continued in public life, later becoming premier of Quebec.

Regardless, people with disabilities are clearly underrepresented in Parliament. One study by Brynne Langford and Mario Levesque estimated that only about 1 per cent of *candidates* for legislative office across Canada (including provincially) were persons with disabilities, well below their proportion in the general population.[18] The number of candidates actually elected is likely even lower.

The *symbolic* power of electing MPs with disabilities is clear, especially for the rest of the population. As Langford and Levesque state, "a greater presence of persons with disabilities in elected office exposes their capabilities to society, which may work towards dispelling some of the stigma surrounding disability."[19] Stephen Fletcher, a quadriplegic MP who served from 2004 to 2015, affirms this:

> People often think if you're in a wheelchair there may be a cognitive problem. People will speak to you louder thinking for some reason that being in a wheelchair affects your hearing. Rather than combating these stereotypes one by one, I thought it best to demonstrate through action that, yes I can door-knock and do all the things that an MP needs to do and I can do it very well.[20]

Parliamentarians with mobility disabilities may face very practical and immediate obstacles of physical access. The Parliament buildings, while now undergoing modernization, are old and accessibility has often been limited.

Legislatures have usually been able, with effort and prompting, to *formally* accommodate legislators with disabilities. For example, Gary Malkowski, a deaf MPP elected in Ontario in 1990, was allowed to bring sign language interpreters onto the legislative floor so that he could follow debates.[21] However, as in many other areas of life, *informal* barriers and restrictions are still constant. Fletcher says, "I'm constantly invited to places for receptions or dinners that are not wheelchair accessible. I find it so rude."[22] However, this may at least raise further awareness. Kevin Murphy, a paraplegic Nova Scotia MLA, states:

> [S]ince I've been sitting around the government caucus table there have been more things happening with regard to people with disabilities, disability policy, the locations of meetings, accessibility of meeting places and accommodations because where I can't go in my wheelchair neither do my colleagues. My colleagues now approach their way of doing business a little bit differently because the level of awareness has increased.[23]

Persons with disabilities can also have a *substantive representation* role, though this is more clearly evident if they are promoted to cabinet. Cabinet ministers with disabilities may be assigned disability portfolios, such as Carla Qualtrough, a blind MP elected in 2015 who was named Minister of Sport and Persons With Disabilities and retained the latter portfolio through subsequent cabinet posts.

However, this risks being seen as tokenism and a belief that a person with one type of disability is an expert on all areas of disability. Fletcher reports that when he was Minister of State for Transport he was able to improve accessibility on ferries and trains. But he also says, "I declined an invitation to be the honorary chair of a standing committee on disability because I don't want to be 'the disability guy.' That's not what my constituents elected me for. They wanted me to focus on things around taxation, immigration and the economy."[24]

Parliamentarians with mental and intellectual disabilities are more difficult to identify. These categories cover a wide range, many of which carry continuing stigma. The last restrictions on voting by people with mental disabilities were only removed federally in 1993. And the line between mental *disabilities* and mental *health* and illness is also fuzzy – disabilities involve an ongoing, chronic condition, while mental health is a status that everyone possesses and that may rise and fall over time, though the relationship and symptoms may overlap. A study of British MPs estimated that MPs were more likely to have mental health problems than the general population, likely linked to the pressures and stress of the job, but it did not specifically identify MPs with mental *disabilities*.[25]

Parliamentarians are often only likely to speak about mental disabilities or mental illness after they have faced a crisis, sometimes involving inappropriate behaviour. Very few speak routinely and openly about disabilities, even relatively common intellectual disabilities such as dyslexia. However there are exceptions, such as former Senator Roméo Dallaire, who was very open about his post-traumatic stress disorder stemming from his military service in Rwanda during the genocide of 1994, both prior to and after his appointment to the Senate in 2005.

Overall, parliamentarians with disabilities are a very diverse group. They appear underrepresented from a descriptive standpoint, though the continuing stigma around mental disabilities in particular makes it difficult to estimate this dimension. But they can be powerful vehicles of both symbolic and substantive representation. Parliamentarians with physical disabilities, especially affecting mobility, can be especially important catalysts for both social awareness and explicit policy change.

LGBT PERSONS

As of 2021, nineteen out LGBT MPs and two senators have served in Parliament.[26] Less known are how many closeted LGBT individuals have also served throughout Canadian history, or are serving today, without publicly disclosing their sexual orientation. Research by Everitt and Camp finds that "whether a candidate is out during an election campaign or not has a substantial negative impact on his or her chance of electoral success, particularly for first-time candidates."[27] Thus for many LGBT politicians, being open about their sexual orientation may reduce their chances of being elected or re-elected, and they face a difficult choice.

The first three open LGBT MPs only revealed their sexual orientation after they had been elected. The first was Svend Robinson. Elected as a New Democrat MP from British Columbia in 1979, he disclosed his sexual orientation as a gay man only in his third parliamentary term, in 1988. The next out politician in 1994 was Réal Ménard, a Bloc Québécois MP elected in 1993. The first lesbian to come out in the Parliament of Canada was Libby Davies, another BC New Democrat, elected in 1997. In 2001, speaking to Robinson's private members' bill to legalize same-sex marriage, Davies mentioned, "almost by accident," that she was in a same-sex relationship.[28] In 2004 Bill Siksay, a gay man, became the first person to be initially elected to the House as an open LGBT person.

LGBT parliamentarians are again powerful instruments of *symbolic representation*, especially when they choose to come out publicly. Robinson's coming out in 1988 made national news, in an era when few LGBT people lived fully out and homophobic comments were widespread in public life. Writing about her own coming out in 2001, Libby Davies notes, "the experience gave me a greater appreciation for what people face when they come out, especially in places where acceptance is difficult, isolated, and even violent. I was a well-established person, a member of Parliament, and I had support from family and friends, but even so, the whole process was challenging and nerve-racking."[29]

They are also instruments of *substantive representation*. Svend Robinson in particular was a skilled parliamentarian and spent twenty-five years in the House of Commons, retiring in 2004. His biographer asserts that "Robinson became the first real link between the unassailable halls of power and gay and lesbian activists in the streets outside.... Acting as something of a broker, Robinson helped to create a network of like-minded gay- and lesbian-rights activists who were seeking to lobby the government. He not only voiced their concerns in the House, but also brought activists to Ottawa so they could provide that voice themselves."[30] And "[w]hen an issue affecting gay and lesbian Canadians hit the news, reporters consistently turned to Robinson for his opinion, and that gave him influence."[31]

Issues and public attitudes have evolved since Robinson's time. Not only are there more open LGBT politicians, but there is a greater acceptance of sexual diversity in Canadian society, including among other parliamentarians. While Robinson laboured alone or with just a few allies, even within his own caucus, many MPs today are – at least in principle – willing to support LGBT rights and to work to promote LGBT issues. However, Manon Tremblay argues for the continuing importance of open LGBT politicians. "Although the support of straight allies is indispensable, only out (and proud) lesbian and gay politicians can descriptively and symbolically represent LGBTQ people, and in terms of substantive representation, only they have the legitimacy to perform a politics of emotion with regard to LGBTQ representation."[32] By politics of emotion, Tremblay means a "capital of legitimacy ... brought by life experiences of marginalization and exclusion."[33]

Most LGBT parliamentarians have been gay white men, with professional-managerial backgrounds very similar to most parliamentarians. Lesbians are less prevalent, just as women are significantly underrepresented in the House (though no longer the Senate). Racialized LGBT MPs and senators are even more rare, and Blake Desjarlais became the first Indigenous queer MP elected, in 2021. Thus gender and racial patterns of underrepresentation are perpetuated within the LGBT community of legislators. Overall, sexual orientation is a changing dimension of parliamentary diversity, with probably the sharpest jump from open discrimination to relative acceptance in recent decades. But this dimension may also replicate other hierarchical patterns and power structures.

WOMEN IN PARLIAMENT

For Parliament's first half-century, women could not even vote in elections, much less stand as candidates. The expansion of the voting franchise to most women in 1917 and 1918 was followed by the first woman MP, Agnes MacPhail, in 1921. The first woman senator was appointed in 1930 after the *Persons* case, discussed below. But further representation was slow. Over the next half century there were never more than five women MPs at a single time. As recently as 1968, while momentous social changes were happening in Canada and internationally and Pierre Trudeau was elected in the wave known as "Trudeaumania," only a single woman was elected to the House of Commons. Flora MacDonald, elected in 1972, writes that "[t]he fact that I was the only woman among the 107 Conservative MPs seems astonishing today."[34]

Early experiences of women in Parliament included unabashed sexism and an unwelcoming environment. When Ellen Fairclough first entered the House chamber after winning a 1950 by-election, she was greeted with an unsolicited kiss by a male MP.[35] Judy LaMarsh, elected in 1960, found there were "many amenities for males – a barbershop, a tailor, a masseur, a steam room, a shoe-shine parlour, and many washrooms – but neither hairdresser nor seamstress nor any other facilities designed" for women.[36] In 1972, Monique Bégin and another newly elected woman MP were prevented from entering the House chamber for the first time by a security guard who did not believe they were parliamentarians, and who tried to send them upstairs to the public galleries.[37] Margaret Mitchell, elected in 1979, writes, "I was shocked at the male-dominated culture" found in Parliament, and "a general air of male superiority dominated the halls of power."[38] Sheila Copps, elected in 1984, was the brunt of numerous sexist comments in the House chamber, including being called a "slut" and told to "quiet down, baby" by a senior cabinet minister. MP Barbara Greene was physically assaulted in the dimly lit parliamentary parking lot in 1989.[39]

Many women parliamentarians, both in the past and today, express discomfort with the traditionally adversarial nature of the House of Commons in particular. Libby Davies, the NDP House Leader from 2003 to 2011, writes:

> I watched many a time as other House leaders duked it out, shouting matches and all. It seemed to me a traditional male way of doing things, and I rejected it. The easiest thing in the world is to sink to that level. Soon enough there's no room to maneuver. It fascinated and disappointed me that hurling insults and making ridiculous challenges, like boys in a sandbox, was considered a mature way of resolving differences. But on Parliament Hill it was the big boys who did it all the time. And the nastier they were, the higher opinion they usually had of themselves.[40]

Some women parliamentarians do appear comfortable in the aggressive parliamentary environment. But most (along with some men) express interest in approaching politics in a more collaborative manner. This can be challenging in practice, as party identities continually exert control. And regardless, women will be *framed* differently. As Sylvia Bashevkin writes, there are many reminders that suggest "female tones don't belong in the dark, woody, masculine recesses of Parliament."[41] Bashevkin identifies how the tone and modulation of women's voices are discussed and sorted either into soft-spoken "non-entities" or conversely "accused of being too 'in your face.'"[42] In Bashevkin's words, "women plus power equals discomfort."[43]

A distinction can be made between *women's* representation and specifically *feminist* representation. Some women parliamentarians do not identify as feminist and/or may disagree on the definition of "feminism," especially in the Conservative Party on issues like abortion rights. This can create conflict, such as in 2017 when Rachael Harder, an anti-abortion Conservative MP, was named chair of the Standing Committee on the Status of Women.

Yet many women's experiences of sexism and harassment are similar regardless of their partisan or feminist positioning. In 2016,

Harder's Conservative colleague Michelle Rempel wrote a blistering attack on the sexist atmosphere of the House of Commons:

> The everyday sexism I face involves confronting the "bitch" epithet when I don't automatically comply with someone's request or capitulate on my position on an issue, confronting assumptions that I have gotten to my station in life by (insert your choice of sexual act) with (insert your choice of man in position of authority), enduring speculation and value judgements about my fertility, and responding to commentary that links my appearance to my competency. It involves my ass being occasionally grabbed as a way to shock me into submission. It involves tokenism. It involves sometimes being written off as not serious when I've clearly proven I am.[44]

Rempel's words draw our attention to the overall experience of women in an institution historically and still dominated by men, regardless of their legislative and policy objectives. They illustrate the growing focus not just on electing and appointing more women and pursuing feminist policy goals, but confronting the institution's foundations and culture as a whole.

To analyse the experience of women in Parliament more fully, we will look first at women in the Senate and then in the House of Commons.

Women in the Senate

The representation of women in the Senate has a dramatic beginning, in the famous *Persons* case. For reasons unfathomable today, the *British North America Act*'s wording that "qualified persons" could be appointed to the Senate was interpreted as applying only to men. Five women, known as the "Famous Five," challenged this in court, leading eventually to the 1929 ruling that women were indeed "persons" and could sit in the Senate. This led to the first appointment of a woman senator, Cairine Wilson, in 1930.

The number of women senators grew very slowly at first, similar to the House of Commons. But in more recent decades, trends in the two chambers have diverged. The growth of women senators was relatively steady from the 1970s all the way to 2016. It then rapidly increased with the change to an independent Senate appointment process, reaching an equal number of men and women in late 2020, though later slipping back to 49 per cent women. In contrast, as we will see below, the House of Commons has seen both rises and plateaus – notably the period from 1997 to 2011 when the proportion of women MPs barely budged from one-fifth – and it remains well below the near-parity in the Senate.

An obvious reason for the contrast is that senators are appointed rather than elected, allowing for a conscious effort to diversify appointments. Additionally, Senate appointments are permanent, leading to lower turnover and more opportunity to build on gains. It is thus useful to look not only at the numbers of women in the Senate, but the *appointment* patterns – and this tells a somewhat more up and down story. Research by Stephanie Mullen finds that up until Pierre Trudeau, every prime minister's Senate appointments were at least 90 per cent men (and, except for Louis St. Laurent, above 95 per cent). Since then, the proportion of women has risen, although not always consistently: 23 per cent of Senate appointments by Brian Mulroney (1984–93) were women, and 44 per cent of Jean Chrétien's (1993–2004), but only 35 per cent for Paul Martin (2004–6) and 31 per cent for Stephen Harper (2006–15).[45] Importantly, Mullen suggests that who was in charge of appointments in the PMO was a factor, with two women under Mulroney and Chrétien being particular champions of appointing more women.[46] (Canada's first woman prime minister, Kim Campbell, made no Senate appointments at all in her short time in power.)

The above focuses on women's *symbolic* and *descriptive* representation in the Senate. What about *substantive* representation – their actual impact? The experiences of women senators have been less documented than women MPs, and are filtered by the general ambiguity of the Senate as an institution, as we explore further in the next chapter. When the basic legitimacy and extent of senators' powers are unclear, it is even more difficult for women senators to establish their roles and seek an impact.

But there are parallels between the Senate's perceived role as a more reflective and less acrimonious body and the documented preference of many women for a more collaborative and less confrontational style of politics. Even before the independent appointment process of

2016, there was evidence that women senators were more able to work across party lines, independent of party.

One of the most famous instances was in 1991, when women senators from both the Liberal and Progressive Conservative parties worked to defeat the PC government's new abortion criminalization legislation that had been passed by the House of Commons. No government has since tried to criminalize abortion. More recently, Elizabeth McCallion suggests that the increase in independent senators in the post-2016 Senate has made it easier for women to cooperate and work together on issues of interest.[47] McCallion identifies removal of gender discrimination in the *Indian Act* and changes to divorce legislation as two high-profile examples of collaboration among women senators in the post-2016 Senate.[48]

Yet the Senate and its potential for women's representation is by no means perfect. Writing in 2013, Mullen noted that while the ratio of women in the Senate was growing (then at 36 per cent), the distribution among committees was varied and comparatively lower among "traditionally male-dominated committees" such as Banking, Trade, and Commerce.[49] It is likely that women senators still labour at a disadvantage in an institution historically built for men. These deep-set barriers and norms are further explored in the next section on women in the House of Commons.

Women in the House

Following the very low numbers up to 1968, the 1970s to 1990s saw a steady rise in women MPs. After the 1972 election, 2 per cent of MPs were women; in 1980, 5 per cent were women; in 1984, 10 per cent; and in 1993, 18 per cent. But this development stalled after the 1997 election, when 21 per cent of elected MPs were women. For the next four elections – 2000 to 2008 – the ratio barely moved at just over one-fifth of the House. It only began to rise again in 2011, with 25 per cent women elected that year, 26 per cent in 2015, 29 per cent in 2019, and 30 per cent in 2021 (see figure 6.1).

The small number and shared experiences of women MPs in the 1970s and 1980s likely contributed to more cross-party solidarity than in more recent times. In 1990, women MPs and senators formed the

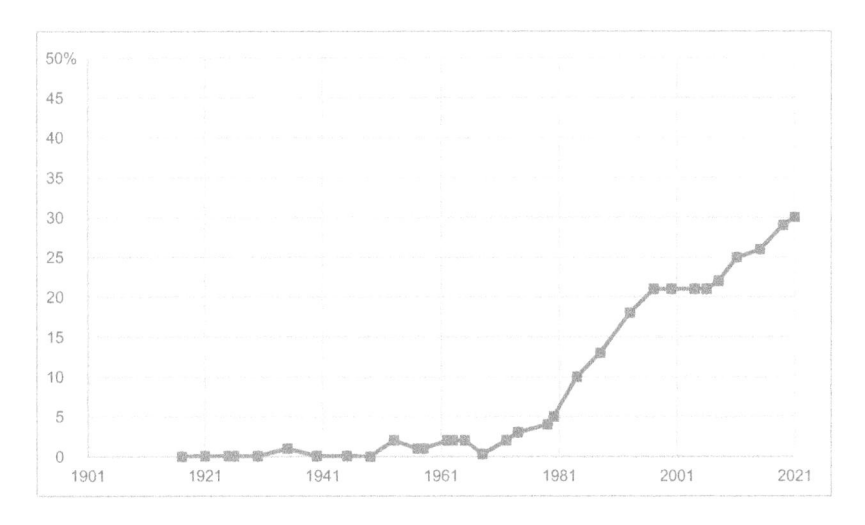

Figure 6.1 Proportion of women members of the House of Commons after each election since 1917, when women were first eligible to be elected

Association of Women Parliamentarians (AWP), whose purpose was not policy and legislative goals, but to address parliamentary culture itself. According to Lisa Young, "the AWP was created in response to negative aspects of parliamentary life experienced by women, including the chauvinism of some of their male colleagues ... this chauvinism bred a sense of solidarity across party lines."[50] Jackie Steele adds that the AWP was created "to discuss women's common experiences, including difficulties in combining family and political life. They managed to make the parliamentary timetable more accommodating for people with family responsibilities by having more frequent week-long breaks and arranging the House to rise in the third week of December. In addition, they pursued basic changes such as having more lights in the parking lot, and prompted a House committee to look at creating sanctions against sexist and racist remarks in the House."[51]

However, the AWP went defunct after the 1993 election, in which the Progressive Conservative and New Democratic parties were nearly obliterated, and MPs in the Bloc Québécois and newly arrived Reform

Party showed less interest. In a 1994 speech to the House on International Women's Day, March 8, Reform MP Deborah Grey stated, "Let us not continue to make these ridiculous delineations between women's issues and men's issues." She went on to say:

> We believe that our party's position is quite different from the traditional parties' positions in that we do not maintain a separate organization for women members. In the Reform Party women are dedicated to the same goals as men. These goals are fiscal, political and constitutional reform. I do not think there are any lines to be drawn between women and men when we look at the things that are happening across the country.[52]

Given this lack of cross-party interest, women in the Liberal Party instead formed their own Liberal Women's Caucus that carried on many of the same conversations, but within Liberal-only structures.

The demise of the AWP illustrates the challenge of addressing the sexist culture of Parliament amid partisan and ideological differences. This remains a difficulty today. As seen above, Conservative women like Michelle Rempel (later Michelle Rempel Garner) report a culture of sexism and sexual harassment, similar to women in other parties. Yet they may not necessarily embrace the full range of policy goals shared by women in other parties, leading to estrangement among women parliamentarians. We return to this point below.

After the steady rise from the 1970s to the early 1990s, the late 1990s and early 2000s were characterized by a discouraging plateau of women's representation in the House. From 1997 to 2011, representation in the House of Commons barely budged at one-fifth of the chamber. While women did consolidate gains in this era, such as increased cabinet appointments and the 2004 establishment of the Standing Committee on the Status of Women, there was a clear lack of momentum compared to the earlier era. Women MPs largely worked within their own party circles rather than the earlier era of modest cross-party cooperation.

The plateau finally ended with the 2011 election of women as 25 per cent of the House of Commons. This increase was driven by the surge of the NDP in Quebec, unexpectedly winning 59 seats, including many won by women. This surge, along with broader attention to sexism in Canadian society, brought a new dynamic to the House and a new focus on issues facing women MPs. Two areas particularly arose: women as mothers, and sexual harassment.

Chapter 4 discussed the general challenge for MPs as parents, and especially the impact of political life and travel on families. However, women MPs have long experienced distinct systemic issues. Long-established parliamentary structures and rules, even if not deliberately gendered, have clearly had unequal impacts that treated MPs who were also mothers differently.

One example arose in 2012, when NDP MP Sana Hassainia attempted to take her infant child into the House chamber in order to participate in a vote. Confusion arose, since rules state that unauthorized persons are not permitted in the chamber (although another MP, Michelle Dockrill, had brought her own newborn for a vote in 1998). The rules were eventually changed to clarify that MPs were permitted to bring in small children. Improvements have been made to make other everyday aspects of the House more family-friendly, from improved child care to high chairs available in the parliamentary dining room like most restaurants.[53]

The concept of parental leave for MPs was a more difficult issue. For most of parliamentary history there was no provision for MPs to take maternity or parental leave. For some, the entire idea of parental leave from one's job made no sense for MPs, given that Parliament is an "employer" in only a loose sense and MPs are not traditional employees. Instead, MPs are elected by their constituency and ultimately accountable to those voters.

On the other hand, the concept of "leave" already existed as MPs were already eligible for short-term sick leave in case of illness – in which case, informal arrangements might be made for other MPs to fulfil any necessary constituency duties. Consequently in 2019, provisions for up to one year of parental leave were established, relieving MPs of all duties on Parliament Hill, though leaving them responsible for arranging coverage of constituency affairs. However, as of 2022 no MPs appear to have taken advantage of this policy. (In 2018 Karina Gould took parental leave from her position as Minister of Democratic Institutions, but this was an unofficial leave prior to the policy for MPs.[54])

Another – dark – dimension of parliamentary life came to the forefront in 2014, when two women NDP MPs reported non-consensual sexual incidents involving two Liberal men MPs.[55] This shed public light on sexism, sexual harassment, and sexual assault on Parliament Hill, for both MPs and staff. Accelerated by broader cultural changes including the #MeToo movement, women began to speak up more about their experiences, like Michelle Rempel's statement in 2016.

The parliamentary atmosphere can be a toxic place that breeds conditions for sexual violence. The intense, deeply competitive atmosphere creates high pressure on individuals to succeed and to please others, regardless of their own instincts and preferences. The political lifestyle, with travel, irregular hours, and separation from family and support circles, along with extensive social events often fueled by alcohol, is disruptive for healthy personal routines. Hierarchy and power are everywhere, as are pressures and insecurities for individuals, at every rung of the ladder. All this increases the vulnerability of victims and the likelihood of predatory and inappropriate behaviour.

Harassment both external and internal to Parliament is a problem. In December 2017, a poll of women MPs found 58 per cent reported they "had personally been the target of one or more forms of sexual misconduct while in office, including inappropriate or unwanted remarks, gestures or text messages of a sexual nature," including three MPs who said they had been the victims of sexual assault.[56] Increasing attention was paid to the treatment of women politicians on social media, which includes sexist comments and threats of sexual violence. Women MPs used their power to shed light not only on their own experiences but on that of staff. New Democrat MP Lauren Liu said in 2017 that "[s]exual harassment, certainly, is almost a daily occurrence.... Almost every single young woman who works on the Hill experiences it."[57]

Parliament struggled to respond as an institution to sexual harassment within itself. Both the House of Commons and the Senate updated their policies in relation to harassment of staff. In the 43rd Parliament from 2015 to 2019, several male MPs were disciplined or expelled from their caucuses after incidents of sexual harassment of their staff, while two senators resigned their seats due to allegations of sexual misconduct. The House of Commons also instituted a harassment policy for incidents *between* MPs, following the 2014 incidents.

Political parties play a mixed role here. As we have repeatedly seen, parties are the dominant players in Parliament, and this means that they hold the strongest overall power to sanction and discipline inappropriate actions – if they choose to do so. The MP-to-MP sexual harassment code vested primary responsibility for disciplining inappropriate actions in party whips who, as we have seen, act on behalf of party leaders and hold a great deal of power over MPs' political lives. Thus, for example, when the two Liberal men MPs were accused of sexual harassment in 2014, then-Liberal leader Justin Trudeau expelled them from caucus, dooming their chances of re-election.

However, objections immediately arose to the code because this responsibility was discretionary, leaving it up to the party hierarchy whether and how to respond.[58] This raised concerns about the vulnerability of victims, especially against perpetrators of high standing and importance in the party.

The loyalty bred in all political parties produces intense pressure not to rock the boat and complain at all. Party remains predominant, and "[t]he culture itself inhibits people from coming forward," said cabinet minister Patty Hajdu in 2018.[59] Raney and Collier critique the "self-regulation" approach as "likely to further reinforce men's institutional advantages over women, allowing (mostly men) to interpret the new rules in ways that will discourage complainants from coming forward and/or enforce discipline against their (mostly male) colleagues as they see fit."[60]

Overall, then, while a great deal of work continues on the priority of electing more women to the House of Commons and increasing the *descriptive representation* of women, more attention is being paid to Parliament Hill itself as an institution and workplace that is deeply gendered and even hostile to women. Important breakthroughs and reforms have taken place in recent years, but more work remains. In the next section, I focus more directly on women's specific activities as legislators and the dimension of *substantive representation*.

Women as Legislators

Analysing the substantive representation of women again puts us amid the central paradox of Parliament – the competition between the logics of representation and governance – and on a larger scale than previous groups discussed above. Is there a critical mass or tipping point at which women representing half the population will be in Parliament in sufficient numbers to effect transformative change? Or will women's issues always be inevitably caught up in the regular struggle between government and opposition that dominates parliamentary business? To what extent can women specifically represent women and women's issues amid the overall prevalence of party discipline?

Women face the common challenges faced by all MPs: multiple roles and competing demands on their time; limited opportunities to pursue individual policy agendas, especially introducing legislation; and a general shortage of legislative time and scrutiny tools amid the overwhelming mass of public business. Like all MPs, and senators as well, they must struggle to find policy openings and opportunities to pursue their goals.

They must also balance their party affiliation with other identities, and they do so in different ways. Some women are more comfortable with strict party discipline than others, and some outright embrace it. Sheila Copps was a prominent Liberal MP from 1984 to 2004, rising to serve as Deputy Prime Minister, and throughout her career strongly prized party loyalty. In 1986 she wrote a strong defence of placing the party first, and implicitly the logic of governance:

> [O]ne of the strongest features of a parliamentary system is party solidarity. If you really believe that your chosen political philosophy is the best vehicle for social change, then your first job is to make sure that your political philosophy and party prevail. Whatever the political philosophy of her choice, a woman in politics must be convinced that her party can best embody positive and social economic changes. In a sense, the vehicle for social change is the party, not the gender.[61]

Copps remained a deeply loyal Liberal partisan after leaving office, and in 2019 criticized Jody Wilson-Raybould for going public with her criticisms of the Trudeau government.[62] In contrast, other women decry the pressure on them to toe the party line[63] in all circumstances, especially on issues affecting women.

As we saw, the early period of cross-party cooperation between women MPs in the 1990s did not last. However, in 2018, a group of

MPs and senators formed the Association of Feminist Parliamentarians (AFP), drawing independent senators and members of all parties except the Conservatives.[64] As suggested by the name, the AFP represents a distinction between *women* parliamentarians and *feminist* parliamentarians. This highlights differences in women's identities and values (and sometimes contested definitions of "feminism"), and women in the Conservative Party do tend to be different from other parties in this regard. Women in the Liberal, New Democratic, Bloc Québécois, and Green parties all generally espouse reproductive rights and other gender and sexuality rights. This is often enforced by official party policies: Justin Trudeau ruled in 2014 that all future Liberal candidates needed to be pro-choice, and the New Democrats have gradually enforced pro-choice views among all their MPs as well. In contrast, the Conservatives have been reluctant to dictate party positions on these issues, given their significant number of social conservative MPs and supporters, including social conservative women.

How can women effect legislative change? International research on women's representation in the past has highlighted the importance of "critical mass" – that the descriptive representation of women would eventually reach a tipping point that would precipitate broad changes and breakthroughs in substantive representation and specifically feminist goals.[65] But more recent theories downplay this idea of a tipping point, and instead highlight the role of "critical actors" – individuals who by their actions or placement can precipitate change and feminist goals. This draws a stronger distinction between descriptive and substantive representation; increases in descriptive representation may or may not correlate with substantive representation and impact itself.

Erica Rayment finds evidence of critical actors in the Canadian Parliament: increases in the number of women elected "did not lead directly to increases in the number of speeches about women in parliamentary debate," and yet "spikes in the substantive representation of women occurred even when the share of women MPs held steady."[66] Rayment suggests that the impact of women and critical actors in the Canadian Parliament, at least for feminist policy objectives, is best seen in *resisting* attempts to roll back feminist gains. Rayment points to the blocking in the Senate of attempts to recriminalize abortion in 1991, mentioned above, and House of Commons resistance to cuts to women's programming in 2006 as examples when women parliamentarians worked as critical actors to resist change.[67]

Feminist institutionalist scholars have also examined the rules, processes, and structures of Parliament and how these affect opportunities for feminist success. The most prominent such institution in Canada is the Standing Committee on the Status of Women. This committee was established as a permanent standing committee in 2004; previously women's issues had been under various committees. Notably, a Sub-Committee on the Status of Women existed from 1989 to 1993 as part of the Standing Committee on Health and Welfare, Social Affairs, Seniors, and the Status of Women. This committee was highly active, especially on gun control and violence against women in the wake of the murder of fourteen women engineering students in Montreal in 1989.[68] Yet it did not continue as a regular part of the committee system.

The Standing Committee on the Status of Women has both emboldened and disappointed many feminists. While dedicated to women's issues, it remains first and foremost a standing committee of the House of Commons and so, like all committees, it is dominated by party. Joan Grace documents the first decade of the committee and notes in particular that while it "articulated a feminist voice," "its existence has not shifted the inequality regime within Parliament.... [I]t is, after all, a legislative committee which functions like all other committees situated within an established parliamentary system."[69] Grace further notes that gender analysis risks being isolated solely to the Status of Women committee, rather than being incorporated more broadly into all committee activities and deliberations, so that "substantive women's equality discussions are likely destined to remain in the gender-focused committee" rather than being mainstreamed more broadly.[70]

Much more research is needed to fully understand women's substantive representation, especially in the overall context of Parliament amid the competing logics of representation and governance. While we can track women's descriptive representation, including barriers and enablers to electing more women, it is more difficult to assess their effect in Parliament itself, given its overall complexities and paradoxes.

Perhaps most importantly, the overall gendered nature of Parliament is receiving attention, including the extent to which the institution itself perpetuates gender inequality and hostility.

RACE

There are both similarities and profound differences between the experiences of women parliamentarians and parliamentarians from racialized groups. Both have been continuously underrepresented in Parliament relative to their share of the general population. Both have experienced discrimination and prejudice – from voters, in their parties, and from fellow parliamentarians. Collectively, their presence challenges the long-standing institutional culture of Parliament as a place for white men. And for women from racial minority groups, many of these burdens are doubled. We saw earlier how Parliament was constructed as a gendered institution. Similarly, racialized parliamentarians report feeling deeply uncomfortable with the setting and its norms; in the words of Celina Caesar-Chavannes, a Black Liberal MP from 2015 to 2019, "navigating spaces that are not accustomed to including people like me."[71] There are also parallels with the experiences of Indigenous parliamentarians.

Yet there are also important differences. One is the changing and complex nature of race in Canada. The racial origins of Canadians are highly diverse, and the very boundaries and meaning of "race" are socially constructed – thus I refer to "racialized" Canadians. It is also essential to distinguish between different racialized groups and their different experiences, and many Canadians have diverse racial backgrounds with more than one heritage; this again complicates the discussion. Racial representation is also a moving benchmark. While parity with men is a clear benchmark for women, the proportion of racialized Canadians in the general population has continually risen over time, and so their proportion in legislatures must also rise simply to keep up.

Notwithstanding the more pervasive forms of prejudice associated with visible forms of difference, a partial link exists between current discussions about racialized MPs and earlier experiences of "ethnic" MPs from European communities outside the dominant British group. In the twentieth century, communities such as Ukrainian Canadians, Italian Canadians, Jewish Canadians, and others sought political representation in a system that did not always seem open to them. These communities have their own stories of prejudice and discrimination. Early "first" representatives from these communities had significant symbolic importance, and their efforts led to further opening up of opportunities to engage in public life and Canadian society. However, we will focus here on the experiences of non-white racialized Canadians. This is not meant to dismiss the experiences of prejudice and discrimination against earlier waves of "ethnic" Canadians, but to focus on the realities of race and parliamentary representation today.

Symbolic

Chapter 4 briefly discussed patterns of ethnic and racial representation including a number of "first" representatives from various groups. As with other groups, there is some evidence that "first" racialized representatives can carry tremendous symbolic power as examples of success and breaking through barriers. Lincoln Alexander, Canada's first Black MP, elected in 1968, wrote in his memoirs that "[w]hen I talk to children in schools, I ask them to repeat after me: 'Lincoln Alexander. He did it. I can. I will.'"[72]

However, this phenomenon is difficult to measure and assess, and easy to overestimate and exaggerate. Alexander also writes, "I soon grew weary of being referred to in the press as the 'black MP.'"[73] Again as with other groups, racialized MPs may have a symbolic power ascribed to them whether they wish it or not. Symbolic power may be ascribed by non-racialized individuals to non-white MPs as examples of "successful diversity" or that "race no longer matters," in a way that actually draws more attention to race; as Laura Jean Kwak phrases it in a study of Douglas Jung, a Chinese-Canadian and Canada's first racialized MP in 1957, "paradoxically raced in the name of racelessness."[74]

Symbolic representative power is thus complex for racialized MPs, especially as they are conscious that in the Canadian parliamentary system they are foremost representatives of their specific electoral district. Lincoln Alexander says, "I told the reporters to call me the MP ready to speak for anyone in my region who suffers from prejudice or some other injustice."[75] Ruby Dhalla, a Liberal MP from 2004 to 2011, said:

> When ... people from the South Asian community or the Italian community get elected, you are an inspiration or role model to others, or those particular communities. But what's really

important is that, first and foremost, we have to remember we are all Canadians and the issues of health care and the issues of child care, the issues of seniors are important to every Canadian across the country regardless of what ethnic background you are from.[76]

Racialized MPs generally resist being seen as "the" spokesperson for their racial community, expected to be able to automatically speak for the community with the definitive word on an issue. Symbolic representation is thus important to some racialized MPs, but it can be overstated.

Descriptive

It is important to track descriptive numbers of racialized parliamentarians and compare this to the general population. But there are methodological challenges. While parliamentary records have long recorded the self-identified gender of parliamentarians and have more recently attempted to identify all Indigenous MPs and senators, there is no similar record of ethnic or racial origins of parliamentarians. Tracking this accurately can be challenging, especially for individuals of more than one racial background, and sensitive, as it ultimately depends on how each person self-identifies. Studies tracking racial representation in Parliament have thus relied on gathering available public information (ideally self-identifying statements by the parliamentarians themselves) to identify and classify individuals' racial background. These methodological challenges mean that studies will sometimes show minor discrepancies on the exact number of racialized MPs or senators.

The most meticulous multi-year studies using consistent criteria have been performed by Jerome Black and his colleagues since 1993 for the House of Commons. According to their figures, the number of racialized MPs rose from 4.4 per cent of the House in 1993 to 15.7 per cent in 2021. But this increase must be viewed in context since, as noted above, the benchmark is constantly moving, reflecting changes in the Canadian population. In 1993, 9 per cent of Canadians were classified under the official Statistics Canada term of "visible minorities," while by the 2021 census the Canadian population had increased to 26.5 per cent "visible minorities." Consequently, racialized Canadians

Table 6.1 Racialized MPs in the House of Commons compared to general population

	1993	1997	2000	2004	2006	2008	2011	2015	2019	2021
# of racialized MPs	13	19	17	22	24	21	28	45	50	53
% of racialized MPs in House	4.4	6.3	5.6	7.1	7.8	6.8	9.0	13.3	14.8	15.7
% of racialized population	9.4	11.2	13.4	14.9	16.2	17.3	19.1	19.1*	22.3	26.5
Ratio		.47	.46	.42	.48	.48	.39	.48	.70	.66	.63

Sources: Jerome Black, "Visible Minority Candidates and MPs in the 2019 Federal Election," *Canadian Parliamentary Review* 43, no. 2 (Summer 2020); Jerome Black, "The 2015 Federal Election: More Visible Minority Candidates and MPs," *Canadian Parliamentary Review* 40, no. 1 (Spring 2017); Jerome Black, "Racial Diversity in the 2011 Federal Election: Visible Minority Candidates and MPs," *Canadian Parliamentary Review* 36, no. 3 (Autumn 2011); Jerome H. Black and Andrew Griffith, "Do MPs Represent Canada's Diversity?" *Policy Options*, January 7, 2022; 2021 census data updated by J. Malloy.
* 2011 data from National Household Survey.

continue to be underrepresented even though the total number of racialized MPs has grown. (Black and co-author Andrew Griffith note that a proportion of the racialized population may be new immigrants not yet eligible to vote or run for office.[77] However, looking solely at Canadian citizens, racialized Canadians are still underrepresented.)

Table 6.1 presents the number of racialized MPs in the House of Commons after each election since 1993, along with their percentage of the overall House and the percentage of racialized people in the Canadian population. The percentage of racialized MPs has steadily grown from 4.4 per cent in 1993 to 15.7 per cent in 2021, only dropping once, in 2008, by 1 per cent. However the percentage of racialized Canadians has also grown, as noted above, from 9.4 per cent in 1993 to 26.5 per cent in 2021.

A complex picture also emerges when looking at different racial groups. Black and Griffith find that South Asian Canadians are the most represented non-European racial group in the Commons, with 7.1 per cent of MPs elected in 2021 being of South Asian origin – higher than their 5.6 per cent proportion of the general population in the 2016 census.[78] Indeed, according to the *Hill Times* newspaper, in 2015 more MPs spoke Punjabi than any other non-official language, with 20 MPs conversant in it.[79] All other groups were underrepresented, some more than others. For example, Black Canadians were 2.6 per cent of MPs, compared to 3.5 per cent of the population, and Chinese Canadians were 2.1 per cent of MPs but 4.6 per cent of the population. Some groups, including Southeast Asian Canadians, Filipino-Canadians, and Japanese-Canadians, had no current MPs at all. Limited data is available on racial diversity in the Senate, especially historically. However, a 2017 study by Andrew Griffith found that 15 per cent of current senators were "visible minorities," slightly above the 13.9 per cent in the House at the time, and that many of these were recently appointed independent senators under the new process.[80]

Racialized representatives tend to have higher educational credentials than other MPs, at least historically. Jerome Black found that 90 per cent of racialized MPs in the 1990s had a university degree, compared to only 70 per cent of all MPs and 50 per cent of MPs with northern/western European heritage.[81] In fact, at the time of that study more racialized MPs (52 per cent) had a second university degree than MPs of northern/western European heritage with a first degree (50 per cent). Similarly, 67 per cent of racialized MPs had a professional occupation compared to 61 per cent of all MPs and 41 per cent of MPs in the northern/western European category. A somewhat more recent study by Laura Jean Kwak of MPs of Asian descent in the 1990s and 2000s found similar patterns of higher educational and professional credentials compared to other MPs.[82] While we lack more recent data, it is unsurprising that racialized minorities who successfully made it to the House of Commons have held considerably more educational and professional credentials than other MPs. It is likely that such high credentials were needed to establish their credibility as viable election candidates.

Also unsurprisingly, women face a double challenge here. While data is limited, in another 1990s study of "ethnic minority" women candidates (including women from non-British/European backgrounds), Jerome Black found that they had the most professional and personal accomplishments compared to any other group running for office – reflecting the "double disadvantage" of expectations placed on them.[83] It is reasonable to assume expectations are similar or even higher for specifically non-European racialized women.

Compared to the extensive literature on the election of women, there is less systematic research on barriers to electing more racialized representatives. While this may unfortunately reflect neglect, it is also explained by the greater complexities at work. Different groups may face different experiences and types of barriers. The highly varying distribution of racialized populations in constituencies is a complicating factor. While every riding has roughly equal numbers of men and women, racialized populations tend to be concentrated in urban ridings and are often sparse in rural and remote districts, creating different contexts and dynamics. Research does suggest that, similar to women, racialized individuals have historically experienced "outsider" challenges of a lack of established networks in parties, and face entrenched incumbents and informal seniority systems with an implicit or explicit message of "wait your turn." Explicit outreach and recruitment efforts and internal allies and champions are often needed to encourage candidates to put their names forward and mount a competitive effort.

Substantive

As with other groups, the most complex dimension of racial representation in Parliament is *substantive* representation. How and in what ways do racialized parliamentarians "represent" issues of specific concern? Can non-racialized MPs and senators also do so? To what extent are they obligated to represent and be a voice for "their group"? And, especially for MPs, what is the effect of the all-powerful dominant factor of party?

Celina Caesar-Chavannes writes that as a Black woman MP, some of her most important activities involved Parliament as an institution, not the legislative process itself:

> I started to understand that the burden of responsibility I was feeling was not a burden at all – it was an opportunity for me to embrace the present and use my position to stir the pot. I loved using my voice to speak about micro-aggressions, body shaming and systemic racism. It was my responsibility, I realized, to bring to the forefront of mainstream politics the whispered conversations people of colour, and in particular Black women, had at water coolers every day.[84]

Caesar-Chavannes saw a key part of her role as being a champion for Black Canadians and other people of colour on Parliament Hill, including staff. "Each time I ran into a woman of colour or a Black staff, they told me that they, too, struggled with feeling excluded or being met with sexist, racist, or microaggressive behavior."[85] For her, the power of being the only Black woman in the House of Commons was both symbolic and substantive, giving her a platform to champion racialized issues in an institution she found very hostile to people of colour. Similarly, Donald Oliver, appointed in 1990 as the first Black man in the Senate (Anne Cools was the first Black woman, appointed in 1984), wrote that "[w]hen I first walked onto Parliament Hill in Ottawa, I saw little or no Black presence of significance in the House of Commons, the Senate, the Library of Parliament, or, most of all, in senior corridors of the Public Service."[86] Oliver writes that he pressed for greater diversity in hiring both in Parliament and government: "I was unrelenting in my task, and I now believe I made a difference."[87]

Research on the legislative activity of racialized MPs in Parliament is limited. Looking at debates, members' statements, and Question Period in 2006–7, Karen Bird finds that racialized MPs in the House of Commons were more likely to speak on racial issues and bring attention to them.[88] Bird found the most frequently discussed issues related to citizenship and immigration, followed by discrimination and violence, cultural diversity, and socio-economic status. She notes, however, that the nature of the constituency is also important – while racialized MPs spoke more on these topics overall, "there is little difference in the kinds of topics addressed by visible minority compared to non-minority MPs from highly diverse ridings."[89] In other words, non-racialized MPs from heavily racialized constituencies still spoke out on racialized issues to a similar extent as racialized MPs, reflecting the nature of their ridings.

Other research by Bird suggests that racialized Canadian *voters* tend to support a trustee model of representation over a delegate model – that is, they feel that MPs should exercise their own judgment rather than simply following the will of their constituents. One obvious reason for this is that people from racial minority populations are wary of the "will of the majority," which has led to discrimination and neglect, both past and present. A trustee model, based on personal judgment rather than majority will, may be more likely to consider and incorporate minority views and rights. But another reason is the complexity of issues including the diversity of social groupings in Canada. As Bird writes, preference for the trustee model "is rooted in minorities' recognition of the intrinsic impossibility of identifying any clear mandate for legislative action on behalf of socially diverse constituencies"[90] and "the vast social heterogeneity of their communities."[91]

However, this can still mean a tremendous amount of expectation rests on racialized MPs, some of it ascribed by individuals *outside* the racial group. As mentioned above, there can be an expectation that a racialized MP "speaks for" their racial group as a whole, and/or even for all racial minorities – both highly offensive concepts. It is reasonable to assume that racialized MPs are generally more likely to address issues of concern to their racial group. But this will differ by individual.

It is also more complicated to identify and assess goals for substantive representation. Though the boundaries of "women's issues" are broad, certain feminist policy goals – especially related to reproductive rights and sexual violence – can act as reliable core indicators of substantive representation. The picture is more complicated for racialized minorities. While we can expect issues of racial prejudice and discrimination to be of common concern, more systemic issues may differ for different racialized groups. And as with women who do not support feminist policy goals, not all racialized MPs will be in agreement on "racial issues."

The Parliamentary Black Caucus is a recent example of organized substantive representation. Formed in 2015 by Black members of the House and Senate, the caucus made headlines in June 2020,[92] at a time of high racial tension in North America, with a call for substantive policy changes through better collection of race-based data to measure discrimination, to support Black owned/run businesses, to improve access to justice and public security, to increase diversity in the public service, and to recognize and support Black Canadian culture and heritage.[93] In this instance, the link between Black MPs and the substantive representation of Black Canadian concerns is very clear. Yet it remains unique. The Parliamentary Black Caucus appears to be the first example of an organization of racialized parliamentarians working collectively on racialized issues, and it is unclear whether it will serve as a precedent for other groups.

As with women MPs, the Conservative Party demonstrates different patterns from other parties when it comes to substantive representation of racial issues. Writing in 2010, Karen Bird found that racialized Conservative MPs (as well as Bloc Québécois MPs) were *more* likely to speak in the House of Commons on racial issues than racialized Liberal or New Democrat MPs. However, non-racialized Conservative MPs were the *least* likely.[94] This may suggest a relegation of racial issues exclusively to racialized MPs, rather than a broader and inclusive embrace by all the party.

In a study of MPs of Asian heritage in the Reform and Conservative parties from 1997 to 2011, Laura Jean Kwak identified a distinct category of "Asian conservatives," and argued that these MPs worked *against* anti-racism goals. Kwak writes that they "serve[d] as agents of legitimization by using the chronicles of their own lives as immigrants and visible minorities to convey reliability and validity in their anti-immigrant and anti-refugee parliamentary statements."[95] This is not to say Conservative MPs did not speak out on such issues; for example, in 2014 (outside Kwak's time of study), Deepak Obhrai, a veteran Conservative MP of South Asian background, spoke against a government bill that would revoke the Canadian citizenship of dual citizens convicted of certain crimes, famously saying "a Canadian is a Canadian is a Canadian."[96]

There is clearly *ascribed* symbolism of racialized MPs; a party can gain overall legitimacy through their words and presence. Lincoln Alexander explained his approach to this: "I seemed [to party leaders] to be just the man to show Canadians the Conservative Party was open to all races and people of all backgrounds. While I realized I was a symbolic candidate, I also felt I could do a great job for the party. So I decided that if the Conservatives wanted to 'use' me, I would use them for my own development."[97]

Ultimately, there is still much to learn about racialized parliamentarians and especially their role in substantive representation. While some frameworks from the study of other groups can be applied here, the dimensions and key questions are not always the same; as with other groups, we must also consider intersectional identities. Particularly limited information is available on *racialized women* parliamentarians, and the extent to which they face dual sets of barriers, and on the experiences and efforts of racialized senators.

We also lack sufficient information on Parliament itself as an institution, and the extent to which its structures and culture discriminate against racialized parliamentarians. Compared to the growing evidence and testimony of women MPs and senators about gendered structures and sexism and sexual harassment, more knowledge is needed about the experiences of racialized parliamentarians. It is a subject ripe for further research and inquiry.

CONCLUSION

Diversity in Parliament is perhaps the most interesting and evolving aspect of the institution, and the aspect most in need of further study. Parliament is no longer exclusively a white man's club. Yet women remain chronically underrepresented, as do people with disabilities and racialized persons. Indigenous parliamentarians play especially complex roles, with a long history of barriers and continuing complexities in their relationship to Parliament. LGBT parliamentarians are increasingly able to be open about their sexual orientation, yet surely some still feel unable to do so, and white gay men remain the most prevalent group.

Where change is just beginning is the institution itself. We have seen much in this chapter about how members of equity-seeking groups feel that Parliament was not built or designed for them, and many were barred entirely from it in the past. They may now be officially welcome, but they still feel like outsiders and interlopers. Some of this can be addressed by policy and administrative changes, such as accessibility accommodations, parental leave, recognition of same-sex partners, etc. But many other aspects are more intangible – the norms and cultural expectations of what an MP looks like, sounds like, and acts like. And some aspects cut to the very heart of the institution, especially the pre-eminence of parties and the combative divide between government and opposition that characterizes the Westminster model and underlies the logic of governance.

Some individual MPs from equity-seeking groups are clearly comfortable with the way the House of Commons works, with strong party discipline and the constant struggle between government and opposition. But others, especially many women, are not. Even if they hold strong ideological convictions, they are dismayed by the degree of artificial conflict and exaggerated competition; the "boys in the sandbox," to use Libby Davies's words. Of course they are not alone; many white men MPs also express exasperation with the prevailing structure and culture. But in the end, it is members of equity-seeking groups that express the most dismay.

The progress of diversity in Parliament is ongoing with many dimensions. The membership of the House of Commons and Senate is likely to continue to diversify, slowly coming closer to resembling Canadian society as a whole. Parliament will continue to update and modernize its practices and policies. Less clear is whether, or at what point, greater diversity in people will lead to truly significant change in the institution itself.

CHAPTER SEVEN

The Senate

The Senate of Canada is an oddity. Appointed rather than elected, it differs from most other modern upper houses, including Australia, which has always had an elected Senate. Its closest counterpart is the House of Lords in Britain, on which it is based. But unlike the Lords, which developed in feudal times and evolved over many centuries, the Senate of Canada was specifically designed from the start. Yet the Senate has long struggled to articulate its exact role and value. What does the Senate do? Does it do what it is supposed to do? And do we even need the Senate?

These questions were asked persistently for many years without satisfying answers. However, significant changes instituted in 2016 have added further complexities and an entirely new set of questions and answers. Prior to 2016, the Senate more or less reflected the general parliamentary tension between the logic of governance and the logic of representation. Now, with the near evisceration of conventional parties as part of its workings, the Senate represents a radical leap forward for the logic of representation. But it is a tentative and uncertain leap, by an unelected body, and the core question of the Senate's value remains. The Senate, the "black sheep of Canada's governing institutions,"[1] adds a puzzle of its own to the overall paradox of Parliament.

BICAMERALISM

The Parliament of Canada is a bicameral legislature, that is, a legislature with two separate chambers, the House of Commons and the Senate. In bicameral parliamentary systems, governments are usually formed based on standings in the larger "lower house" (in Canada, the House of Commons), while the other chamber (such as the Senate) is typically called the "upper house" and may have a different configuration of seats with fewer government members.

David Smith writes that bicameralism is "a concept in search of a theory."[2] Why does a legislature need two houses? Other large federal countries like the United States, Australia, and Germany also have bicameral legislatures. But they are also found in smaller unitary countries like Ireland or the Netherlands. Subnational bicameralism is also common outside of Canada. All but one American state has a bicameral legislature, as does every Australian state except Queensland. Yet no Canadian province is currently bicameral; the last was Quebec, which abolished its upper house in 1968. New Zealand, a unitary state but built on the Westminster model, had an upper house, the Legislative Council, until 1951. The use of bicameralism is thus irregular. There are patterns, but not consistent ones. The exact purpose of bicameralism – and thus the purpose of the Senate – is elusive.

One commonly given reason for bicameralism is that it serves as a check and balance on powerful governments dominating the lower house. Upper houses are seen as more thoughtful and less impetuous – thus the long-standing ascription of the Canadian Senate as the chamber of "sober second thought." In the terminology of Bagehot (see chapter 2), the House of Lords even in 1867 was fading as an "efficient" body and was becoming part of the "dignified" part of government – there to ratify and smooth decisions, not make them. Similarly in the United States, the smaller Senate has long been seen as the more reflective and thoughtful chamber compared to the larger House of Representatives.

The second reason for bicameralism is that, especially in federal countries, upper houses are seen as important instruments of regional representation. In both the American and Australian senates, each state has the same number of senators regardless of population – a measure specifically designed to counteract the power of representation by population in the lower houses. The German *Bundesrat* is also anchored on the regional principle, consisting of members appointed directly by state (*lander*) governments rather than directly elected.

The Canadian Senate reflects both of these impulses – a body of sober second thought and an instrument of regional representation. But its achievements in both dimensions are often elusive. It does not always stand up well in bicameralism's ongoing search for a theory to justify its existence. In fact, the Canadian Senate often seems more like a solution shopping for a problem to solve.

In this chapter I will show how the perceived strengths, deficiencies, and ascribed potential of the Senate have risen and fallen through the years. For all the talk of Senate reform, exactly why we need a Senate – especially an *unelected* Senate – is not always clear. The reforms of 2016 have moved the Senate into a new era that is still evolving. But they have only doubled down on the basic question of why we need a Senate at all. On the other hand, those who call for abolition of the Senate may overestimate the ability of the House of Commons to suddenly carry the legislative burden alone.

The origins of bicameralism are strongly elitist, most notably in the UK House of Lords, a body specifically designed to represent the aristocracy. The Senate traces its genesis to that chamber as well as the provincial legislative councils in pre-Confederation times – bodies also appointed from the colonial elite of the day. Even in the nineteenth century when "democracy" was already limited to white men, upper houses were meant to retain some control over the "masses." This is most blatant in the 1867 constitutional rule that Senate appointments were limited to men over thirty years of age owning $4000 in "real property" (typically land); the age and financial requirements remain today, even though the dollar figure has never been adjusted. In modern times, whatever their other strengths, upper houses, even elected ones, are by their very design meant to deflect and dilute simple representation by population, and thus the overall collective will of the majority of voters. For this reason, the New Democratic Party of Canada has consistently called for abolition of the Senate and refused to endorse the concept of NDP senators.

The Senate's unelected status and near-unlimited terms pose a permanent image problem for the institution. Whether or not senators are more prone to misdeeds and scandals than members of the House of Commons, their often long tenures and unelected status give them an air of unaccountability compared to MPs, who must face re-election on a regular basis. A series of high-profile expense scandals in the mid-2010s was particularly damaging for the Senate, along with struggles to remove senators for racist statements and sexual misconduct. Again, senators are not necessarily more prone to outrageous or controversial behaviour than MPs. But they do not face regular review through election, and thus are perceived to be less accountable.

Nevertheless, the Senate of Canada takes its job and ethical standards seriously, as do the vast majority of senators. It has, especially in recent years, developed an acute self-awareness of its own image and attempted to respond with internal reforms and better communications. And its appointed nature can be a strength, allowing greater and more diverse representation than in the House, especially of women where it now far surpasses the House.

The Canadian legislative process might be poorer and weaker without the Senate. While it is possible that abolishing the Senate would prompt the House of Commons to improve itself and fill any gaps, this is a speculative gamble. Bicameralism may rest on weak theoretical grounds. But it is a phenomenon likely here to stay – even if the exact purpose of the Senate often remains unclear.

A BRIEF DESCRIPTION OF THE SENATE

The Senate is significantly different in composition from the House of Commons, especially after 2016, and mildly different in procedures and processes. Let's review some of its key characteristics:

- *Seats and Regional Formula:* The Senate has 105 seats, according to an imperfect regional formula. The original 1867 design allocated twenty-four seats to Ontario, twenty-four to Quebec, and twenty-four to the Maritime provinces of Nova Scotia and New Brunswick (twelve seats each; when Prince Edward Island joined Confederation six years later, each gave up two seats to maintain the overall regional number of twenty-four). Over time, a similar package of twenty-four seats was gradually allocated to Western Canada, which meant only six per province. Newfoundland and Labrador also received six seats in 1949 (so that Atlantic Canada now has thirty seats, more than any other region), and each territory also has one seat. This formula obviously disadvantages Western provinces, especially populous Alberta and British Columbia, with six Senate seats apiece compared to ten for Nova Scotia and New Brunswick despite their much smaller populations, and twenty-four for the large provinces of Ontario and Quebec. But despite much discussion, the formula remains unchanged.

– *Appointment:* Senators are formally appointed by the Governor General in council; that is, on the advice of the prime minister. For nearly all of Canadian history, this was a powerful tool of prime ministers to appoint party (and personal) loyalists, and the vast majority of Senate appointments were supporters of the prime minister's party. Senators retained their partisan affiliations, sitting with House MPs in party caucuses and generally maintaining the same party cohesion and discipline. The reform experiments of the late twentieth and early twenty-first centuries provided some brief exceptions, including the appointment of five elected senators from Alberta. Paul Martin was also noteworthy for appointing some senators affiliated with other parties during his brief term in office, as did Pierre Trudeau in the late 1970s, both in times when the Liberals already overwhelmingly dominated the chamber.

– Until 1965 senators were appointed for life. They must now retire at age seventy-five but otherwise have no term limits (despite Stephen Harper's attempt to introduce limits, discussed below). These near-permanent terms created a permanent legacy "overhang" in the Senate – meaning that the appointees from a party stayed in the Senate long after that party had been defeated in the House. When a party came to power, it typically faced a Senate full of partisans from the now-defeated party, which only dwindled as those senators retired. For example, when Brian Mulroney's Conservatives were elected in 1984, almost three-quarters of the Senate was filled by members of the Liberal Party, which had been in power for most of the previous two decades. Despite Mulroney immediately beginning to appoint Conservatives as Liberals retired, the Liberal majority – the overhang – remained until 1990. Then when

Jean Chrétien's Liberals came to power in 1993, the Senate retained a Conservative majority – an opposite overhang – until 1996.
- This partisan system was radically upset in 2016 by the newly elected Trudeau government, which instituted a new system of independent appointments of senators, with no role for political parties. This quickly transformed the institution, in part because Trudeau's predecessor Stephen Harper had left a large number of vacancies unfilled. Within two years "independent senators" had become the largest category in the chamber. Critics, especially the Conservative Party, argue the Trudeau-appointed independents are Liberals in all but name, however. We return to this below.
- *Organization:* Until 2016, the dominance of parties meant the Senate was nearly as disciplined as the House. Senators typically voted along party lines, and the prime minister appointed a leader of their party's senators, assisted by a whip, who piloted government legislation through the chamber. A significant shift happened under Justin Trudeau in 2014, even before the larger changes, when he removed all senators from the Liberal parliamentary caucus. This meant when he took office in 2015 he had no affiliated senators available to represent the government and to steer its legislative agenda through the chamber. Instead, Trudeau appointed a Representative of the Government to oversee its interests, along with a deputy and a whip (termed "Government Liaison"). But there is no government caucus accompanying these leaders. And as we see below, the post-2016 Senate has been a shifting morass, with both traditional party groups and fluid and shifting new organizations, particularly the Independent Senators Group.
- *Process:* The general legislative process in the Senate is similar to the House, with three readings of bills, standing committees, opportunities for private members' bills (called Senate Public Bills), and even a Question Period. Procedural rules and the standing committee system are somewhat different, but overall the chambers are not that dissimilar. Like the House, the Senate has a Clerk and a considerable bureaucracy, though somewhat differently organized. A chief difference often noted, both past and present, is the somewhat more relaxed and consensual nature of the Senate, with fewer restrictions on speaking times and a typically more genteel bargaining atmosphere.

HISTORY OF THE SENATE

At the time of Confederation there was likely no question about including a Senate. After all, Britain had an upper house, and bicameral legislatures were familiar and customary in colonial Canada. Though little known today, the founding provinces except Ontario even retained upper houses themselves, known as "legislative councils," some into the twentieth century. Manitoba created an upper house when it was founded in 1870, though it was abolished soon after in 1876. New Brunswick kept its legislative council until 1891, Nova Scotia until 1928, and the Quebec upper house was not abolished until 1968. The New Zealand Parliament and Australian legislatures were also created with upper houses (though the Queensland legislative council was abolished in 1922). The question in 1867 was not whether to have two houses of Parliament; the more unconventional question would have been to consider only having one.

The importance of the Senate is sometimes noted in that six of the fourteen days of the 1864 Quebec Conference were devoted entirely to its design.[3] These deliberations have been pored over by scholars and Senate reformers, attempting to unlock the exact purpose of the Senate and the intentions behind its design. But there is little doubt that a Senate simply made obvious sense to the Fathers of Confederation. Bicameralism, appointment rather than election, and the entire notion of "sober second thought" came naturally to these elites, themselves creating a country behind largely closed doors. And the regional seat formula of the Senate was part of a deal between the existing colonies, with the Maritimes wary of the growing power and strength of Ontario and Quebec, and French-speaking Quebecers concerned about protecting their religious and linguistic rights.

Making the Senate appointed also made sense because of the fear of deadlock. The Province of Canada (today's Ontario and Quebec) had experimented with an elected legislative council in the 1850s, but it proved unwieldy as it became unclear who held ultimate power. Tensions in the United States that led to the American Civil War also underlay Canadian fears about giving power to an upper house that could fully block the will of the majority. Appointment made it clear that the lower elected house, the House of Commons, retained primary democratic legitimacy, as in Britain. Furthermore, the Senate was specifically constrained from introducing money bills that involved public spending, thus affirming that the Commons held the "power of the purse."

Still, by making appointments without term limits, defeated governments could live on through the legacy "overhang" of past appointments that dogged their successors. Problems began as early as Prime Minister Alexander Mackenzie (1873–8), "who became frustrated with the Conservative majority in the Senate after it defeated some important bills during his first administration."[4] The long Conservative reign from 1878 to 1896, followed by a Liberal regime from 1896 to 1911, ensured that Senate appointments continued to be lopsided.

In 1913, the Liberal-dominated Senate refused to pass a Conservative government bill on naval spending. Not long before in Britain, a showdown over a budget bill led to the *Parliament Act* of 1911 and the curbing of the power of the House of Lords, in particular removing its right to veto money bills. While the 1913 naval spending bill came close, there was no similar pivotal moment in Canada. Nevertheless, the activism of the Senate in standing up to the House of Commons slowly retreated.[5]

By the mid-twentieth century, the Senate had more or less evolved into its modern form as a legislative body of indirect, not direct, power. It avoided direct confrontation with governments and the elected House, favouring the image of reflection and "sober second thought" but rarely or never actually vetoing and stopping legislation of consequence. Senate committees cultivated an image of careful deep study of bills, focusing on wording and technical considerations rather than ideological content. In the 1970s the Senate began a process of "pre-study" of bills while they were still in the Commons; this allowed senators to communicate concerns and possible amendments before legislation was finalized in the House. Some senators began to be noted for expertise in specific areas, such as David Croll, a leading proponent of anti-poverty measures.

Nevertheless, the 1970s represented a low point for the Canadian Senate. Its appointed and elitist nature appeared more and more out of touch. The unabashed use of Senate appointments as patronage awards for the party faithful meant a wide variety in quality, and the ambiguous purpose of the chamber gave it little purpose or discipline. Thus Jackson and Atkinson observed in 1980 that "[t]he work of the

Senate is performed by a few diligent Senators," while overall "[t]he image of the Senate is such that none of the functions of integration, representation, and legitimation are performed with success."[6]

The late twentieth century saw a reasserted Senate, once again due to the overhang of previous government appointments. In 1988, the Liberal-dominated Senate refused to pass the free trade bill of the Mulroney Conservative government, leading to the 1988 federal election, won by the Conservatives. Two years later, Liberal senators again refused to pass the government's Goods and Services Tax (GST) legislation, forcing Mulroney to use an extraordinary clause in the 1867 constitution and appoint eight additional Conservative senators to pass the GST bill. In 1994 after the change in government, the Conservatives got their revenge by voting down a Liberal government bill related to airport privatization. The Senate also had moments independent of party, vetoing an abortion bill by a single vote in 1991. These controversial actions showed, for better or worse, that the Senate did have power and purpose. And it fueled what had become by this time a perennial Canadian debate: Senate reform.

SENATE REFORM

Senate reform is not new. R.A. Mackay's book, *The Unreformed Senate of Canada*, first appeared in 1926.[7] In 2003, Jack Stillborn published a study titled "Forty Years of Not Reforming the Senate."[8] It chronicled several decades of late twentieth century studies and proposals to reform the Senate, none of which had come to fruition.

The heart of the issue, observed Stillborn, was that "discussions of Senate reform in Canada have suffered from a chronic lack of adequately specific attention to the problem that reform is intended to remedy."[9] Senate reform, in other words, was a solution shopping for a problem to solve, and the actual problem the Senate was meant to solve kept shifting. Reform debates, Stillborn remarked, were "dominated by relatively transitory assumptions about what is needed and how it should be achieved." Similarly, David Smith wrote, also in 2003, that "commentary on the Senate of Canada is strongly negative although not necessarily united in its cause for complaint."[10] Emmett Macfarlane wrote in 2021 that "[u]ltimately, reform of the Senate has failed over the course of a century and a half in part due to wildly disparate ideas about what the Senate should be (and whether it should exist at all)."[11]

Early and mid-twentieth century reform discussion tended to concentrate on whether a second chamber was needed at all. The Co-operative Commonwealth Federation party and its successor, the NDP, stood from the start for abolition of the Senate. Bicameralism began to go out of fashion; as noted, all provincial upper houses were abolished by 1968 and New Zealand got rid of its legislative council in 1951. The Senate seemed superfluous and without purpose, except its derided role as a retirement home for politicians. Thus Mackay wrote in a revised version of *The Unreformed Senate* in 1963 that the Senate could not win no matter what it did:

> The role of the Senate has been a recurring political problem almost since Confederation. If a Government measure fails to pass the Senate when its majority happens to be of the opposite party to that of the Government of the day, the Government majority and the faithful party press hurl a torrent of abuse upon it. If it rejects or drastically amends a bill for social or moral reform, it is condemned by impatient reformers as reactionary, autocratic, and perhaps immoral. If it is quiescent, it is assumed to be simply a fifth wheel on the governmental coach.[12]

In the 1960s and 1970s, the Senate began to be seen not simply as passively useless, but perhaps an active *problem*. Criticism focused on the business and corporate connections of senators. Most notable was Colin Campbell's 1978 critique, *The Canadian Senate: A Lobby from Within*, that noted the close ties between many senators and Canadian business.[13] Campbell argued that the Senate's focus on "technical review" rather than substantive policy debates allowed senators to quietly craft the details of legislation in advantageous ways. He called this a "one-sided review" in a system "which bends over backwards to ensure that business has preferential access to the policy process."[14] He further asserted that "[t]he Senate primarily protects the interests of major businesses and financial concerns. To do this, it regularly challenges, delays, and at times amends or deletes legislative provisions that might endanger major business and financial concerns, or might overlook 'good' business practice."[15] Similarly, Jackson and Atkinson echo this with their 1980 observation that "a small portion of the Senate's membership is actively engaged in challenging, delaying, and amending any government legislation which may be detrimental to major business and financial concerns."[16] The problem of the Senate was thus its elitism and business ties.

However, at the same time as these criticisms, an urgent phenomenon was arising in Canada: national unity. The rise of Quebec separatism along with Western alienation produced great pressures on Canadian national institutions. This awoke a long-dormant interest in the Senate's regional structure, and its potential role in federalism and mediating national unity discussions.

The Senate was now not merely a problem, but a possible *solution* to other problems. Some suggested the Senate become a "House of Provinces" fashioned on the German *Bundesrat* with its appointees from the German states.[17] In 1978 the federal government of Pierre Trudeau proposed a somewhat similar House of the Federation, and the idea was also advocated in 1979 by the Task Force on Canadian Unity (the Pepin-Robarts Commission) as an instrument of "intrastate federalism" as opposed to the "interstate" struggles between federal and provincial leaders and governments mentioned in chapter 2.[18] Thus Smith notes that "[a]t the end of the 1970s, the problem the second chamber needed to repair had nothing to do with the question of accountability and everything to do with improving federal-provincial relations."[19]

One reform not advocated was direct election of senators. This was likely influenced by a crisis in Australia in 1975. In the Australian incident, the Labor government of the day held a majority in the lower House of Representatives, but the opposition Liberals and their allies controlled the elected Senate. The Liberals in the Senate repeatedly blocked "supply" and the approval of spending by the government. This draining deadlock continued until the Governor General shockingly dismissed the Labor prime minister, Gough Whitlam, and appointed the Liberal leader, Malcolm Fraser, as his replacement. Fraser promptly called and won an election, but "the Dismissal," as it is known, shook Australian political foundations to the core. This deadlock between two elected houses likely discouraged interest in an elected Canadian Senate, and 1970s Canadian reformers preferred to retain an appointed model, such as the German practice of appointments through state legislatures.

But reform dynamics shifted again. The continuing rise of Western alienation in the 1980s, fueled by the perceived failure of existing federal institutions to protect Western interests, led to a relatively novel but powerful Western interest in Senate reform. This was best seen in the goals of the Reform Party of Canada, founded in 1987, whose top priority in its Statement of Principles was a "Triple E Senate" – elected, effective, and equal.[20] A Triple E senate closely resembled the Australian model – with seats distributed equally by province regardless of population, directly elected by voters, and with clear and effective powers. For Senate reformers concerned with Central Canadian dominance in the House of Commons, the power to stand up to the House and risk deadlock was desirable, rather than something to be avoided.

It is difficult to overstate the importance of Senate reform in Western Canada in the late twentieth century, where it was "a staple of Western Canadian political discourse."[21] It was a top priority especially for Alberta, which held an election for a vacant Senate seat in 1989, though the province had no power to make the appointment. The winner, Stan Waters, was eventually seated in 1990 by Prime Minister Brian Mulroney as part of the overall constitutional bargaining over the Meech Lake Accord. Alberta held further Senate elections from 1998 to 2012, and again in 2021. Four of the winners were seated by the Harper government, including Bert Brown, notable for once plowing a field with the words "Triple E Senate or Else."

The Senate and its defenders began to respond as well. Displaying awareness of its poor image, the institution and individual senators engaged in Senate reform discussions, typically emphasizing (1) the strengths of the current model and (2) the risks and complexities of reform. Above all, they emphasized how the Senate made up for deficiencies in the House of Commons. This was articulated by Senator Serge Joyal in 2003 in a fervent defence of the institution:

> The dominant political culture seems to have effectively neutered the House of Commons.... The Senate is markedly different from the House of Commons in its structure and practices. Because the government cannot be brought down by the Senate, there is no need for senators to abandon strongly held convictions and yield

to their Party Whip. As they do not campaign for office, senators are not captive to their respective parties for promotions and political favours. In light of the qualifications of its members, the Senate is actually better equipped to hold the executive government accountable for its policies and conduct than is the House of Commons.[22]

In this view, the Senate was a solution to yet another problem, this time the House of Commons itself. Defences of the Senate focused on the allegedly better quality and depth of its inquiries and legislative review. They also noted the generally better record of diversity in the Senate compared to the House. While the House of Commons was stuck at one-fifth women's representation from 1997 to 2011, the number of women in the Senate continued to increase and surpass the House. The appointment of Indigenous senators was also historically similar to or somewhat higher than Indigenous MPs.[23] Historic data is less available on racialized senators, though the first Black woman senator, Anne Cools, was appointed in 1984, while the House only saw its first Black woman elected in 1993, Jean Augustine. (The first Black male MP was Lincoln Alexander, elected in 1968; the first Black male senator was Don Oliver, appointed in 1990, six years after Cools). Again, though perhaps more implicitly than explicitly, the Senate was presented as a solution to another problem of Canadian democracy – underrepresentation of equity-seeking groups.

An underlying assumption of nearly all reform discussions from the 1970s to the 2000s was that Senate reform needed to be done wholesale. Individual tinkering was seen as risky and leading to further problems. Prime Minister Paul Martin said in 2004: "I have long been an advocate of Senate reform. However, I do not believe ... that doing Senate reform piecemeal really would bring us the desired result. In fact, what it would quite well do is, in fact, simply exacerbate a number of the problems. So ... what I think we should do is to look at Senate reform but look at it in its entirety."[24] This assumption that significant Senate reform had to be all-or-nothing paralyzed actual attempts at reform for many years.

Both Stephen Harper and Justin Trudeau rejected the all-or-nothing approach, though in two very different forms. Frustrated by the continuing paralysis of the debate, both went ahead and unilaterally attempted to make *partial* changes on their own, though only Trudeau's were successful.

During his time in power, Harper repeatedly introduced bills to change aspects of the Senate. The last attempt was in 2011 when he proposed two changes: to limit senators to a single nine-year term, and to allow for provinces to hold consultative elections. These and their predecessors were controversial, both for their substance and over the constitutional procedural issue of whether Harper needed to seek provincial consent to enact them. Eventually the Supreme Court of Canada ruled in 2014 that Harper could not proceed without provincial consent.[25] Harper then abandoned attempts at reform entirely and refused to appoint any more senators to replace retirements and other departures, meaning that by the time he left office in 2015 the Senate had twenty-two vacant seats.

Justin Trudeau took a different approach, targeting a different aspect. Harper's reforms focused on the lack of a provincial link to the Senate and the perception of unaccountability due to unlimited terms. Trudeau instead focused on the inherent partisanship of the Senate, including the problem of legacy overhang that allowed the dead hand of past governments to keep control, as they did in the 1980s and 1990s.

Having already expelled senators from the Liberal parliamentary caucus in 2014, in 2016 Trudeau created a new independent mechanism to solicit applications and appoint senators with no partisan affiliation. Because Harper had left a large number of vacancies, the Trudeau reforms had an immediate effect. By 2019, a majority of senators had no partisan affiliation, a stunningly rapid change unimaginable prior to 2015. It also placed the Senate in unknown waters.

THE SENATE SINCE 2016

Since 2016 the Canadian Senate has changed rapidly. In early 2016 the Trudeau government established the Independent Advisory Board for Senate Appointments (IAB) to make "non-binding, merit-based recommendations to the prime minister on Senate appointments."[26] The first seven appointments under the new system were made in March 2016, and by the end of the year twenty-seven appointments – over a quarter of the entire chamber – had already been made.[27] While many appointees were already active in public life in some way, very few had a partisan political background; those that did were not necessarily Liberals, such as Frances Lankin, a former Ontario NDP cabinet minister. Instead, they were generally people of substantive professional accomplishments. By the end of Trudeau's first term in 2019, fifty appointments had been made under the new process – nearly half of the entire Senate.

The new crop of senators were diverse. A majority of new appointments were women, so that the Senate reached gender parity in 2020 (though lapsing back to 49 per cent for a time in 2021).[28] Racial diversity was also evident, although not dramatically. VandenBeukel finds that appointments of racialized minorities actually started earlier under the Harper government, and increased further but not dramatically after 2016.[29] More distinctive was the increase in Indigenous senators. After seeing fifteen senators of First Nations, Inuit, or Métis origin appointed during the first 148 years of Canadian history, ten were appointed between 2016 and 2021.[30] Overall, this record gives credence to the argument that an appointed Senate can lead to greater diversity and a chamber that looks more like Canada than the elected House of Commons.

The new appointment process can be seen as a triumph for the logic of representation and specifically a "trustee" model of legislators that emphasizes legislators exercising their own considered judgment. Senators have been appointed based on their personal merits, without obvious partisan filters. Facing neither electoral pressures nor party discipline, they can theoretically exercise their best judgment on each aspect of Senate business, acting only in the best interests of Canadians.

On the other hand, many Conservatives in particular argue that these new appointments are largely Liberals in all but name. As we will see below, senators appointed after 2016 have generally supported the Liberal government agenda. Critics also argue that the new process favours a certain type of Canadian – drawing almost exclusively from the educated, professional class. Senators may be in this sense well qualified for their jobs but, even more than the House of Commons, they are not necessarily representative of the occupational and class diversity of Canada.

Appointment reforms also meant changes were needed in the organization of the Senate, and here we encounter the logic of governance. As we saw above, throughout its history, Senate organization and proceedings operated along traditional party lines similar to the House of Commons. (A few pre-2016 senators sat as "independents," each typically for exceptional reasons.) Like the House of Commons, the basic organization and processes of the Senate were built around the organizing principle of political parties. But now a new mechanism was needed to coordinate the growing number of independent senators and incorporate them into the proceedings of the Senate.

In 2016 the first group of new senators along with several veterans formed the Independent Senators Group (ISG), and most newly appointed senators afterward joined the ISG. In 2017 the Senate rules were rewritten to recognize this and other "groups" in the chamber and allocate resources and opportunities similar to a regular party caucus. But importantly, the ISG served only as a coordinating body, and took no position on any issues or legislation. Meanwhile, Conservative senators continued business much as usual, retaining a caucus and hierarchical leadership positions. The dwindling number of Liberal senators, no longer welcome in Trudeau's caucus, mostly retained their partisan identity and were known, somewhat confusingly, as "Senate Liberals" despite having no affiliation with the Liberal government.

Dynamics became further complicated. Some independent senators declined to join the ISG, seeing it as a fledgling party in its own right. In 2019, a new group called the Canadian Senators Group, comprising some former Conservatives along with independents, was formed, particularly to address regional issues. Meanwhile the Senate Liberals, dwindling because of retirements, changed their name to the Progressive Senators Group in late 2019. Some independent senators joined this group, and the numbers of all these new groups have fluctuated as individuals switch affiliations.

In the past partisan era, governments had appointed a Government Leader in the Senate to organize government business in the chamber, similar to the Commons's House Leader. Lacking any official Liberal senators, Prime Minister Trudeau appointed a Government Representative instead, tapping a former public servant, Peter Harder. Harder faced a very different task than his predecessors, who were normally supported by all the caucus members in the governing party. Instead, supplemented only by a deputy and "government liaison" (whip), he was responsible for piloting government legislation through the Senate and generally speaking for all that the government did – without a caucus backing him up and providing the normal predictability of the logic of governance.

Thus by the end of the Trudeau government's first term in 2019, Senate organization had become deeply complex. A radical experiment in the logic of representation had created a chamber where power was widely dispersed with no one truly in charge. The ISG was the largest group, yet by definition not one that could actually order and discipline the chamber. Furthermore, the Conservative Party was skeptical of the entire process, arguing that most "independent" appointees were aligned with the views of the Liberal government, even if not active party members. Thus Andrew Scheer, Conservative leader from 2017 to 2020, pledged to return to the old system and appoint "Conservative senators who would implement the Conservative vision for Canada," while affirming a preference for elected senators.[31]

Conservative skepticism of the independence of the new crop of senators is fueled by their voting patterns. In a study of Senate voting from 2015 to 2019, VandenBeukel et al. found that senators belonging to the ISG voted more in favour of Liberal government bills than did senators from the dwindling Senate Liberal caucus.[32] Given this apparent enthusiasm for the Liberal agenda, Conservatives naturally have been skeptical that these are truly "independents" representing the full political spectrum. However, an alternative interpretation is that the new crop of senators are deferential to the elected government and House of Commons, knowing the limitations of their appointed status.

Elizabeth McCallion supports the latter argument by focusing on amendments to bills, separate from votes on the overall bill. She finds a much higher rate after 2016 of proposed and accepted amendments to bills in the Senate, and argues that senators use amendments as a tool to exercise independence – while still ultimately deferring to government. McCallion writes: "Newly appointed senators see their job as challenging the government by amending bills, but generally they defer to the elected government's will when it comes time to vote at Third Reading" and that "this might explain the discrepancy" between VandenBeukel et al.'s data and her own.[33]

Indeed, the Senate is more assertive than its recent predecessors in being more willing to amend bills as well as slow them or send them back to the House. This included high-profile bills on assisted dying and cannabis reform. This was undoubtedly frustrating for the government, and possibly for members of the House of Commons. However, it did not lead to paralysis. A pattern emerged in which Senate amendments were either accepted by the House – suggesting the Senate's input had improved the bill – or they were rejected by the House, and the Senate then acquiesced and passed the original legislation. Macfarlane concluded in 2019 that "[a]lthough there are clear signs that a more independent Senate has made the legislative process more challenging and complex from the government's perspective, it has not been unduly obstructionist."[34]

The true colours of the post-2016 Senate remain to be tested. McCallion writes: "There has only been a Liberal government since the reforms, so it is uncertain whether the high Senate amendment rate will continue when a Conservative government takes power and senators regain access to the government caucus (or when Conservatives regain a majority in the Senate)."[35] As to the question of whether independent senators are really Liberals in all but name, VandenBeukel observes that "the question of senatorial independence cannot be conclusively answered under the current circumstances.... The true test of this can only come when there is a change in government. At that point, the voting records of senators ought to offer a much more reliable test of their independence."[36] Emmett Macfarlane concurs: "The real test of the non-partisan behavior of the Trudeau-appointed independents is a long-term one."[37]

Thus while its appointment patterns and membership have transformed, the overall Senate still largely plays its historic function as a reflective body that defers to the elected House of Commons. What remains to be seen is whether the Senate will behave similarly under a non-Liberal government, especially if that government returns to appointing partisan senators. It may finally prove whether independent senators are truly independent and not Liberals in all but name.

THE FUTURE OF THE SENATE

Over time the Canadian Senate has moved from an assertive elite body, to an ignored backwater, to a solution shopping for a problem to solve, and to a radical experiment in the logic of representation. Decades of talk but inaction were broken in 2016 by an open-ended foray whose contours are still developing. Never before has the future of the Senate been so unclear.

It is possible that the Senate will continue to develop into a trustee-style dream team of noble and accomplished citizens, working together to improve public policy without regard to partisan interests and advantage. At the same time, conscious of their unelected status, these idealized senators would ultimately defer to the wishes of the elected government of the day, which retains both ultimate power and ultimate accountability. This would be a happy resolution of the parliamentary paradox and a reconciliation of the logics of representation and governance – ensuring full voicing of diverse interests, yet also ensuring parliamentary business flows and decisions are made.

On the other hand, the lack of party control could lead to a new and alarming era of lack of Senate accountability. A body run entirely by the logic of representation, unbound and undisciplined by parties and the logic of governance, and yet possessing vital power, is concerning, and a possible ticking time bomb. The organic rise of the Independent Senators Group demonstrated the need for some sort of organization to guide and allocate resources for senators without party affiliation. But the rise and evolution of other groups suggests an ongoing instability, while the ISG leadership is, by design, highly constrained in how much it can speak for its membership.

Increasingly, no one controls the Canadian Senate, which is refreshing in good times but could be perilous in crisis. The 1975 Australian deadlock looms as a bogeyman for some. That incident involved clashes between parties in which leaders at least retained control of their legislators. A deadlock between the Canadian House and a Senate of independent but undisciplined members could be even more chaotic and irresolvable. Having said this, a single complete deadlock comparable to the Australian incident is unlikely; in fact, the Australian deadlock was only possible because it involved highly organized parties that stuck together as they squared off against each other. In any event, similar showdowns already occurred in Canada in 1988 and 1990 over free trade and the GST, and Parliament and Canadian governance survived.

More concerning is a slow-burning insurrection if the Senate chips away at the House's authority, without a corresponding accountability in the upper chamber. The Senate may also still develop a future "overhang" with an overwhelming body of Liberal-appointed "independent" senators one day facing a government of another party, perhaps committed to returning to appointing its own partisans.

Perhaps the most encouraging aspect of the new Senate is its gender parity. Elizabeth McCallion finds "evidence of heightened feminist activity in the Canadian Senate as the number of women senators rises."[38] As discussed in chapter 6, one example given by McCallion is efforts to eliminate sex discrimination in the *Indian Act*, where feminist senators worked with Indigenous women to overcome resistance in the government and House of Commons. The lack of strong party lines may encourage greater cooperation among women (and men) than in the House of Commons, while diminishing Parliament's traditionally competitive and aggressive atmosphere. This may also hold promise for Indigenous senators and racialized senators as well.

But the post-2015 Senate also does little to fulfil dreams of regional representation, at least in the way envisaged by the 1980s' Reform Party and other Triple-E enthusiasts. There is little evidence of regionally driven voting patterns or development of regional blocs, especially for Western Canadian interests. And the odd distribution of Senate seats still disadvantages the Western provinces, and is unlikely to change without major constitutional reform.

We can return to the question at the beginning of this chapter: Is a second chamber truly necessary? Recall Smith's observation that "bicameralism is a concept in search of a theory." It remains unclear whether the Senate is truly necessary at all. But abolishment is unlikely, and very difficult constitutionally.

Ultimately the Senate is a paradox within the larger paradox of Parliament. Created in a different context and time, it has been simultaneously a problem and yet also posited as a solution to other problems of Canadian democracy and government. Long run as a variation on the logic of governance, it has switched to a foundation based on the logic of representation. This has put it on a new journey that may end in enlightenment, the status quo, or disaster.

CHAPTER EIGHT

Scrutiny

Scrutiny is the traditional heart of Parliament. Modern expectations of Parliament often focus on its power to make laws and to voice new policy ideas. But the medieval origins of Parliament had little to do with coming up with ideas itself. Rather it focused on *scrutinizing* the ideas and actions of the state, voicing grievances, and holding the government to account. The great moments of English constitutional history involve establishing Parliament's power of approval over government actions, and scrutiny of those actions.

Most important has been the "power of the purse" – the hard-fought ability of Parliament to approve taxes and spending. But Parliament does not actually initiate spending or generally set policy. That is the purview of the government: the executive. Under the "strong executive" order that characterizes our system, governments hold primary power and then take responsibility for that power. As Janet Ajzenstat writes, designers specifically recommended that governments have exclusive control over "money bills": "The money bill principle would have had the effect of establishing executive independence, while at the same time enabling the popular house to curb the excesses of the executive branch."[1]

Scrutiny is thus about examining government actions, not initiating the actions themselves. And it is most importantly – though by no means exclusively – about money. This chapter looks especially at Parliament's role in the budget and financial processes of government.

But scrutiny also covers all areas of government actions, including activities that do not automatically require legislative approval. Most important in recent years is Parliament's growing role in foreign policy and security and defence matters.

A key theme of this chapter is that while scrutiny can be elegant in theory, it is difficult to apply in practice. Scrutiny in the Canadian Parliament is regularly decried as weak and inadequate. Former Conservative Brent Rathgeber resigned from his party caucus in 2013 partly over concerns about government spending, and later wrote, "Parliament's ability to perform its role of government oversight has declined to the point that it is entirely ineffective."[2] Like much else about Parliament, this is not a new argument. In a famous 1976 statement, then-Auditor-General of Canada J.J. Macdonell said, "I am deeply concerned that Parliament – and indeed the Government – has lost, or is close to losing, effective control of the public purse."[3]

As with all things parliamentary, the exact concerns about scrutiny have shifted over time. During the Liberal governments of the 1990s and 2000s, particular concern was given to a supposed breakdown of ministerial responsibility at the expense of public servants. In the Conservative government of 2006–15, focus shifted to Parliament's access to information, especially a showdown over Afghan detainee documents in 2010 and a successful non-confidence motion in 2011 over access to defence spending contracts. Under the Justin Trudeau government, especially during the COVID-19 pandemic, great concern arose about the ability of Parliament to track the sudden enormous jump in public spending, as well as over information regarding the firing of two government scientists. But the overall themes and concerns have not really changed. Parliamentary scrutiny is perennially considered to be weak and overly politicized, and MPs are viewed as often uninterested in and/or ineffective at it.

Scrutiny is a bedrock concept in the logic of governance. By drawing a sharp distinction between the actions of government and holding government to account, the logic of governance gives governments freedom to act, but also, through scrutiny, little ability to escape responsibility. Scrutiny fits naturally with the division between government and opposition, and with the natural teamplay and competition of political parties. But scrutiny need not be inherently partisan, and it can also fit with the logic of representation, allowing MPs to voice individual perspectives, concerns, and grievances. Still, as already mentioned, applying the theory of scrutiny can be difficult in practice.

SCRUTINY IN THEORY VERSUS PRACTICE

Scrutiny is retrospective more than forward-looking. It emphasizes the past, though it may also focus on steps to avoid problems in the future. It does not make decisions itself, but demands that decision-makers account for their choices and actions. This idea of oversight that is separate from decision-making is an important concept in most large organizations and industries, such as through boards of directors or audit and accreditation bodies.

Scrutiny is closely linked to the principle of *responsibility*, which has two distinct elements relevant to the Canadian political system. One is the concept of *collective* responsibility, in which ministers are expected to stand together and be accountable for all actions of the government. While an ordinary government MP can, at some personal political risk, criticize their own leader or ministers, constitutional conventions strongly hold that a cabinet minister cannot do so in the same way. This is collective responsibility – the cabinet must stick together, rather than turning on each other. The second is individual *ministerial* responsibility, which emphasizes the role of each minister to account for anything within their areas of responsibility, not just for their own personal actions. This is the basic principle of Question Period – ministers must respond to questions about anything to do with their portfolios, and a simple denial of personal knowledge or complicity is inadequate.

But taking the theory of scrutiny and applying it in practice is difficult. What does it mean exactly to "account" and "take responsibility"? Where is the precise line between oversight and involvement in decision-making? How much responsibility must a minister take for decisions they didn't make themselves? How far can and should Parliament go in its quest to know what happened? These are perennial challenges for scrutiny.

For the most traditional champions of the logic of governance, scrutiny works best in pure form, hand-in-hand with the overall concentration of power in Parliament. They call for a stark and clear distinction between government and opposition, in which government holds all the power. When this clarity exists, it is argued, governments cannot squirm away and escape scrutiny and accountability for their actions. They hold the power, meaning they carry the accountability. They cannot shift blame onto the opposition, renegade MPs, public servants, or anyone else. They stand and/or fall on their own actions.

Sharon Sutherland argues strongly for this kind of concentrated accountability that leaves no room for shades of grey.[4] She contends that Parliament is not equipped to deal with complicated issues without exploiting and distorting them for partisan gain, writing that "the dominant Opposition parties and House committees are too partisan to devote real effort to protecting the public interest in good government,"[5] and "the kind and amount of scrutiny provided by House standing committees cannot in principle meet rationalistic standards for completeness of coverage of policy and administration."[6]

For Sutherland, scrutiny works best in brute force on a large scale, such as through Question Period, in which boundaries are well-established and the government and opposition clash in their normal opposing ways. In this way, scrutiny is driven by the natural forces of partisanship. The opposition will always be opportunistic and the government inevitably defensive, so these self-seeking behaviours may as well be harnessed rather than attempting to override or ignore them. Nuance and subtlety are seen as dangerous, because they provide loopholes and confusion that are easily exploited.

But this purist approach leaves little autonomy for MPs, again making them merely foot soldiers in the clash between government and opposition. Following the logic of representation, MPs unsurprisingly want to feel useful and to have an individual impact, for their own self-esteem and to build their careers and tell voters that they have accomplished things. They want more nuance, not less. Former parliamentary budget officer Kevin Page asserts that "we need to fix the system under which our MPs and senators scrutinize spending, as the current system is untenable. Many MPs with whom I have had discussions over the past 10 years do not feel inspired to do their jobs because they are not permitted to make changes."[7] Rather than merely being overseers, MPs want to have some part in decisions.

Consequently, while purist defenders like Sutherland remain, other discussions of scrutiny wrestle with how to balance the theory of concentrated accountability, based in the logic of governance, with the messier subtleties and practice of the logic of representation. But doing this in practice is difficult, for at least five reasons.

First is the vast complexity of government. Parliament has 338 MPs (including government ministers) along with 105 senators, but they oversee hundreds of billions of dollars of spending and the activities of hundreds of thousands of public servants. The challenge of "overload" is long-standing. Government seems to continually grow both bigger and more complex, surpassing any attempt to keep on top of it. MPs of all ideological stripes admit that it is impossible to monitor everything, let alone hold it all to account. In turn, governments might argue that MPs are too quick to jump to conclusions on things they do not fully understand. Regardless, parliamentarians cannot keep track of the full complexity of government and must select priorities.

Second and related is the imbalance of resources. While parliamentarians have come a long way from the mid-twentieth century when MPs had no staff or research assistance at all, their resources for scrutiny remain limited. MPs' assistants, caucus research bureaus, and the Library of Parliament all support MPs in their scrutiny duties. But capacity for deep and long-term research is largely absent. There is a significant amount of *indirect* support, most notably through the Auditor-General and more recent officers of Parliament, as discussed below. Governments have also made efforts to streamline and simplify reporting, to help MPs more easily digest information. But MPs remain limited in the available resources that they can apply to scrutiny.

A third reason is the competing demands on MPs' time and energy. As we saw in chapter 4, MPs hold many responsibilities, and even the most diligent can only spend a limited time absorbing and thinking about scrutiny issues. And while scrutiny may be at the heart of our parliamentary system, it is often not very rewarding work, especially on an individual level. A 1990s' survey of MPs found they ranked "scrutinizing government" the lowest of five roles compared to "policy" and "helping constituents," and there is little reason to think this has changed.[8] Scrutiny can sometimes be very tedious work, especially looking for substantive long-term issues rather than explosive but minor items. Furthermore, the focus on *oversight* rather than actually participating in decisions is unmotivating for many MPs who are already restless and searching for meaningful impact. And yet a considerable amount of the scrutiny process, such as the estimates, is a fixed part of the parliamentary calendar, making MPs go through the motions of work they find inconsequential.

Fourth, the public and electorate do not necessarily reward scrutiny. It is often difficult to understand and can involve technical interpretations, complexities, and shades of grey, rather than clear-cut choices between right and wrong. Small but outrageous matters can receive more attention than complex ones, even if the latter are much more significant in the long run.

One of the most famous incidents in the Harper government was the revelation that cabinet minister Bev Oda had stayed at an expensive London, England hotel, where her expenses included $16 for a glass of orange juice.[9] Some of Oda's other actions, such as controversy over whether she had revised a document to imply a deputy minister's approval, did not catch fire in the public imagination in the same way as taxpayers having to pay a costly hotel bill and $16 for a glass of orange juice.

Scrutiny is also rooted in deeper questions about the role of government and competing values. One reason that scrutiny can fixate on small things like a $16 glass of orange juice is not simply its simplicity, but the lack of disagreement on its questionableness. In contrast, inquiries into complex defence procurement contracts costing tens of billions of dollars inevitably raise deep and larger questions in which reasonable observers may disagree, such as over the role of the military, foreign policy commitments, and regional dimensions like the distribution of bases and shipbuilding contracts. Answers are far less clear-cut.

Scrutiny can also feel unrewarding because the payoff for any one individual to start doing it is minimal. In rare cases, an individual MP has gained a high profile for doggedly pursuing an issue. But even when a MP does find something significant, the collective is likely to soon overshadow the individual, as the pack – led by opposition party leaders – takes over. Since MPs largely rise and fall on their party label rather than individual effort anyway, there is little political profit in building deep scrutiny expertise as an individual MP. In fact, work scrutinizing a complex government issue in Ottawa can take away from effort on a more narrow constituency issue that is more likely to deliver crucial personal votes.

A fifth and the most complex reason is that MPs are not alone in scrutinizing government. Journalists, interest groups, activists, and others also see themselves in this role. This is essential to remember in any discussion about the historic role of Parliament in holding government to account. In the twentieth century, the mass media increasingly saw itself in this role as well, assisted by innovations like the Access to Information Act that gave anyone, not just parliamentarians, access to government documents. This has expanded even more in the twenty-first century. Online technology and digitized information now provide easy access to what used to be held only in bulky printed form in Ottawa, and activists and wonks can use this information to create their own websites and databases to disseminate information even further. Social media also allows quick transmission of information and incidents without relying on MPs, or journalists, as intermediaries. Relatedly, MPs are also aware that this scrutiny is also on them, not just on government. Parliamentarians investigating government spending and actions must be equally ready for scrutiny of their own behaviour.

These five reasons mean that parliamentary scrutiny is more opportunistic than systematic, and will always be. MPs (and senators) do not and realistically cannot operate alone in their function of scrutiny, even though they and Parliament may be evaluated in those terms. Instead, they are part of a larger, highly imperfect system that attempts to hold government to account, and as public figures they are themselves held to account as well.

Scrutiny is also deeply *political*, and it serves little purpose to deny or ignore this. MPs are not disinterested evaluators. They are human and ambitious – for their ideals, for their parties, and for themselves. This returns us to Sutherland's arguments above, that scrutiny must recognize the inevitable self-interest of all actors involved. For the opposition, the purpose of scrutiny is always to nail the government to the wall, to embarrass and humiliate it, in the hope of electoral gain and replacing the government, or at least surpassing the other opposition parties. For the government, it is to defend its actions and to deflect and dilute criticism, and ideally squelch it entirely. For individual MPs on both sides, it is to build profiles and careers, whether as crusading opposition MPs or as dogged government backbenchers who nimbly defend the government to prove their loyalty and worthiness of promotion.

In earlier chapters I discussed how the Canadian House of Commons is compared unfavourably to its British counterpart. Many of these concern scrutiny – such as the lack of meaningful government backbencher questions in Question Period, or the weakness of Canadian parliamentary committees – and especially scrutiny by government MPs. In Canada scrutiny is almost exclusively an opposition pursuit. Government MPs spend far more energy defending the government than scrutinizing it, though this is not necessarily by their own choice. Scrutiny is very much anchored in the logic of governance; the logic of representation, unless it happens to coincide with party interest, is only weakly present.

In contrast, British MPs and committees do have a clearer record of independence, cross-party cooperation, and holding the government's feet to the fire. The reasons for this are heavily debated, and some have been covered in earlier chapters. British MPs may be more aggressive because of safer electoral districts and a larger chamber with fewer opportunities for promotion. Giving the Speaker control over Question Time gives more opportunity for backbenchers to ask uncomfortable questions to ministers. There may be a stronger ongoing culture of scrutiny in Britain that empowers and socializes new MPs in a different way than in Canada. The relative strength of British scrutiny is even counterintuitive when considering the reasons above, since the British government is even larger and more complex, while its MPs are often less resourced than Canadians.

On the other hand, as discussed in chapter 2, in Britain Parliament is indisputably the most important political institution, while in Canada both the courts and federalism have long played significant and consequential roles, including in the area of scrutiny (especially with the *Charter of Rights and Freedoms*). Only recently have British courts begun to play similar roles. While it should not be overstated, Britain has long seemed ahead of Canada in parliamentary scrutiny, but there may also be other reasons for this. Regardless, once again British parliamentarians seem to have found a better reconciliation between the logic of representation and the logic of governance when it comes to scrutiny.

PARLIAMENT AND MONEY

Money is a special category in parliamentary business. As discussed in earlier chapters, Parliament historically held the power of supply, in which it had to approve any government spending, as well as power over introducing or raising taxes. This outright veto was exchanged in 1968 for "opposition days" in the parliamentary calendar and a modern committee system. But Parliament still retains multiple areas of input over government spending.

In turn, government still holds the sole power of introducing money bills that call for taxation or spending; private members and the Senate cannot do so. Signalling the special importance of taxation, governments wishing to introduce or change taxes must first introduce a "ways and means" motion – essentially a warning that the government will be introducing taxation legislation. These motions correspond with the overall "strong executive" design and the principle that the government initiates and decides, while Parliament oversees and approves the decisions.

Parliament follows an annual fiscal cycle.[10] In March, governments must present "estimates" of planned spending for the fiscal year, organized by departments and agencies. These are then referred to the corresponding standing committee for review. But typically this review is rudimentary since the estimates are deemed accepted by committees at the end of May, regardless of the committee's activity, after which they go through a similar automatic acceptance by the House on June 30. Former Commons law clerk Rob Walsh describes the process in blunt terms:

> A committee, whether it has reported back to the House or not, will be deemed to have done so on 31 May. Typically, a standing committee meets with the responsible minister, accompanied by a few departmental officials, once in the March to May period to consider the main estimates of the department. There is an exchange between committee members and the minister and the officials, which usually takes two hours. Shortly afterward the committee reports to the House that it "has considered" the main estimates, without any comment or recommended alterations. Committee reports are not allowed to comment on any of

the estimates they reviewed but report only on the votes taken. In other words, it's a "yes" or "no" on each of the estimates – and it's never "no."[11]

The estimates process has never been satisfying. Jackson and Atkinson wrote in 1980 that "[m]eetings on estimates are the worst attended of all types of committee meetings."[12] C.E.S. Franks observed in 1987 that "the [estimates] process has had a large element of futility."[13] No less than the sitting clerk of the House of Commons, Robert Marleau, referred in 1992 to "the dismal, farcical, absolutely silly exercise of review of estimates and supply…. Passing billions of dollars under some form of closure at the last minute, on June 30, is hardly a rational way of passing supply legislation."[14] And problems existed well before the 1968 changes. Jack Stillborn writes that "[d]issatisfaction among parliamentarians with the form and substance of Parliament's role concerning the estimates dates back virtually to Confederation."[15]

The estimates are also a prime example of the limits of technical reform to address deep underlying issues in the paradox of Parliament. Various adjustments have been made over the years to try to enhance the estimates process. For example, since 1997 departments have been required to present a Report on Plans and Priorities and a Departmental Performance Report in the spring and fall respectively, and in 2001 the opposition was given the power to select two departments annually for deeper scrutiny. But, as Brodie suggests, "committee scrutiny of the estimates never lived up [to] these hopes,"[16] and Walsh remarks that "the information setting out the Government's proposed expenditures is both overwhelming and uninformative for parliamentary purposes."[17] This is not to say that honest and significant undertakings have not been made to find a workable system. The challenge, clearly, is the ability of parliamentarians to perform reasonable oversight of giant government operations, within a partisan environment, under any conditions.

In contrast to the perpetual backwater of the estimates, the budget and budget speech are among the highest profile events in the parliamentary calendar. The annual budget speech by the Minister of Finance to the House of Commons is a dramatic, nationally watched event in which the House of Commons is on full display. Particular emphasis has long been given to budgetary secrecy; by convention, no details should be revealed before they are presented to Parliament (though also because of the possible effect on financial markets). While governments tend to leak many of the provisions beforehand anyway, the budget speech in the House of Commons still stands as the pivotal moment. In 2003 the Ontario provincial government experimented with holding its budget speech outside the legislature at a factory, to deep disapproval – thus reasserting that in Canada the budget speech is a legislative event.

And yet it is not. Unlike the estimates, the budget speech is merely customary, and is not required in the Standing Orders (though the overall budget debate is).[18] From the viewpoint of parliamentary procedure the budget speech has no special relevance; the more significant action is the motion customarily introduced just before the speech "That this House approve in general the budgetary policy of the government." The budget speech itself is the follow-up in support of the motion. The motion and the formal budget implementation bill – increasingly a massive document as we saw in chapter 5's discussion of omnibus bills – are the true documents that must be approved by Parliament and upon which a government can rise or fall. The budget speech is thus a parliamentary event that has little to do with Parliament itself beyond the symbolic act of presenting it in the chamber, and budget debates follow the customary patterns of government and opposition mobilizing for and against consent.

The contrast between the mostly ignored minutiae of the estimates and the high-profile budget shows how parliamentary power is primarily collective and blunt. MPs can bring down entire governments through the budget, which is considered a confidence motion. But they have limited power to fine-tune specific spending. In practical reality, parliamentary scrutiny comes too late in the process to matter much. Geneviève Tellier writes: "Budgets are written by people in a few decision-making centres situated at the top of the government apparatus, close to the political power, at the expense of elected representatives' participation in the budgetary process. And yet our democratic institutions place parliamentarians at the heart of the process."[19] Donald Savoie pessimistically says: "I know of no one who is prepared to make the case that Parliament is able to hold the government to account on budget matters or that MPs play a meaningful role in reviewing the government's spending plans. However, I know many credible voices who argue the contrary."[20]

A potential middle ground was developed in the 1990s with the tradition of "pre-budget hearings" by the House of Commons Standing Committee on Finance. These are normally held in the fall, prior to the budget being introduced in late winter, and have been adopted in many provincial legislatures as well. The pre-budget hearings are an opportunity for interest groups and other stakeholders to present their case in a high-profile national forum. But as with all committee proceedings, their effect is mostly indirect. For most witnesses, the hearings are a forum to make their case to the government and the public; the committee itself is only the host vehicle. Governments themselves can use the hearings to test ideas. While the pre-budget hearings are considered far more rewarding work than the estimates, and probably are the most prestigious of all committee activities in Parliament, they are still of modest, indirect significance in the overall policy process. As well, this function is not really scrutiny at all, since the focus is on new spending rather than examining past spending – though this forward-looking spotlight on new things greatly increases its appeal for MPs and the media alike.

Two other Commons committees are primarily tasked with scrutiny functions. One is the Standing Committee on Public Accounts, which primarily examines matters related to the Auditor-General's report. As we saw in chapter 5, the public accounts committee stands apart from other committees, with an opposition chair since 1957 and a national and international network of similar legislative committees. But despite its long-standing special status, Public Accounts is not necessarily a popular assignment, because it is solely a *scrutiny* committee. The changes it does achieve are often technical and apolitical, with little public notice. Another committee, the Standing Committee on Government Operations and Estimates, was created in 2002. This committee has a very broad mandate to review all aspects of government administration and operations, including the estimates process. But like the public accounts committee, its work is often technical, and it is again not necessarily sought by MPs as an opportunity. The House and Senate additionally share a Standing Joint Committee for the Scrutiny of Regulations, which also labours in relative obscurity.

The basic principle is clear: financial scrutiny is a major but sometimes underwhelming aspect of Parliament. MPs rarely find it rewarding; the most significant impacts are often technical and lack newsworthiness, and high-profile activities like the budget speech or pre-budget hearings are symbolically important but less substantive in other ways. The weakness of financial scrutiny in the Canadian Parliament suggests it does not even fully live up to the ideals of the logic of governance, and it certainly leaves limited room for the pursuit of the logic of representation.

OFFICERS OF PARLIAMENT

Over the course of its history Parliament has developed a range of specialized arms-length offices to carry out a range of activities. These followed from the long-standing Auditor-General, established in 1878 to review and approve the annual public accounts. Two other officers were created in the next century: the Chief Electoral Officer, created in 1920, and the Commissioner of Official Languages, created in 1969 with the introduction of official bilingualism. The Office of the Auditor-General (OAG) was considerably overhauled in the 1970s to add a strong investigatory power – to review not just whether revenue and spending were correctly accounted for, but whether taxpayers received "value for money." This opened up a new world of investigations, making the Auditor-General a much more public figure and known in the media as the "taxpayers' watchdog." OAG reports can receive considerable media attention, particularly if they contain obvious examples of egregious spending. Largely overlooked was that these are technically reports *to Parliament* and fall to the public accounts committee for follow-up and action.

Further officers were created beginning in the 1980s. The introduction of access to information legislation prompted creation of the Information Commissioner in 1983; simultaneously, concerns about privacy of information led to the Privacy Commissioner. Three offices broadly dealing with ethical issues were created in the 2000s: the Conflict of Interest and Ethics Commissioner (overseeing issues for MPs and ministers), the Commissioner of Lobbying, and the Public Sector Integrity Commissioner (for public servant "whistleblowers"); some of these replaced earlier, somewhat different, offices. A ninth officer, the Parliamentary Budget Officer, arose in a more complicated way and is discussed in detail below.

The officers of Parliament are both a unified category and a sprawling collection with little in common with each other. For many years it was not even clear how many there were. An authoritative study in 2003 estimated there were "six to eight" depending on how their mandates and reporting relationships were understood.[21] More recently it is generally agreed that there are the nine listed above.[22] (Another entity, the Commissioner of the Environment and Sustainable Development, is housed within the Office of the Auditor-General and is not considered an independent officer equivalent to the others.)

The system of parliamentary officers is an eclectic mess because each was created at a different time to fulfil a specialized purpose, rather than as a comprehensive network. They remain often very different from one another. Some have clear operational responsibilities, such as approving the public accounts, administering access to information appeals, or registering and tracking all lobbying activity. Others are solely complaint driven, like the Conflict of Interest and Ethics Commissioner or the Public Sector Integrity Commissioner. Some investigate broad policy areas, like the Privacy and the Official Languages commissioners; some are limited to specialized inquiries. Officers may have a combination of the above responsibilities. They also vary considerably in size from the hundreds of staff in the Office of the Auditor-General to much smaller operations.

The one thing they all have in common is that they are responsible to Parliament, not to the Government of Canada. Technically, every officer is a servant of Parliament. Yet as arms-length officers they operate on their own and in practice are widely seen by the public as "independent" from everything, possibly including Parliament. This poses both opportunities and challenges for MPs, who may feel overshadowed or eclipsed by these nominal "servants."

Officers typically bring considerable professional expertise and experience to their specific portfolio, but negligible political background. The Auditor-General, always a professional accountant, in particular enjoys considerable public legitimacy and esteem as a disinterested evaluator of government spending, with the resources and expertise to carry out detailed investigations and evaluations. In contrast, as we have seen, MPs feel both underresourced and too pressured by party discipline to do any real scrutiny not driven by partisan considerations.

Some observers, notably Donald Savoie, argue that officers have ballooned out of control and "they now appear to function as free agents accountable to no one."[23] Sharon Sutherland has long been a particular critic of the Auditor-General, saying the office holds "what may be the loosest and most incomplete set of responsibilities for a state auditor in existence."[24] In Savoie's view, "Parliament has contributed to its own decline by effectively outsourcing the scrutiny function to independent officers."

However, the relationship is at least somewhat balanced. Most officers report or liaise through an appropriate standing committee, and ideally there is a good working relationship between the two.[25] Typically, committees may hold hearings to discuss officers' reports; this gives an opportunity both for the officers to repeat their findings and for MPs to amplify and take on the issue themselves.

In most cases a committee-officer relationship is shaped by the overriding issue facing all standing committees: autonomy versus relevance. Many discussions with parliamentary officers take place with relatively little public notice, because the issues are either not contentious or are a low priority for the government and other observers. In contrast, when an issue is more high-profile or downright explosive, committees are more likely to polarize along partisan lines and filter the officer's findings through those dimensions. If Parliament has outsourced its scrutiny role to the officers, it may be because Parliament itself struggles to fulfil the role.

The complexities of officers of Parliament are illustrated by the saga of the most recently created officer: the Parliamentary Budget Officer (PBO). The PBO was created in 2006 by the newly elected Harper government. This was one of several financial accountability reforms promised by the Conservatives after the spectacular Liberal "sponsorship scandal" of the early 2000s, in which public money was siphoned off to Liberal-connected advertising agencies. These reforms introduced or strengthened other officers of Parliament, namely the Commissioner of Lobbying, the Public Sector Integrity Commissioner, and the Conflict of Interest and Ethics Commissioner.

Unlike the others, the creation of the Parliamentary Budget Officer was not directly in response to the scandal. Instead it was an entirely new office intended to support MPs in researching and understanding government budgets. This was distinct from the Auditor-General, whose mandate is solely retrospective, reviewing past government spending and the public accounts. In contrast, the PBO was to provide forward-looking forecasts and analysis on government spending before or as it happened. Kevin Page, a long-time public servant, was appointed as the first Parliamentary Budget Officer in 2008.

But the status of the PBO and Kevin Page soon proved unclear. The Officer was administratively housed in the Library of Parliament, alongside the long-standing Research Branch that provided general research support for all parliamentarians and committees, and Page was expected to report to the Parliamentary Librarian. However, Page balked at this, arguing that his office needed to be fully independent, with the same status as fully established officers like the Auditor-General.

This led to a surprisingly public feud with the then-Librarian of Parliament.[26] A critical difference was that the Library provided its research in a scrupulously neutral manner, and was always careful not to provide evaluations that could be seen as overly critical or favouring one political perspective. However, Page openly criticized the government as the PBO, in a way that challenged the traditional discreet neutrality of the regular parliamentary bureaucracy.

Throughout his mandate, Page clashed with the Conservative government over the scope of his authority and access to information. This was in addition to his actual reports, which were often highly critical of government spending and forecasts.[27] The issue became very politicized. The opposition, which made much use of the critical reports for its own attacks, generally took the PBO's side and championed a wide mandate for the office. The government – which ironically had created the office in the first place – was more resistant. The bitter situation raged throughout Page's five-year term. He did not seek renewal in 2013, after which he published a book, *Unaccountable*, highly critical of the Harper government.[28]

Page's successors as PBO were less outspoken and did not have the same high profile. The change in government from the

Conservatives to the Liberals in 2015 also allowed for a reset of the relationship. In a predictable development, in 2016 the PBO issued a report criticizing a lack of transparency in the Liberal budget and the Liberals pushed back, while the Conservative Party now argued the PBO needed more freedom to do its job![29] Fortunately, the relationship never again descended into the highly personal, bitter fight between Page and the Conservative government. By the time of the appointment of the next PBO in 2018, the office had become institutionalized, with legislation finally passed in 2017 affirming the PBO as an independent officer equivalent to the Auditor-General and others.[30]

The story of the PBO illustrates larger issues with officers of Parliament. The office started with a flawed design and lacked clarity about its basic independence. Since there is no master framework for officers of Parliament anyway, it was difficult to ascertain where the PBO fit. The office became highly personalized around its first incumbent, yet without his persistence and obstinacy it would likely have faded away rather than becoming fully independent.

And attitudes depended on what side of Parliament one sat. The PBO was created as a Conservative election promise, yet once in power the Conservatives became the focus of its criticisms and became increasingly exasperated at their own creation. In turn, the opposition found little or no fault with the PBO, since it scrutinized government and not itself – until the Liberals came to power and became the new focus of the PBO, at which point they found the office's demands inconvenient.

Officers of Parliament are clearly here to stay, though their exact number and configuration are likely to continue evolving in the future. But they remain an exceptional and somewhat unclear aspect of Parliament. They do not fit neatly into the logic of either governance or representation. They work for parliamentarians, but are largely independent even of Parliament. Officers' relationships with Parliament are *symbiotic* more than *dependent* – that is, each side uses the relationship for its own ends. And because their focus is the scrutiny of government, officers will typically be more popular on the opposition than the government benches, regardless of which party is in power, as an extension of the overall parliamentary game between government and opposition.

PARLIAMENTARY SCRUTINY: HOW FAR CAN IT GO?

Another of the great tensions in Parliament's scrutiny role is the extent of Parliament's powers to hold government and individuals to account. How far can Parliament go? How much access should it have to relevant information? How wide should its scope and focus be? To what extent can it focus on individuals, particularly public servants as opposed to elected officials? How far can it dig to get to the bottom of things?

As mentioned, this debate has taken various forms over the years. In the early 2000s, significant discussions arose over the concept of ministerial responsibility and the ability of Parliament to hold public servants directly to account. This shifted later to debates about Parliament's access to information, especially in the post-9/11 security world, and its role in military deployments to Afghanistan. Later, the COVID-19 pandemic provoked emergency debates about Parliament's basic ability to operate and hold government to account amid an unprecedented crisis.

In each instance, the debate is not really between the logic of representation and the logic of governance. Rather, it is primarily a discussion *within* the logic of governance, with the role and freedom of individual MPs a secondary concern. The logic of governance stresses the principle that government makes decisions and is then held accountable to Parliament *for* these decisions. But, once again, what exactly does the theory of accountability mean in practice?

This debate is most clearly seen in the concept of *ministerial responsibility*. As we saw earlier, the core principle of ministerial responsibility is simple: that government ministers are *responsible* for activities within their portfolio, allowing them to take both credit and blame for anything under their watch. This is a comprehensive, institutional responsibility, distinct from more personal errors when ministers are found to have personally committed inappropriate or questionable actions and are pressured to resign. For example, in 2008 when Minister of Foreign Affairs Maxime Bernier was found to have mishandled secret documents, he resigned for his personal error. In one of the most infamous Canadian political scandals, Fisheries Minister John Fraser resigned in 1985 after approving "tainted tuna" for sale after it had been rejected by his department's inspectors. In both cases, the minister had personally committed the action that led to their resignation.

But the broader principle of ministerial responsibility is also to be accountable for things not in the personal control of ministers. This is a deeply complex and multifaceted concept. It is rooted in a mix of executive, legislative, and judicial power and authority and, like other aspects of Parliament, it blends legal and statutory written rules with more unwritten political conventions. Considerable scholarship has been written on the concept and its exact meaning and implications. Our focus is on *Parliament's* role in ministerial responsibility, and two broad issues are most relevant.

The first broad issue is the distinction in responsibility between accounting and resigning. It is not uncommon for opposition MPs to demand ministers resign for a wide array of issues under their responsibility. Yet it is extremely rare for ministers to do so, and unlikely that the opposition actually expects them to resign. Rather, this is part of the ongoing scrutiny game between the two sides. Ministerial responsibility does not necessarily mean losing their job, but rather answering questions and accounting for and explaining the government's actions. This is seen on an everyday basis in Question Period, and also in the media.

One of the most exemplary and high-profile examples of ministerial responsibility in Canadian history was in 2000, in what was known as the "grants and contributions" scandal. This was spurred by an internal audit in the then-Human Resources and Development Canada (HRDC) department that found insufficient documentation for approximately a billion dollars of HRDC funds transferred to other organizations. This quickly exploded in the media and Parliament as "the billion dollar boondoggle." The Minister of HRDC, Jane Stewart, took responsibility for the issue. She never resigned, but was the focus of repeated questions in the House of Commons, parliamentary committees, and the media. The issue dominated headlines for months, though in the end only a small portion of money was found to have been actually misspent.

However, the problem had not happened on Stewart's watch. She was newly appointed to the HRDC portfolio, and the audit's findings covered the time of the previous minister. While her predecessor remained in cabinet in a different portfolio, Stewart was now the face of the department and had to answer for decisions that happened before she arrived. Furthermore, despite the total sum of money, which made it such a high-profile "boondoggle," the lack of documentation was a relatively low-level administrative matter in which a minister would not be expected to have personal involvement. Nevertheless, Stewart stood up and repeatedly took responsibility for the problem and for fixing it, to the likely detriment of her political career.

The second broad issue for ministerial responsibility is the role of public servants and other actors. How far can Parliament go *beyond* ministers into government departments themselves? This issue arose in the HRDC scandal and several other inquiries of the era. MPs were frustrated that the exclusive focus on the minister, despite their lack of personal culpability, left parliamentarians uninformed and unsatisfied because they felt they could not truly get to the bottom of the issue. The minister took overall responsibility, but it was the public servants who had taken the actions and who seemingly held the facts. In some cases, public servants were called before committees in what many felt was an interrogation of their actions, and were "named and blamed" in public debates. This led to a considerable discussion in the 1990s and early 2000s about ministerial responsibility, and specifically whether it remained an effective principle to allow meaningful parliamentary scrutiny. Some reformers argued for a more nuanced, multi-stage version in which public servants would be more directly accountable to Parliament.

Yet others resisted. One of the strongest champions of concentrated accountability, as introduced earlier, was Sharon Sutherland. In these debates Sutherland championed the simplicity of concentrated accountability, arguing that individual ministerial responsibility creates a "timeless focal point for legal, political and administrative responsiveness" within Parliament.[31] In contrast, she was highly skeptical of Parliament's ability to interact with public servants and to deal with nuanced and complex issues through anything but blunt force and a partisan lens. Sutherland recognized that MPs were political actors, and that the opposition would inevitably look to find fault with the government by any means it could, while the government would defend itself. In her view, accountability should flow *with* political forces rather than try to counteract them.

Others argued, however, that while Sutherland's position was clear and simple, it was unsatisfying, both for parliamentarians who did seek more nuanced roles and ultimately for the better oversight and improvement of government. Simply loading responsibility on ministers meant that actual blame and accountability were elusive. Donald Savoie argued that the increasing complexity of governance and the complex role of senior public servants meant that "career officials can no longer quietly operate away from political debate and citizens' scrutiny."[32] C.E.S. Franks in particular advocated for adopting the British practice of "accounting officers" in which heads of departments were given specific authority, and thus also direct responsibility, for administrative matters under their command.[33] David Smith captures the issue that, as with much else about Parliament, there was a gap between elegant theory and public demand and expectations: "For the public especially, the traditional boundaries of the debate are disappointing and confusing since they do not admit of public expectations. Modern emphasis upon openness, responsiveness and transparency fits awkwardly with a convention whose practice is determined by shifting calculations of partisan advantage."[34]

This debate died down following the election of the Harper government in 2006 and its introduction of accountability reforms that partly followed reformers' suggestions, including the accounting officer concept. Ministerial responsibility was less of an issue under the Harper government, possibly because the Harper Conservatives held a tight rein over communications even from ministers themselves, let alone public servants – very different from the leaky sieve of the Liberal era. Instead, debate began to shift to different dimensions: Parliament's role in military and foreign policy, and its access to information.

Parliament and War

The September 11, 2001 terror attacks and the subsequent "global war on terrorism" placed a new dimension on parliamentary scrutiny – how far could Parliament go in matters of national security? Prior to 2001, Parliament's role in security matters, particularly overseas military deployments, was checkered and uneven, with no clear precedent. While Parliament did vote to declare war on Germany in 1939 at the start of the Second World War, the constitutional precedent was unclear. Parliament did not vote on UN peacekeeping deployments in the twentieth century, and only vaguely affirmed Canada's participation in the 1991 Gulf War after hostilities had already started. It also showed itself to be deferential, if not always willingly, in domestic security matters, such as by approving use of the War Measures Act in 1970 during the October Crisis, a vote that was opposed only by the New Democratic Party.

But responses to the 9/11 attacks and the Canadian military mission to Afghanistan led to a new parliamentary interest in security and defence matters. Parliamentary committees began to hold inquiries and scrutinize government and military actions in more detail. This new interest also evoked calls for reforms that argued for a more non-partisan, less politicized approach to scrutiny of security and defence issues. As Philippe Lagassé puts it, "An underlying assumption of these criticisms is that empowering MPs and parliamentary committees and encouraging a non-partisan approach to military questions will improve Canadian defence accountability."[35] However, like Sutherland, Lagassé notes the fundamental reality of partisanship and the divide between government and opposition. Like Sutherland, he argues for *harnessing* rather than attempting to resist or erase partisan forces, stating: "Reforms that dilute ministerial responsibility and the adversarial character of the House of Commons will weaken rather than strengthen defence accountability. Indeed, reinforcing ministerial responsibility and encouraging partisan competition could bolster Canadian defence accountability."[36]

The Afghanistan missions eventually saw a new parliamentary involvement with voting on military missions. As noted, Parliament had little involvement in approving military deployments beyond the declaration of war in the Second World War. Parliament did not vote on the initial deployment to Afghanistan in 2002, nor on the decision to not join the American invasion of Iraq in 2003. However, in 2006, the newly elected Harper government held a House of Commons vote on whether to extend the Afghanistan mission until 2009, past its scheduled 2007 end date. A second vote was held in 2008 to extend the mission to 2011. This practice of voting on active military deployments continued for other missions to Libya and Syria and was continued by the Trudeau government after 2015.

While nominally a win for parliamentary autonomy, these votes are concerning in other ways, especially through the lens of scrutiny. They blur the line between *decisions* and *scrutiny* of decisions by implicating Parliament itself in the decisions. Boucher and Nossal argue that the Afghanistan votes politicized the military mission, as "the Harper government realized the partisan political benefits that could be reaped by submitting combat missions to the House of Commons."[37] The first Afghanistan vote in particular was extraordinarily close – 149 to 145 – and badly split the Liberal Party, while allowing the government to claim parliamentary support in what was a very complex and controversial conflict. Lagassé has been particularly critical of the House of Commons' involvement in voting on military deployments, arguing that the votes badly mixed executive and legislative authority.[38] Writing with Norman Hillmer, he says:

> [Stephen Harper's] intention was not to give the House the power to decide, but to increase the perceived legitimacy of his government's decision. By bringing the extensions to a vote, moreover, the Harper government blurred understandings of which body – the executive or the legislature – was responsible for the decision. The votes allowed the executive to launder controversial policies through the Commons, giving the impression that MPs were making the decisions, rather than the government alone. This in turn meant that the House could be made to share the blame, or be used to deflect criticisms of the government, as the popularity of the mission fell. This strategy was especially effective because a portion of Liberal MPs voted for the extension in 2006 and the entire Liberal caucus voted with the government in 2008.[39]

Ian Brodie, chief of staff to Stephen Harper from 2006 to 2008, pushes back against this argument, saying that such worries were "groundless."[40] "[T]he prospect of the parliamentary vote improved the government's oversight of the mission, but it did not stop the Liberals or anyone else from criticizing the mission in the House and elsewhere."[41] Brodie argues the votes were important in establishing legitimacy for what were important but controversial operations, enhancing rather than compromising the place of Parliament.

A more recent example of parliamentary involvement in foreign policy took place in 2021, when the Conservatives made an opposition day motion condemning Chinese government activities against the Uighur people as constituting genocide. The opposition parties immediately endorsed the motion, but the government equivocated, worried about upsetting Canada-China relations and prospects for the release of two Canadians then detained in China, even though the motion was only symbolic and did not change Canadian law or policies. In the end, the cabinet abstained from voting, while many Liberal backbenchers endorsed the motion, which passed unanimously. Again, criticisms arose about the politicization of foreign policy, especially amid complex diplomatic negotiations over the detained Canadians. Is Parliament an appropriate instrument in such cases?

Unlike other dimensions of Parliament, party discipline itself is rarely targeted or lamented in these debates about scrutiny of foreign, defence, and security policy. With some exceptions like the Liberals in 2006, parties generally move in lockstep on major foreign policy issues given their importance. Thus, the typical arguments of the logic of representation – which tends to valorize the individual MP and constituency and group representation – are less in play here. Furthermore, few would argue that parliamentarians themselves should be designing and directing policy here, which is clearly the purview of the government, public servants, and military officials. Rather, the arguments are more within the logic of governance itself – how far and how detailed can Parliament get in approving and scrutinizing the actions of government?

As with the ministerial responsibility argument, there is a compelling simplicity and elegance to the notion of concentrated rather than diluted power. If authority and responsibility are clearly and exclusively concentrated in government and government ministers, there is no room for them to hide. They cannot blame others and must take the full brunt of scrutiny, both for overall decisions and the details within them. In this sense Parliament secures *more* authority and legitimacy if it decides *less*, because it then does not get mired in complexity by mixing decisions with scrutiny of those decisions.

But what then is the use of this dignified authority, if it cannot be used for much? There is also an argument for a messier approach that spreads power around, giving MPs and the public a greater sense of involvement and say in critical decisions. The fact that military and foreign policy issues in the twenty-first century are increasingly amorphous and complex gives weight to *both* perspectives: either that the issues are so complex and multifaceted that governments must be given exclusive room to decide and manoeuvre, or that they are so important and value-laden that Canadians must have more say through their elected representatives.

Parliament's Access to Documents

A related aspect of the question of how far Parliament can go in its scrutiny function is its powers to access all information – its power "to send for persons, papers and records." This covers both government and private individuals. Serious problems over summoning people are rare, though not unheard of. Conflict over "papers and records" are more common. As Rob Walsh dryly notes, "generally governments do not like to hand over documents, particularly if they contain information that may have political implications."[42] At the same time, there may be reasonable grounds – such as national security, personal privacy, or commercial sensitivity – why documents might not be shared, especially in a fully public forum.

This has provoked many conflicts between Parliament and government. The most important in recent history were two disputes in 2010 and 2011 during the Harper government, and another in 2021 under the Trudeau government. These are important not only in the precedents they set, but also in how party positions were reversed, demonstrating the inherent cyclicality of parliamentary disputes.

The first in 2010 was over the "detainee documents" – information about Afghans captured or detained by the Canadian military before being handed over to other authorities and possibly mistreated. The government refused to release documents requested by a parliamentary committee, citing security concerns. The issue expanded and eventually led to a formal request by opposition MPs to the Speaker of the House to affirm parliamentary supremacy. In a major ruling, Speaker Peter Milliken affirmed this right that Parliament had the unfettered and ultimate privilege to request and receive any papers or records it desired, regardless of government objections or concerns. However, Milliken did suggest that the government and opposition negotiate a mechanism to accommodate any genuine security concerns, which was done. Heather MacIvor criticizes the latter concession for implicitly curbing parliamentary supremacy: "Now that a majority of MPs have agreed that the government can withhold cabinet documents and legal advice, it will be very difficult for any future speaker to repeat Milliken's sweeping assertion of privilege."[43]

The issue returned over the costs of purchasing F-35 fighter jets. In late 2010 the Standing Committee on Finance requested that the government supply information on the costs of a number of initiatives, including the F-35 procurement. The government pushed back, citing cabinet confidence. This eventually led to a ruling by the Speaker that the government was *prima facie* (that is, likely) breaching the privileges of the House, referring the matter to a committee for further investigation. This prompted a motion of non-confidence by the Liberals that passed on March 25, 2011, triggering a general election in which the Conservatives won a majority for the first time. The curious result then was that the Conservative government was found to be possibly violating the rights of Parliament, and yet the electorate gave them a majority government.

The 2011 showdown is important for any discussion of scrutiny, as it combines both *parliamentary* and *electoral* elements into a closely linked single episode. As we have repeatedly seen, some argue that Parliament's role should be blunt rather than nuanced, harnessing natural partisan forces and ultimately letting voters decide. This is exactly what happened in 2011. By going to an election which it then won, the government could claim vindication of its actions, regardless of any concerns about parliamentary rights and privilege. This was a blow to many champions of parliamentary scrutiny, especially given that the opposition parties had triggered the non-confidence vote and election, seemingly confident that voters would share their outrage over the government's evasiveness. And while voters may have had concerns, when they looked at the available options in the election, the Conservatives were most popular.

A decade later in 2021, another showdown developed between the government and the House of Commons. But now the positions were reversed and a Liberal government was in power. The issue was about two scientists fired from a Winnipeg government laboratory, and more specifically *why* they had been fired. The government resisted full disclosure of the reasons for the firings, citing national security concerns. The opposition argued that the government was trying to hide embarrassing information and errors. As in 2010 and 2011, the government was in a minority position, and so the opposition parties were able to cooperate and pass motions demanding disclosure of the documents. This clearly pitted "the will of the House" against the government.

However, while the earlier disputes were largely resolved by a Speaker's ruling and a general election respectively, the 2021 situation escalated into new territory. After repeated failures by the two sides to agree on a compromise, in June 2021 the president of the Public Health Agency of Canada, which oversaw the government lab, was summoned to appear in the House of Commons chamber and produce the relevant documents. While calling a person "before the bar" (a physical metal bar that sits in the chamber opposite the Speaker) is an ancient parliamentary tradition, it had not been done since 1913 in Canada for a non-parliamentarian. (In 1991 and 2002 MPs were called to the bar after misbehaving in the House.)[44] The president appeared without the documents and was admonished by the Speaker for defying the will of the House. This calling-out of a public servant is concerning, and returns us to earlier discussions about the degree to which Parliament can and should directly hold public servants to account. The agency head was clearly following the will of the government, not necessarily his own, and yet was directly targeted. However, the government moved into disturbing territory of its own by seeking a court order preventing the release of the documents, naming the House Speaker as the respondent.[45] This was also shocking and raised constitutional questions about the relationship among parliamentary supremacy, executive discretion, and the role of the courts.

The court application was dropped after the 2021 election was called, and the dissolution of the House terminated the parliamentary motions as well. However, the inconclusive election result of another Liberal minority meant the issue was not resolved, in the way that the 2011 election and Conservative majority victory had provided a clear reset of the whole matter, and it continued to drag out with no consensus.

Much of the Winnipeg lab struggle revolved around the status of a body called the National Security and Intelligence Committee of

Parliamentarians (NSICOP). The NSICOP was created in 2017, after years of discussion about how parliamentarians could effectively oversee activities that involved sensitive national security information, and following previous temporary committees, including the one struck in 2010 to oversee the Afghan detainee documents.[46] Committee members are all MPs or senators who hold enhanced security clearances and are bound to secrecy about the committee's work.

But despite its name and membership, the NSICOP is not a truly parliamentary committee, under the jurisdiction of the House and/or Senate. Rather, it is an instrument of the government – the executive – with its members named directly by the prime minister and its administration and work supported directly by government, not parliamentary, resources. In contrast, similar committees in the United Kingdom, Australia, and New Zealand are all clearly committees of Parliament.[47]

In the 2021 lab scientist controversy, the government offered to provide the documents to the NSICOP, arguing this was the appropriate way to submit to parliamentary scrutiny while maintaining national security. But the opposition Conservatives rejected this compromise, arguing that the committee was too beholden to government and secrecy rules and insufficient to investigate the matter. MP Michael Chong said, "The purpose of the committee is the general review of government national security and intelligence policies, it is not a committee set up to review mistakes that the government has made."[48]

These incidents are certainly not the only clashes between Parliament and government over access to documents and information. However, the three described here – in 2010 and 2011 under a Conservative government, and in 2021 under a Liberal one – truly qualify as "showdowns." Both sides dug in, and the disagreement pushed Parliament into new or rarely visited territory. And they illustrate the challenge of parliamentary scrutiny of national security issues. When information and the ways in which it has been obtained are sensitive or secret, it is reasonable that some precautions be taken to maintain the secrecy of Canada's national security apparatus. But it is also reasonable to disagree on the necessary level of secrecy and precautions, since there is a long history in Canada and in other countries of governments misusing "national security" as a cover for mistakes.

The showdowns also highlight two enduring principles about parliamentary scrutiny in Canada. One is the continuing lack of institutional maturity in the Canadian Parliament. While other countries have also seen clashes over parliamentary access to information, Canada's continuing inability to set up a truly parliamentary body to examine national security issues is embarrassing in its immaturity. Governments have been able to dig their heels in and resist increasingly blunt Parliamentary tools, such as calling public servants to the bar of the House. But MPs must also take blame here for the extent to which these incidents are polarized and politicized. Neither government nor opposition MPs did much to cooperate on a common front that represents Parliament; rather they simply stuck to their government and opposition teams and ratcheted up the conflict.

The second principle is the cyclicality of scrutiny and Parliament itself. In 2010 and 2011 it was a Liberal opposition championing the rights of Parliament against a Conservative government; in 2021 it was a Conservative opposition standing up for the institution against a Liberal government (in both cases, the New Democrats and Bloc Québécois were also part of the opposition side). While there are differences in the specific cases, the overall pattern is striking. Scrutiny is political and opportunistic, and whatever politicians may say, their approach to it inevitably depends on what side of the House they sit.

CONCLUSION

Though backed by elegant theories and rhetoric, the actual business of scrutiny can feel like a thankless task for parliamentarians. Like debates, scrutiny is part of a larger picture, in which parliamentarians contribute, expose, reveal, and defend, all as part of the larger political system and struggles. But their own autonomy and direct impact is limited. Similarly, as with other aspects of parliamentary reform, there have been many attempts to improve scrutiny tools and functions, some of which have been effective but generally have not lived up to aspirations.

Parliament may be the supreme body for scrutiny and holding government to account. But it is arguably not very well-equipped for the task, nor are parliamentarians necessarily interested in many aspects of scrutiny given the limited reward. And even when governments evade scrutiny, such as over the F-35 procurement in 2011 that led to the vote of non-confidence, the electorate may still reward them, as voters did in the 2011 election.

Much of the debate around scrutiny is within the logic of governance, asking questions about how far Parliament can go, how involved it should be in decisions, and how clear the lines must be. There is less room for the logic of representation and the role of individual MPs, though, as noted, this is an area where Canada does seem to lag the United Kingdom, with Canadian government MPs particularly restricted from holding government to account too aggressively. And some of the most active work is done by officers of Parliament, outside the normal parliamentary processes entirely. Overall, scrutiny is core to Parliament, but often underwhelming in practice.

CHAPTER NINE

The Future of Parliament

This final chapter considers the future of Parliament. But rather than speculating about new developments or issuing a list of possible reforms, it will look at how Parliament has adapted to change in the past. This gives us clues to the future of Parliament.

When we look at how Parliament has dealt with change and disruption in the past, it is striking how much the institution is able to absorb change, rather than be changed itself. I have argued that Parliament operates with two logics: the logic of governance and the logic of representation. These are perennial, and competition and friction between the two logics drives the evolution of Parliament. Any external development or disruption, rather than changing the institution, inevitably gets drawn into the existing paradox of Parliament.

An immediate example of disruption, and absorbing that disruption, is Parliament's adaptation to COVID-19. When the global pandemic was declared in March 2020, Parliament at first moved quickly to adapt to the immediate crisis. In a time of great uncertainty, the leadership of the parties reached extraordinary all-party agreements to suspend regular sittings and to give the government powers to respond to the crisis. This was not without disagreement, especially when the Liberal government originally proposed that it be given extensive taxation and spending powers until the end of 2021. The opposition strongly resisted, and an all-night sitting of a small number of socially distanced MPs on 24–25 March 2020 was required to reach a compromise. This fast response illustrates the logic of governance at its best – the ability of Parliament to flexibly adapt to circumstances and make quick and clear decisions, after give and take between well-organized government and opposition sides.[1]

But as the pandemic continued, the consensus splintered. After the initial success in socially distanced emergency sittings, Parliament struggled to establish a system for remote participation.[2] The parties disagreed sharply, and it took several months to agree on a permanent arrangement for House and Senate proceedings and committees. And ultimately, while the lifestyles and working arrangements of parliamentarians and staff transformed for a time, as they did for most Canadians under pandemic restrictions, the familiar institutional patterns soon emerged. The House of Commons, operating remotely and later in a hybrid arrangement, acted almost exactly as it had before, with the same patterns of government-opposition conflict and minority brinkmanship, though more muted when MPs spoke from remote screens. If there was a change, it was most likely in the diminution of informal contact behind the scenes. Instead, the dependence on technology may have prioritized the formal proceedings and the performance aspect of Parliament even more than before.

Thus, while COVID-19 had significant practical impacts on the daily routines of Parliament and parliamentarians, the institution itself remained resilient and largely unchanged. The perpetual struggle between government and opposition proceeded much as always, and actors lapsed into their familiar roles. Parliament absorbed change, far more than it was changed itself.

This returns us to the future of Parliament. Bold predictions about the future of Parliament are almost never fulfilled. Whether it is procedural reforms, technological advancements, changes in the demographic cohort of MPs, or other developments, including COVID-19, the fundamental paradox of Parliament largely continues. Parliament does evolve and change. But the change is gradual, and rarely linear or fully predictable.

Chapter 2 traced the evolution of parliamentary reform and how issues were cyclical, change sometimes caused new problems, and nearly all reform ideas have been founded on inadequate conceptions of the overall purpose of Parliament. In the end, reforms and attempts at reform tend to show the resilience of the institution and the fundamental persistence of the two logics.

To consider the future of Parliament, I will look at how the institution has dealt with change in the past. In the following sections I examine change and disruption to Parliament through three prisms: technological, the changing composition of MPs, and citizen attitudes. Again we see the resilience of the logics, and the continuing paradox of Parliament

TECHNOLOGICAL

Parliament has been affected by many technological developments over the years. The most critical have been communication technologies. But there are also others, such as the advent of air travel that allowed MPs to return to even the most distant constituencies for the weekend, rather than travelling for days on the train and spending months at a time in Ottawa.

The development of the telephone, long-distance calling, and other technologies all shaped the workings of Parliament and government, both on an everyday basis like any other workplace, but also in its ability to connect across the vast country of Canada. For example, the telephone may have contributed modestly to an undermining of MPs' claims to be exclusive spokespersons for their part of Canada. Such claims could be undermined when ministers and party officials could use long-distance calling to take their own instant soundings of opinion.

Little research has been conducted on the impact of radio and radio journalism on Parliament. But the rise of national television news in the 1960s has been identified as a key aspect of the third national party system. Television's need for images likely accelerated the primacy of party leaders as the unparalleled face of their party. National news broadcasts gradually led to a homogenization of coverage, as "Canadian politics" became synonymous with the day's events in Ottawa, broadcast nightly across the country. As in the United States and other countries, television changed *politics* by emphasizing images over words and evoking a range of emotional reactions unconnected to the actual speeches and actions of politicians.

Yet how much did television shape *Parliament*? This remains debated, especially the specific effect of introducing television cameras in the House of Commons in 1977. But looking at the introduction of television decades ago gives us insights to how twenty-first-century technologies affect Parliament, and how the logics of representation and governance persist amid the promise and hopes surrounding technological change.

Televised proceedings were introduced in the House of Commons in 1977, slightly before the official televising of the US Congress and well before the British House of Commons introduced TV cameras in 1989. As discussed in earlier chapters, some critics have blamed the introduction of television for contributing to Parliament's ills, leading to style over substance, the paramountcy of Question Period, and a general decline in the reverence of the proceedings.

Yet television clearly had positive effects. While it may have ill-served a few old-fashioned orators who sounded better than they looked on camera, television also curbed many more undistinguished speakers. Speeches became more focused and MPs' comportment likely improved. As one analyst remarked, the presence of television cameras now meant "[m]embers must be careful not to doze off, bury their heads in a newspaper, or have inappropriate expressions on their face if they are near someone who is speaking."[3] A 1978–9 survey of MPs immediately after the introduction of television found MPs reported both positive and negative effects.[4] Some felt it had led to public disapproval of MPs' behaviour and a loss of respect for Parliament, but others said it had led to increased decorum and better preparation of MPs for debates, as well as greater public knowledge and interest in Parliament. Some felt it did not really change actual behaviour but merely gave new outlets; one MP said "the publicity hounds were that way before TV was installed."[5]

In fact, far from undermining Parliament, television may have given it a new life. "Televising the house has put its proceedings back into the news," remarked C.E.S. Franks in 1987.[6] MPs quickly realized the value of being seen on TV, even if speaking in an obscure debate to a nearly empty chamber. Parliament became visually alive and available to Canadians. Robertson says that "[b]efore the introduction of television, most news reports relied on Members repeating their speeches or comments outside the House of Commons. Today, it is far more likely that actual audio-visual clips from Question Period or debates will be used in news reports."[7] The public became familiar with basic aspects of parliamentary procedure. The House chamber, previously a room far away in Ottawa only visible in photographs, became a familiar and lively sight. In contrast, the Senate resisted bringing cameras in for decades, and did not introduce regular televised proceedings until 2019.[8]

The televising of proceedings likely increased the already growing prominence of Question Period as the highlight of the parliamentary day and the key arena for performance, especially for opposition leaders and MPs. Indeed, Franks noted in the 1980s that "media interest in debates has declined," in part because Question Period was the undisputed highlight of the parliamentary day.[9] On the other hand, as we saw in chapter 5, Question Period was already well covered before television, and a comprehensive study in 2015 found no evidence that television had led to an increase in leaders' participation in Question Period over MPs, somewhat contrary to conventional wisdom.[10]

In short, while television certainly changed the House of Commons, it did not transform it in the ways fully envisioned either by proponents or detractors. Rather, the institution and its underlying norms and existing practices prevailed. Any changes have been long-term and/or difficult to disaggregate from other changes in the institution and society.

The rise in the 1990s of digital technology, online communication, and the internet posed another technological challenge for Parliament. Unlike the introduction of televised House proceedings in 1977, the effect of the internet on Parliament was more gradual and in tandem with the general spread of new communication technologies at the turn of the century. Email and websites arose in the 1990s, while social media such as Facebook and Twitter came later in the 2000s. And like television, the internet changed Parliament, but again in ways that were not necessarily anticipated and sometimes both under- and over-estimated.

In the fledgling online years, there was optimism about the power of technology to invigorate the logic of representation – giving MPs and constituents more power to directly communicate with each other. Indeed, the Reform Party's 1990s ideas about constituency-based voting were partly predicated on the increasing availability of electronic technologies at the time, such as landline telephone touch-tone polling that could survey constituents much more quickly than regular mail.[11] The internet seemed to have considerable potential for strengthening direct MP-citizen connections, reducing the power of political parties as well as traditional media gatekeepers.

While taken for granted today, individual websites were at the time a remarkable new platform that allowed members to promote themselves and update constituents at little cost. Entrepreneurial MPs began to experiment with blogs, instant messaging, and other new tools. For at least some heady technophile visionaries, this foretold a transformation of Parliament and a radical shift in favour of the logic of representation – the ability of MPs to truly be voices for their constituency in Parliament.

But some argued MPs themselves would be eclipsed by a new wave of "e-democracy." If citizens could communicate directly with government, was Parliament needed at all? Paul G. Thomas wrote in 2000 that "[o]f all the institutions and actors involved with the Canadian policy process, Parliament may have the most to lose in terms of the impacts of the new technologies."[12] Thomas suggested that technology would allow governments and citizens alike to bypass parliamentarians and engage directly with each other. He wrote: "If the new technologies make plebiscitary democracy and bureaucratic responsiveness the more prevailing pattern, there could be less and less reliance upon elected (MPs) and appointed (senators) representatives in Parliament as channels of communication with governments and as liaison agents with the bureaucracy on behalf of citizens."[13] British authors Chadwick and May similarly suggested in 2003 that "e-government potentially blurs the distinction between executive and legislative functions by creating opportunities for citizens *as citizens* to have direct political influence upon public bureaucracies in ways that have not existed before"[14] – that is, again potentially cutting out parliaments as middle actors.

Yet neither of these predictions – one empowering and one bypassing MPs – came to pass. Both were rooted in the logic of representation, seeing Parliament primarily as a voice for citizens and constituencies. But the logic of governance and the power of parties increasingly asserted themselves as well.

A key issue was technical capacity. While some MPs were early enthusiasts, many others (and their untrained staff) struggled with the unfamiliar new technology. Parliament itself offered limited support in these early years. One issue was the unclear status of websites – were they political or parliamentary? Lacking clear precedents, the House of Commons was reluctant to host or support sites that carried partisan messaging, which crossed the already sometimes blurry line between parliamentary-funded activities (such as constituency offices) and partisan activity. This lack of consistent resources and support blunted and obscured attempts by most MPs to build truly personalized and well-maintained sites. On the other hand, party caucus offices were more likely to have the necessary resources; in the early 2000s the Canadian Alliance was particularly proactive at an early stage in supplying MPs with a template to build basic sites; naturally this meant the websites all looked much the same and conformed to the party brand.[15] The distribution of resources and support for online activity thus could reinforce, rather than dilute, the power of the party over most MPs.

Furthermore, the logic of governance and the Westminster model of concentrated accountability also asserted themselves more directly, both for Parliament and within government itself. Amanda Clarke and others have shown how ideas of networked and decentralized governance have been no match for the long-standing hierarchies and accountability systems that concentrate power and responsibility in ministers and the cabinet.[16] This extended to Parliament more generally. MPs may have had more communication tools with which to engage the public. But these had little effect on the rules and structures of parliamentary business, which remained dominated by parties and the core struggle between government and opposition.

MPs could communicate more and in different ways, but their actual job didn't change. We saw in chapter 8 that Parliament's long-standing role has been to *review* government actions, not participate in the actions themselves. So, enthusiastic predictions that MPs could engage in accelerated forms of digital, networked participation and policy formulation made little sense when this had never been a primary role for MPs in the first place. Again, MPs are not short of ideas; they are short of opportunities to turn them into action.

Consequently, despite initial excitement and dreams, the use of digital technology was shaped by the institutional norms of

Parliament, rather than changing the norms themselves. Parliamentary business and dynamics remained much the same. For some, this led to further arguments, as Jeffrey Roy wrote in 2010, about "the need to broadly rethink the entire Westminster model, since one can reasonably ask whether a system designed in the nineteenth century is sufficiently robust to meet the challenges of the 21st."[17] But this merely adds more voices to the ongoing calls for systemic parliamentary reform. In the meantime, the existing structure and its existing logics continued.

As technology evolved, the logic of governance and the importance of collective discipline likely *accelerated*, far from the original hopes of the logic of representation. The rise of social media such as Facebook, Twitter, and YouTube, and the increasing prevalence of smartphones, initially led again to enthusiasm about their potential for individual MPs. But Alex Marland argues convincingly that the rise of social media, far from empowering MPs from the shackles of parties, has accelerated and invigorated party discipline.[18] The ubiquity and universality of social media means statements and actions can be quickly disseminated and reposted, losing context and spiraling out of anyone's control. We saw in chapter 3 how statements by Conservative MP David Wilks in a BC restaurant quickly went viral across the country and provoked an immediate and heavy response from party leaders. Similar incidents, and the fear of such incidents, discourage MPs from going "off-message" in their social media posts and again encourage conformity. MPs certainly have made great use of social media to build their individual profiles, but almost always within the boundaries of party discipline. This inevitably then contributes to the larger and well-documented effect of social media in reinforcing and entrenching existing opinions, more than changing them.

In the end, while social media and the constant parade of new digital technologies and platforms have become basic tools for MPs, they, like television before them, have had limited effect on the underlying foundations and norms of Parliament. Parliament and the competing logics have shaped their use far more than they have shaped Parliament. This demonstrates the overall continuing resiliency of Parliament, for better or worse, and its capacity to resist, slow, and/or redirect forces of change.

CHANGE IN MEMBERSHIP

Another form of possible change to Parliament is the nature of the people in it – the members themselves. In chapter 6 I discussed the growing diversity of parliamentarians, with gradually more people from equity-seeking groups elected and appointed to the two chambers. But predictions of a critical mass or transformation of the institution through more diversity have not yet come to pass.

As with technology, we can see how a greater diversity of MPs has produced overall changes in the culture and working conditions of Parliament, similar to changes in society as a whole. But it is difficult to see how past changes in Parliament's membership have led to transformation, disruption, or other major changes to the way Parliament has always done business. Gender and race are profoundly different dimensions of change, compared to the evolution of the type of white men in the chamber. Still, past waves of change in the composition of the House of Commons have not fulfilled predictions of change in the institution.

Youth is a perennial hope. There is always optimism that a new generation of younger MPs will challenge staid existing norms, and no longer be patient with the contradictions and paradox of Parliament. But this has likely been said for many decades, from war veterans in the 1940s and 1950s, to baby boomers in the 1970s and 1980s, to Generation X in the early twenty-first century, followed by millennials and future generations to come. Yet there is no evidence that a "youth surge" of MPs in their 20s and 30s in any era has led directly to meaningful institutional change.

It is possible that a *lack of youth* may inhibit parties' ability to perform in Parliament; J.P. Lewis posits that the difficulties of the Liberal transition from Jean Chrétien to Paul Martin in the early 2000s were linked to the relatively mature Liberal caucus and lack of new and younger blood.[19] But overall, young MPs may in fact be *more likely* to reinforce and maintain parliamentary norms of party discipline and the logic of governance, because the ones that make it to Parliament are ambitious and typically already have extensive and early partisan political involvement. They are there to climb the ladder, not destroy it. There is also occasional speculation about the effect on Parliament of shifts in the regional distribution of seats, the ever-growing proportion of urban MPs, shifts in occupational and educational backgrounds, etc. But these shifts are gradual, and change, if there is any, is gradual as well.

High turnover and the arrival of a wave of new MPs not yet socialized into the institution might also suggest a special opportunity for disruption and big change in Parliament. But historical examples again show only modest adjustments. We are fortunate to have a careful study by David Docherty of the biggest reset in Canadian parliamentary history in 1993, when 67 per cent of MPs were newly elected. In Docherty's study, evocatively titled *Mr. Smith Goes to Ottawa* in reflection of the 1939 American film about an innocent new member of Congress, he finds that again the institution overwhelmingly shaped the newcomers, rather than the other way around.[20]

On the other hand, the 1984 Progressive Conservative landslide with many new MPs and a huge Conservative backbench did spur the McGrath Committee, which as we saw in chapter 2 brought significant reforms, though not to the extent some had hoped. The election of the Justin Trudeau government in 2015 also saw a considerable influx of new MPs and a new tone, but it is difficult to pinpoint abrupt new changes to the institution. The Senate, of course, has radically shifted in character and organization, but that is due to a complete overhaul of its entire appointment process, introduced externally. The change to the institution came first, before the change in its membership.

The sudden arrival of new parties in large numbers in the House of Commons might signify sufficient disruption to change parliamentary ways. But new parties have not been able to change old ways, even though the two most obvious examples, the Progressives in 1921 and the Reform Party in 1993, were founded with the goal of radically changing the political system. We saw in chapters 2 and 3 how the Reform Party's ideas were gradually worn down or proved unworkable, leading the party to conform more and more to existing norms. The Progressives, who won 58 seats of the 235 Commons seats in 1921 and became the second largest party in the House, also failed to make a substantive impact, in part because of their lack of internal organization and cohesion.

Where new parties do have a possible impact on the future of the House is simply by increasing the *number* of parties in the House. The 1921 election of the Progressives broke the simple two-party dichotomy between Liberals and Conservatives and was the beginning of the multi-party Canadian Parliament, with subsequent "third parties" of the CCF/NDP, Social Credit and Creditistes, the Bloc Québécois, Reform, and (in modest numbers so far) the Green Party. This long-standing multi-party system has shaped the Canadian Parliament in distinct ways from its Westminster counterparts in Britain and Australia, particularly by making minority government a regular event in Canada unlike those other countries.

The instability of minority government and the generally more competitive atmosphere of a multi-party Parliament may also lead to greater partisanship and less freedom for backbench MPs. But as Jean-François Godbout argues (see chapter 3), the causal arrow is unclear. It may have been harsh parliamentary discipline and rules that actually precipitated the multi-party system in the first place.[21] And since 1993, party standings have certainly changed the way the House is administered,[22] but have not transformed the overall patterns of the institution. Again, as with technology, when we look at the influx of new members and actors in Parliament, there is much more evidence of Parliament shaping and absorbing change, rather than disruptive change shaping Parliament.

CITIZEN ATTITUDES

The final and most possibly drastic form of disruption is citizen attitudes. Parliament, like all governing institutions, ultimately depends on the consent of the governed. The twenty-first century has seen highly disruptive challenges to governing institutions and conventional governing norms. In 2022, the "trucker convoy" protest against vaccination mandates and COVID-19 measures led to protestors parking big-rig trucks and demonstrating for three weeks in downtown Ottawa in front of the Parliament buildings. The United States saw an actual physical attack on its legislative institutions in the invasion and sacking of the US Capitol in 2021. Could Parliament ultimately lose the confidence of citizens and be permanently overwhelmed or disrupted as an institution?

Canadian parliamentary institutions have been under pressure before. The election of the Progressive Party in 1921 followed a series of disruptions including the 1919 Winnipeg General Strike, the sudden election of farmers' parties to government in Alberta and Ontario, and other developments that for some appeared to herald a crisis and breakdown in parliamentary government and institutions. The subsequent hardships of the 1930s also seemed to signal possible disruptions, including challenges to the entire capitalist system as outlined in the Regina Manifesto of 1933. Yet this discontent subsided, captured in part by the rise of new political parties like Social Credit and the CCF, forerunner of the NDP, that chose to engage in political change through parliamentary means. The disruptors ultimately chose to work in and with Parliament, rather than undermine or shatter it.

Some of the most important parliamentary reforms in Canadian history took place in 1968, a year of widespread unrest and social disruption throughout the Western world. But it is difficult to draw a direct link between social protests of the era and the institutional overhaul of Parliament. And while the economic recession and malaise of the 1970s led some elites to worry about government "overload" and sparked the Auditor-General's famous remark (see chapter 8) that Parliament was "close to losing control of the public purse," there is again little evidence of disruptive citizen attitudes against the entire institution of Parliament. This period was one of substantive reform and updating: establishing the modern committee systems, making MPs full time with increased resources, introducing television, and streamlining debates and procedure. But these changes were arguably driven more by MPs themselves, rather than propelled by a broad citizen movement of discontent.

A different picture emerged in the 1990s. Known by Neil Nevitte's term "the decline of deference,"[23] polling data and studies found rising levels of disillusionment and discontent with government, as well as other establishments like business corporations, organized religion, and educational institutions. This took concrete form in a steady decrease in voting after 1988, symbolizing that Canadians no longer felt obligated to participate in their most basic and important chance to shape Parliament. Thus Lisa Young wrote in 1998 that "over the past three decades, Parliament and political parties have both become increasingly unpopular, as citizens' discontent with the Canadian political process has mounted."[24] Some of this discontent was captured in the Reform Party, with its ideals of constituency-directed voting, lack of hierarchy in the parliamentary caucus, and promotion of referendums and other instruments of direct democracy, all enabled by the fledgling rise of digital technology as discussed.

But looking back on this 1990s discontent, especially as embodied by the Reform Party, it is striking how much of it focused on *institutional reform* – that is, it still had faith in the underlying institutions of parliamentary democracy themselves. The issue was simply that they were not working well. Much of this was driven by the logic of representation and a belief that party discipline and the excesses of the logic of governance were the problem. While some ideas like referendums set Parliament aside entirely, there was still a general faith in the institution itself. Similarly, concerns about a "democratic deficit" in the early 2000s again focused on how to fix the institution, not discard it.

The 2010s saw a different type of movement, manifested internationally particularly in the Trump presidency in the United States and the 2016 Brexit referendum in the United Kingdom. In those international examples, citizens did not show a yearning for the reform and improvement of representative institutions, but more an incoherent fury that surpassed reason or logic, as seen in the attack on the US Capitol. American politics in particular has steadily polarized since the 1990s, with increasingly bitter partisan divides between politicians and between citizens. This has led to repeated deadlocks between presidents and Congress, and near breakdowns in the functioning of the overall system, as the disrespect between the actors spills over into disrespect of the system itself.

While Canadian politics has seen polarization and disruption, it has not seen the same near breakdown of democratic institutions and the rule of law. And while Canadians do display ongoing skepticism of Parliament, political parties, and government, it is not clear that this is *increasing* as a cause of concern. In fact, some studies show relative stability and trust in parliamentary institutions and sometimes even increases.[25] And after declining from 1993 to 2008 (with one uptick in 2006), Canadian voting rates improved in the 2010s, though dropping again in 2021.

Ironically for many reformers that champion the logic of representation and more freedom for MPs, the logic of governance may be the most powerful force preserving Parliament from descending into chaos and paralysis. The discipline, hierarchy, and accountability inherent to the logic of governance allows party leaders to retain control, steering their caucuses toward coherence rather than anarchy, through trade-offs, deliberation, and compromise. The logic of representation, if left unchecked, could lead to gradually more extreme voices, and choke off incentives to compromise and moderate. In contrast, the logic of governance can channel and preclude more vivid and undemocratic forms of anger.

In Canada, the greater threat to Parliament is not American-style anger and fury but rather apathy. Every call for parliamentary reform is, somewhat ironically, an implicit vote of confidence in the institution, because it indicates that Parliament matters enough to be fixed and improved. More concerning is when Canadians disengage and indicate they do not really care one way or another about Parliament at all. This is the real danger for the future of Parliament – not that it will be targeted for change by citizen unrest, or plagued by poorly thought out reforms, but that it will be seen not to matter at all.

CONCLUSION

The future of Parliament is unknown. But experience tells us it will look much like the past and present. Parliament does change and adapt. But it is gradual, and the institution absorbs change far more than it is shaped by change. There is little doubt that the fundamental structures and the long-standing themes and dynamics of the Parliament of Canada will continue into the future.

This book has argued that the Canadian Parliament is a paradox. It can only be properly understood by recognizing that it operates according to two disparate, colliding logics: one of representation and one of governance. For many decades, there has been an uneasy tension between the two, and different aspects of Parliament may reflect one or the other.

Parliament works well as a system. It provides both decisions and scrutiny. Its testing fire produces a "mobilization of consent" that legitimizes state activity and connects it to democracy and the people. It is the focal point of political activity in Canada – if not actual power – and its activities draw together the nation. The flexibility and adaptability of the Westminster model may be overstated at times, but it does show an ability to adapt to crises and new developments, and to avoid permanent paralysis or deadlock.

Less clear is how Parliament works for individuals. The contradictions and tensions of Parliament require 338 MPs to each play individual roles that often feel futile and meaningless. Historically the same contradictions held even more true for senators, though this may change in the era of independent senators. The great bulk of parliamentary debate in both houses is forgettable. Committees embody the pathologies of the larger institution rather than serve as a refuge from them, and must always wrestle with the endless dilemma of autonomy or relevance. A vast professional bureaucracy serves Parliament in every way it can, yet much of its work is ultimately predictable and routine because so much is prescribed and set by higher forces. And voters and constituents ask whether this expensive institution is needed, if so much of its activity is determined simply by election results once every four years.

Together, the system works, and overall it works well. But it requires the work of many who struggle to see how their individual contribution makes a difference. Many have seen this gap between the institution and the individual, and tried to close it. Some reforms have worked and some have not; some have created new problems requiring new reforms.

Yet Parliament has in many ways improved over the years. The Parliament of Canada is arguably in stronger and better shape in the twenty-first century than in the twentieth, when party voting was equally high, but MPs were part-time with minimal resources and tools for influence. Government has grown immeasurably, but so has Parliament, which has never been more professional and sophisticated than it is today. The Senate still struggles for legitimacy but is far more vigorous and relevant after its 2016 reforms, though with an unknown future. Parliament is also a tremendously more diverse place, though still not fully reflective of Canadian society. And it has evolved with technological change, in both positive and negative ways.

For over a century and a half, Parliament has lurched and adapted to changes in Canadian society. And yet in many ways it remains fundamentally the same. Because at the heart of Parliament remains a fundamental paradox – an institution that both represents and governs.

Notes

1 The Paradox

1. Robert Jackson and Michael M. Atkinson, *The Canadian Legislative System*, 2nd ed. (Toronto: Gage, 1980), 3.
2. David C. Docherty, *Mr. Smith Goes to Ottawa: Life in the House of Commons* (Vancouver: UBC Press, 1997), 5.
3. David Smith, *The People's House of Commons: Theories of Democracy in Contention* (Toronto: University of Toronto Press, 2007), 9.
4. Jackson and Atkinson, *The Canadian Legislative System*, 3.
5. C.E.S. Franks, *The Parliament of Canada* (Toronto: University of Toronto Press, 1987), 6.
6. Liberal Party of Canada, *A New Plan for a Strong Middle Class* (2015). Archived at https://web.archive.org/web/20161105074044/https://liberal.ca/files/2015/10/New-plan-for-a-strong-middle-class.pdf.
7. Thomas Axworthy, "Everything Old Is New Again: Observations on Parliamentary Reform" (Kingston: Queen's University Centre for the Study of Democracy, 2008).
8. Monique Begin, *Ladies, Upstairs! My Life in Politics and After* (Montreal and Kingston: McGill-Queen's University Press, 2018), 102.
9. Celina Caesar-Chavannes, *Can You Hear Me Now? How I Found My Voice and Learned to Live with Passion and Purpose* (Toronto: Random House Canada, 2021), 246.
10. Canada. Parliament. House of Commons. *Debates*, 43rd Parliament, 2nd Session, vol. 150, no. 118 (June 15, 2021): 8511.
11. Graeme Truelove, "Afterword: The Champion," in *Queering Representation: LGBTQ People and Electoral Politics in Canada*, ed. Manon Tremblay (Vancouver: UBC Press, 2019), 321.

12 Michael Chong, Scott Simms, and Kennedy Stewart, "Conclusion," in *Turning Parliament Inside Out: Practical Ideas for Reforming Canada's Democracy*, ed. Michael Chong, Scott Simms, and Kennedy Stewart (Vancouver: Douglas+McIntyre, 2017), 155.
13 Robert L. Stanfield, "The Present State of the Legislative Process in Canada: Myths and Realities," in *The Legislative Process in Canada: The Need for Reform*, ed. W.A.W. Neilson and J.C. MacPherson (Montreal: Institute for Research on Public Policy, 1978), 41.
14 Axworthy, "Everything Old Is New Again," 49.
15 Richard G. Price and Harold D. Clarke, "Television in the House of Commons," in *Parliament, Policy and Representation*, ed. Harold D. Clarke, Colin Campbell, F.Q. Quo, and Arthur Goddard (Toronto: Methuen, 1980), 58–83.
16 J.R. Mallory, "Parliament: Every Reform Creates a New Problem," *Journal of Canadian Studies* 14, no. 2 (Summer 1979): 26–34, https://muse.jhu.edu/article/675452/pdf.
17 David C. Docherty, *Legislatures* (Vancouver: UBC Press, 2005), 5.
18 Jackson and Atkinson, *The Canadian Legislative System*, 9.
19 Gerhard Loewenberg, *On Legislatures: The Puzzle of Representation* (London: Routledge, 2011).
20 "Legislature" and "parliament" can be seen as mutually exclusive terms and concepts, describing two different types of representative institutions and systems of government. However, in practice they are often used interchangeably. In the past, at least some provinces referred to their representative bodies as "parliaments" (e.g., "the Ontario Parliament"). Now they identify as legislative assemblies or legislatures (the latter concept includes the Crown) – except in Quebec (National Assembly) and Nova Scotia and Newfoundland and Labrador (House of Assembly). In contrast, their closest comparators, Australian states, still identify themselves as parliaments (e.g., "the Parliament of Queensland"). Ontario legislators are titled "Members of Provincial Parliament" (MPPs) while other provinces refer to "Members of the Legislative Assembly" (MLA) (or MNA in Quebec and MHA in Newfoundland and Labrador; members of the Nova Scotia House of Assembly are referred to as MLAs). In short, overall usage is inconsistent, though the Parliament of Canada is normally referred to only as a parliament, and this book follows that custom.
21 A.H. Birch, *Representative and Responsible Government* (Toronto: University of Toronto Press, 1964).
22 Franks, *The Parliament of Canada*.
23 Gerhard Loewenberg, "Paradoxes of Legislatures," *Daedalus* 136, no. 3 (Summer 2007): 56.
24 Loewenberg, *On Legislatures*, 13.
25 Libby Davies, *Outside In: A Political Memoir* (Toronto: Between the Lines, 2019), 179.

2 Historical Foundations and the Competing Logics

1. For a general overview see Suzanne Von Der Porten, "Canadian Indigenous Governance Literature: A Review," *AlterNative: An International Journal of Indigenous Peoples* 8, no. 1 (March 2012): 1–14, https://doi.org/10.1177/117718011200800101. For examples of Indigenous governance and decision-making, see Kahente Horn-Miller, "What Does Indigenous Participatory Democracy Look Like? Kahnawà:ke's Community Decision Making Process," *Review of Constitutional Studies* 18 (2013): 111–32, https://www.constitutionalstudies.ca/wp-content/uploads/2019/08/05_Horn-Miller-1-1.pdf; Taiaiake Alfred, "From Sovereignty to Freedom: Towards an Indigenous Political Discourse," *Indigenous Affairs*, March 2001, 22–34; Taiaiake Alfred, *Peace, Power, Righteousness: An Indigenous Manifesto*, 2nd ed. (Don Mills, ON: Oxford University Press, 2009); and Sâkihitowin Awâsis, "'Anishinaabe Time': Temporalities and Impact Assessment in Pipeline Reviews," *Journal of Political Ecology* 27 (2020): 830–52, https://doi.org/10.2458/v27i1.23236. See also Michael Morden, "Indigenizing Parliament," *Canadian Parliamentary Review* 39, no. 2 (Summer 2016): 24–33, http://www.revparl.ca/english/issue.asp?param=227&art=1694, and Tim Mercer, "The Two-Row Wampum: Has This Metaphor for Co-Existence Run Its Course?," *Canadian Parliamentary Review*, Summer 2019, 21–8, http://www.revparl.ca/english/issue.asp?param=239&art=1852.
2. Erica Neeganagwedgin, "The Land since Time Immemorial: A Review of the Assimilation Policies on Indigenous Peoples through Canada's Indian Act," *ab-Original* 3, no. 1 (September 1, 2019): 136–42, https://doi.org/10.5325/aboriginal.3.1.0136.
3. Assembly of First Nations, "Enfranchisement" (Legal Affairs and Justice Fact Sheet, January 2020), https://www.afn.ca/wp-content/uploads/2020/01/12-19-02-06-AFN-Fact-Sheet-Enfranchisement-final-reviewed.pdf.
4. Louis Riel's electoral career was short but complex as he was elected to the House of Commons three times in less than twelve months for the riding of Provencher. He was acclaimed with no opponents in a by-election in October 1873, elected in the general election of January 1874, and again acclaimed in a by-election in September 1874 after his first expulsion from the House. Library of Parliament, "Louis Riel, M.P.: Electoral History," https://lop.parl.ca/sites/ParlInfo/default/en_CA/People/Profile?personId=12738.
5. Len Marchand and Matt Hughes, *Breaking Trail* (Prince George, BC: Caitlin Press, 2000), 86.
6. Kiera L. Ladner and Michael McCrossan, *The Electoral Participation of Aboriginal People* (Working Paper Series on Electoral Participation and Outreach Practices, Elections Canada, 2007), https://elections.ca/res/rec/part/paper/aboriginal/aboriginal_e.pdf.

7 The Parliament of the United Kingdom was formed in 1800 as a merger between the Parliament of Ireland and Parliament of Great Britain; the latter was itself created in 1707 by combining the Parliaments of England and Scotland. For simplicity, this book will use the terms "British Parliament" and "UK Parliament" interchangeably, in line with modern usage today.

8 See F. Leslie Seidle and Louis Massicote, eds., *Taking Stock of 150 Years of Responsible Government in Canada* (Ottawa: Canadian Study of Parliament Group, 1999).

9 See, for example, Janet Ajzenstat, Paul Romney, Ian Gentles, and William D. Gairdner, *Canada's Founding Debates* (Toronto: University of Toronto Press, 2003).

10 Janet Ajzenstat, "Modern Mixed Government: A Liberal Defence of Inequality," *Canadian Journal of Political Science* 18, no. 1 (March 1985): 119–34, https://www.jstor.org/stable/3227912.

11 Ajzenstat, "Modern Mixed Government," 120.

12 Janet Ajzenstat, "The Constitutionalism of Etienne Parent and Joseph Howe," in *Canadian Constitutionalism: 1791–1991*, ed. J. Ajzenstat (Ottawa: Canadian Study of Parliament Group, 1991), 173, http://cspg-gcep.ca/pdf/1991_11-e.pdf.

13 Walter Bagehot, *The English Constitution* (Cambridge: Cambridge University Press, 2001), 8–9.

14 Bagehot, *The English Constitution*, 10.

15 Dennis Baker, *Not Quite Supreme: The Courts and Coordinate Constitutional Interpretation* (Montreal and Kingston: McGill-Queen's University Press, 2010).

16 Ian Brodie, *At the Centre of Government: The Prime Minister and the Limits of Political Power* (Montreal and Kingston: McGill-Queen's University Press, 2018), 179.

17 For contemporary discussion of the Crown see D. Michael Jackson and Philippe Lagassé, eds., *Canada and the Crown: Essays in Constitutional Monarchy* (Montreal and Kingston: McGill-Queen's University Press, 2014).

18 David Smith, *The Invisible Crown: The First Principle of Canadian Government* (Toronto: University of Toronto Press, 1995).

19 Government of Canada, Privy Council Office, "About the Speech from the Throne," October 22, 2020, https://www.canada.ca/en/privy-council/campaigns/speech-throne/info-speech-from-throne.html.

20 Bagehot, *The English Constitution*, 34.

21 C.E.S. Franks, *The Parliament of Canada* (Toronto: University of Toronto Press, 1987), 19.

22 Jennifer Smith, "Democracy and the House of Commons at the Millennium," *Canadian Public Administration* 42, no. 4 (Winter 1999): 413, https://doi.org/10.1111/j.1754-7121.1999.tb02034.x.

23 Jonathan Malloy, *The "Responsible Government" Approach and Its Effect on Canadian Legislative Studies* (Ottawa: Canadian Study of

Parliament Group, 2002), http://cspg-gcep.ca/pdf/Parliamentary_Perspectives_5_2002_e.pdf.
24 Franks, *The Parliament of Canada*, 202.
25 Gerhard Loewenberg, "Paradoxes of Legislatures," *Daedalus* 136, no. 3 (Summer 2007): 56.
26 J.R. Mallory, "Parliament: Every Reform Creates a New Problem," *Journal of Canadian Studies* 14, no. 2 (1979): 26–34, https://muse.jhu.edu/article/675452/pdf.
27 David C. Docherty, *Mr. Smith Goes to Ottawa: Life in the House of Commons* (Vancouver: UBC Press, 1997), xx.
28 Paul G. Thomas, "Parliament and the Public Service," in *Handbook of Canadian Public Administration*, 2nd ed., ed. Christopher Dunn (Toronto: Oxford University Press, 2010), 113.
29 C.E.S. Franks, "The Dilemma of the Standing Committees of the Canadian House of Commons," *Canadian Journal of Political Science* 4, no. 4 (December 1971): 461–76, https://doi.org/10.1017/S0008423900029991.
30 Peter MacLeod, "The Constituency Project Ten Years On," *Canadian Parliamentary Review*, Summer 2014, 38, http://www.revparl.ca/english/issue.asp?param=219&art=1591.
31 Jonathan Malloy, "Reconciling Expectations and Reality in House of Commons Committees: The Case of the 1989 GST Inquiry," *Canadian Public Administration* 39, no. 3 (September 1996): 314–35, https://doi.org/10.1111/j.1754-7121.1996.tb00135.x.
32 S.L. Sutherland, "The Al-Mashat Affair: Administrative Accountability in Parliamentary Institutions," *Canadian Public Administration* 34, no. 4 (December 1991): 603, https://doi.org/10.1111/j.1754-7121.1991.tb01487.x.
33 Michael M. Atkinson and David C. Docherty, "Moving Right Along: The Roots of Amateurism in the Canadian House of Commons," *Canadian Journal of Political Science* 25, no. 2 (June 1992): 295–318, https://doi.org/10.1017/S0008423900003991.
34 Jennifer Smith, "Democracy and the House of Commons," 399.
35 Jonathan Malloy, "More Than a Terrain of Struggle: Parliament as Ideological Instrument and Objective under Conservatism," in *Blueprint: Conservative Parties and Their Impact on Canadian Politics*, ed. J. Everitt and J.-P. Lewis (Toronto: University of Toronto Press, 2017), 242–63.
36 Peter Aucoin and Lori Turnbull, "The Democratic Deficit: Paul Martin and Parliamentary Reform," *Canadian Public Administration* 46, no. 4 (December 2003): 443, https://doi.org/10.1111/j.1754-7121.2003.tb01586.x.
37 Peter H. Russell, *Two Cheers for Minority Government* (Toronto: Emond Montgomery, 2008).
38 Brian Laghi, "Harper Buys Time: Coalition Firms Up," *Globe and Mail*, November 29, 2008, https://www.theglobeandmail.com/news/politics/harper-buys-time-coalition-firms-up/article25582123/.
39 Tom Flanagan, "Only Voters Have the Right to Decide on the Coalition," *Globe and Mail*, January 9, 2009, https://www.theglobeandmail.com

/opinion/only-voters-have-the-right-to-decide-on-the-coalition/article782719/.
40 Brodie, *At the Centre of Government*, 159.
41 Peter Aucoin, Lori Turnbull, and Mark Jarvis, *Democratizing the Constitution: Reforming Responsible Government* (Toronto: Emond Montgomery, 2011), 91.
42 See, for example, Aucoin et al., *Democratizing the Constitution*; Peter H. Russell and Lorne Sossin, *Parliamentary Democracy in Crisis* (Toronto: University of Toronto Press, 2009).
43 "Zero Support from MLAs for Motion to Introduce Party Politics in N.W.T.," *CBC News*, October 30, 2018, https://www.cbc.ca/news/canada/north/party-politics-motion-kieron-testart-1.4884189.
44 Graham White, "Westminster in the Arctic: The Adaptation of British Parliamentarism in the Northwest Territories," *Canadian Journal of Political Science* 24, no. 3 (1991): 499–523, https://doi.org/10.1017/S0008423900022666.
45 R.A.W. Rhodes, John Wanna, and Patrick Weller, *Comparing Westminster* (Sydney: Oxford University Press, 2009).
46 David Smith, *The People's House of Commons* (Toronto: University of Toronto Press, 2007), 13.
47 Donald J. Savoie, *Democracy in Canada: The Disintegration of Our Institutions* (Montreal and Kingston: McGill-Queen's University Press, 2019), 178.
48 Savoie, *Democracy in Canada*, 10.
49 Donald V. Smiley, "Federalism and the Legislative Process in Canada," in *The Legislative Process in Canada: The Need for Reform*, ed. William A.W. Neilson and James C. MacPherson (Toronto: Butterworth, 1978), 73–87. See also D.V. Smiley, "The Structural Problem of Canadian Federalism," *Canadian Public Administration* 14, no. 3 (1971): 326–43, https://doi.org/10.1111/j.1754-7121.1971.tb00284.x.
50 David Smith, *The People's House of Commons*.

3 Parties

1 Jean-François Godbout, *Lost on Division: Party Unity in the Canadian Parliament* (Toronto: University of Toronto Press, 2020).
2 Peter Russell, *Two Cheers for Minority Government* (Toronto: Emond Montgomery, 2008).
3 R.K. Carty, "Three Canadian Party Systems," in *Canadian Political Party Systems: A Reader*, ed. R.K. Carty (Peterborough, ON: Broadview Press, 1992), 563–90.
4 Godbout, *Lost on Division*, 6.
5 Jean-François Godbout and Bjørn Høyland, "The Emergence of Parties in the Canadian House of Commons (1867–1908)," *Canadian Journal of*

Political Science 46, no. 4 (December 2013): 773–97, https://doi.org/10.1017/S0008423913000632.
6 R.K. Carty and W. Cross, "Political Parties and the Practice of Brokerage Politics," in *The Oxford Handbook of Canadian Politics* (New York: Oxford University Press, 2010), 191.
7 William Cross, "Party Membership in Canada," in *Party Members and Activists*, ed. Emilie van Haute and Anika Gauja (London: Routledge, 2015), 50–65.
8 Kennedy Stewart, "Empowering the Backbench: The Story of Electronic Petitions," in *Turning Parliament Inside Out: Practical Ideas for Reforming Canada's Democracy*, ed. Michael Chong, Scott Simms, and Kennedy Stewart (Vancouver: Douglas+McIntyre, 2017), 60.
9 Quoted in Gloria Galloway, "Is Canada's Party Discipline the Strictest in the World? Experts Say Yes," *Globe and Mail*, February 7, 2013, https://www.theglobeandmail.com/news/politics/is-canadas-party-discipline-the-strictest-in-the-world-experts-say-yes/article8313261/.
10 Alison Loat and Michael MacMillan, *Tragedy in the Commons: Former Members of Parliament Speak Out about Canada's Failing Democracy* (Toronto: Random House, 2014), 194.
11 Royce Koop, "Room in Politics for Diversity of Thought," *Winnipeg Free Press*, December 11, 2020, https://www.winnipegfreepress.com/opinion/analysis/room-in-politics-for-diversity-of-thought-573364981.html.
12 Alex Marland, *Whipped: Party Discipline in Canada* (Vancouver: UBC Press, 2020), 4.
13 Ulrich Sieberer, "Party Unity in Parliamentary Democracies: A Comparative Analysis," *Journal of Legislative Studies* 12, no. 2 (2006): 150–78, https://doi.org/10.1080/13572330600739413.
14 Sam Depauw and Shane Martin, "Legislative Party Discipline and Cohesion in Comparative Perspective," in *Intra-Party Politics and Coalition Governments*, ed. Daniela Giannetti and Kenneth Benoit (London: Routledge, 2009), 103–20.
15 Jonathan Malloy, "High Discipline, Low Cohesion? The Uncertain Patterns of Canadian Parliamentary Party Groups," *Journal of Legislative Studies* 9, no. 4 (2003): 116–29, https://doi.org/10.1080/1357233042000306290.
16 Marland, *Whipped: Party Discipline in Canada*.
17 Marland, *Whipped: Party Discipline in Canada*, 121.
18 Rachel Aiello, "Long-Serving Tory MP Says Scheer Dropped Him from Critic Role over Pro-Cannabis Position," *CTV News*, December 31, 2019, https://www.ctvnews.ca/politics/long-serving-tory-mp-says-scheer-dropped-him-from-critic-role-over-pro-cannabis-position-1.4748896?.
19 Paul E.J. Thomas, Adelina Petit-Vouriot, and Michael Morden, "House Inspection: A Retrospective of the 42nd Parliament" (Toronto: Samara

20 Marland, *Whipped: Party Discipline in Canada*, 86.
21 Ian Brodie, *At the Centre of Government: The Prime Minister and the Limits of Political Power* (Montreal and Kingston: McGill-Queen's University Press, 2018), 46.
22 Alex Marland, "Whip It, Good: Whips Embody the Best and Worst of Party Discipline," *Globe and Mail*, September 18, 2020, https://www.theglobeandmail.com/opinion/article-whip-it-good-whips-embody-the-best-and-worst-of-party-discipline/.
23 Garth Turner, *Sheeple: Caucus Confidential in Stephen Harper's Ottawa* (Toronto: Key Porter Books, 2009).
24 Tonda MacCharles, "Conservative MP David Wilks Breaks Ranks and Says Budget Bill Should Be Split Up," *Toronto Star*, May 23, 2012, https://www.thestar.com/news/canada/2012/05/23/conservative_mp_david_wilks_breaks_ranks_and_says_budget_bill_should_be_split_up.html.
25 Marland, *Whipped: Party Discipline in Canada*, 53–5.
26 Peter Aucoin, Lori Turnbull, and Mark Jarvis, *Democratizing the Constitution* (Toronto: Emond Montgomery, 2011), 19, 135–6.
27 David C. Docherty, *Mr. Smith Goes to Ottawa: Life in the House of Commons* (Vancouver: UBC Press, 1997), 164–7.
28 Michael Chong, "Rebalancing Power in Ottawa: Committee Reform," in *Turning Parliament Inside Out: Practical Ideas for Reforming Canada's Democracy*, ed. Michael Chong, Scott Simms, and Kennedy Stewart (Vancouver: Douglas+McIntyre, 2017), 81.
29 Samara Centre for Democracy, "The Reform Act," https://www.samaracanada.com/research/political-leadership/the-reform-act.
30 Ian Campbell, "Liberal Caucus Votes Unanimously against Reform Act Measures," *Hill Times*, November 11, 2021, https://www.hilltimes.com/2021/11/11/liberal-caucus-votes-unanimously-against-reform-act-measures/327963.
31 Stephanie Taylor, "Conservative MPs Vote to Give Themselves Power to Oust O'Toole," *National Observer*, October 6, 2021, https://www.nationalobserver.com/2021/10/06/news/otoole-conservative-caucus-united-despite-vote-giving-mps-power-oust-him.
32 C.E.S. Franks, *The Parliament of Canada* (Toronto: University of Toronto Press, 1987), 4.
33 Godbout, *Lost on Division*.
34 David Smith, *The People's House of Commons*, 82.
35 The three are Leonard Jones (1974), Tony Roman (1984), and Andre Arthur (2006). In 2021, Kevin Vuong was elected technically as a Liberal candidate, though the party had disavowed him shortly before Election Day due to sexual harassment allegations. Nevertheless he was elected, likely due to advance voting before the allegations and expulsion were known. He thus

immediately sat as an independent but was not elected with that status. It is unlikely voters would have elected him as an independent.
36 Brent Rathgeber, *Irresponsible Government: The Decline of Parliamentary Democracy in Canada* (Toronto: Dundurn Press, 2014).
37 Russell, *Two Cheers for Minority Government*.
38 Canadian Press, "CP's News Story of the Year: The Conservative Majority," *iPolitics*, December 26, 2011, https://www.ipolitics.ca/news/cps-news-story-of-the-year-the-conservative-majority.
39 Russell, *Two Cheers for Minority Government*.

4 MPs

1 Alison Loat and Michael MacMillan, *Tragedy in the Commons: Former Members of Parliament Speak Out about Canada's Failing Democracy* (Toronto: Random House, 2014), 85.
2 David Smith, *The People's House of Commons* (Toronto: University of Toronto Press, 2007), 14.
3 Samara Canada, *The Accidental Citizen?* (Toronto: Samara Centre for Democracy, 2010), 7, https://www.samaracanada.com/research/political-leadership/mp-exit-interviews/volume-i/the-accidental-citizen-report.
4 Samara Canada, *The Accidental Citizen?*, 8, 11.
5 Barry Campbell, "A Legend Is Born," *The Walrus*, March 2008, https://thewalrus.ca/a-legend-is-born/.
6 Loat and MacMillan, *Tragedy in the Commons*, 24.
7 David Docherty, "To Run or Not to Run?," *Canadian Parliamentary Review* 24, no. 1 (2001): 16–23, http://www.revparl.ca/english/issue.asp?param=78&art=205.
8 Docherty, "To Run or Not to Run?," 16.
9 Royce Koop and Amanda Bittner, "Parachuted into Parliament: Candidate Nomination, Appointed Candidates, and Legislative Roles in Canada," *Journal of Elections, Public Opinion and Parties* 21, no. 4 (2011): 431–52, https://doi.org/10.1080/17457289.2011.609297.
10 Rosemary Barton, "Ruth Ellen Brosseau's Rise from Paper Candidate to NDP Star," *CBC News*, May 14, 2014, https://www.cbc.ca/news/politics/ruth-ellen-brosseau-s-rise-from-paper-candidate-to-ndp-star-1.2640310.
11 C.E.S. Franks, *The Parliament of Canada* (Toronto: University of Toronto Press, 1987), 67.
12 Susan Delacourt, "Politicians Now More Likely to Be Businessmen Than Lawyers," *Toronto Star*, February 1, 2013, https://www.thestar.com/news/insight/2013/02/01/politicians_now_more_likely_to_be_businessmen_than_lawyers.html.
13 N. Guppy, S. Freeman, and S. Buchan, "Research Notes/Notes de recherche," *Canadian Review of Sociology/Revue canadienne de sociologie* 24 (1987): 417–30.
14 Postmedia News, "New Parliament Younger, More Diverse: Study," *National Post*, June 30, 2011.

15 Tamsin McMahon, "The REALLY New Democrats," *National Post*, May 4, 2011, https://nationalpost.com/news/canada/the-really-new-democrats; Chris Fox, "Rookie NDP MPs Reflect on Spending Their Early 20s on Parliament Hill," *CP24*, May 19, 2015; Eric Andrew-Gee, "Rookie MP at 20, Laurin Liu Now Fights to Hold NDP Ground in Quebec," *Globe and Mail*, August 10, 2015, https://www.theglobeandmail.com/news/politics/elections/rookie-mp-at-20-laurin-liu-now-fights-to-hold-ndp-ground-in-quebec/article25917312/.
16 Loat and MacMillan, *Tragedy in the Commons*, 62–3.
17 "Newly Elected MPs Attend 'Boot Camp' Before Parliament Resumes," *CTV News*, November 9, 2015, https://www.ctvnews.ca/politics/newly-elected-mps-attend-boot-camp-before-parliament-resumes-1.2649359; "Fresh-faced MPs Arrive in Ottawa for Orientation Day," *CTV News*, October 29, 2019, https://www.ctvnews.ca/politics/fresh-faced-mps-arrive-in-ottawa-for-orientation-day-1.4660499; Sarah Turnbull, "First-time MPs Get First Taste of Their New Jobs," *CTV News*, September 27, 2021, https://www.ctvnews.ca/politics/first-time-mps-get-first-taste-of-their-new-jobs-1.5602371.
18 Gordon Aiken, *The Backbencher: Trials and Tribulations of a Member of Parliament* (Toronto: McClelland and Stewart, 1974), 49.
19 Jody Wilson-Raybould, *"Indian" in the Cabinet: Speaking Truth to Power* (Toronto: Harper Collins, 2021), 116.
20 Franks, *Parliament of Canada*, 76.
21 David C. Docherty, *Mr. Smith Goes to Ottawa: Life in the House of Commons* (Vancouver: UBC Press, 1997), 50.
22 Docherty, *Mr. Smith Goes to Ottawa*, xxi.
23 Loat and MacMillan, *Tragedy in the Commons*, 85.
24 Royce Koop, Kelly Blidook, and Heather Bastedo, *Representation in Action: Canadian MPs in the Constituencies* (Vancouver: UBC Press, 2018).
25 Koop, Blidook, and Bastedo, *Representation in Action*, 3.
26 Peter MacLeod, "The Constituency Project Ten Years On," *Canadian Parliamentary Review*, Summer 2014, 36–9, http://www.revparl.ca/english/issue.asp?param=219&art=1591. See also Peter MacLeod, "How to Organize an Effective Constituency Office," *Canadian Parliamentary Review*, Spring 2006, 9–12, http://www.revparl.ca/english/issue.asp?param=173&art=1177.
27 Koop, Blidook, and Bastedo, *Representation in Action*, 177.
28 Lincoln Alexander, *"Go to School, You're a Little Black Boy": The Honourable Lincoln M. Alexander; A Memoir*, with Herb Shoveller (Toronto: Dundurn Press, 2010), 111.
29 Terhas Ghebretecle, Michael Morden, Jane Hilderman, and Kendall Anderson, "Beyond the Barbecue: Reimagining Constituency Work for Local Democratic Engagement" (Toronto: Samara Centre for Democracy, 2018), https://www.samaracanada.com/docs/default-source/reports/beyond-the-barbecue---by-the-samara-centre-for-democracy.pdf?sfvrsn=25a1012f_4.
30 Loat and MacMillan, *Tragedy in the Commons*, 93.

31 Rebecca Zandbergen, "Regardless of Political Stripe, MPs Say They're Fielding Vile Calls from Belligerent Constituents," *CBC News*, February 16, 2022, https://www.cbc.ca/news/canada/london/regardless-of-political-stripe-mps-say-they-re-fielding-vile-calls-from-belligerent-constituents-1.6353480.
32 In one of the most definitive studies on the "personal vote" in Canada, Blais et al. found the local candidate made a difference for 5 per cent of Canadian voters: 6 per cent outside of Quebec and 2 per cent inside of Quebec. André Blais, Elisabeth Gidengil, Agnieszka Dobrzynska, Neil Nevitte, and Richard Nadeau, "Does the Local Candidate Matter? Candidate Effects in the Canadian Election of 2000," *Canadian Journal of Political Science* 36, no. 3 (2003): 657–64, https://www.cambridge.org/core/journals/canadian-journal-of-political-science-revue-canadienne-de-science-politique/article/does-the-local-candidate-matter-candidate-effects-in-the-canadian-election-of-2000/9E0027D9ABC436C4357C37F570DEF903. Using experimental methods, Roy and Alcantara suggest strong local candidates may increase vote share, but generally for voters who already favour the candidate's party. Jason Roy and Christopher Alcantara, "The Candidate Effect: Does the Local Candidate Matter?," *Journal of Elections, Public Opinion and Parties* 25, no. 2 (2015): 195–214, https://doi.org/10.1080/17457289.2014.925461.
33 Loat and MacMillan, *Tragedy in the Commons*, 231.
34 Ghebretecle et al., "Beyond the Barbecue," 28
35 Ghebretecle et al., "Beyond the Barbecue," 30.
36 MacLeod, "The Constituency Project Ten Years On."
37 Peter L. McCreath, *The People's Choice: The Inside Story of Being an MP* (Tantallon, NS: Four East, 1995), 56.
38 Elizabeth Goodyear-Grant, "The House of Commons Should Continue to Be a Hybrid Workplace, Even after the Pandemic," *Globe and Mail*, June 10, 2022, https://www.theglobeandmail.com/opinion/article-the-house-of-commons-should-continue-to-be-a-hybrid-workplace-even/.
39 Julie Smyth, "Why Are Divorce Rates So High for MPs?," *Maclean's*, October 30, 2013, https://www.macleans.ca/news/canada/why-are-divorce-rates-so-high-for-mps/.
40 Docherty, "To Run or Not to Run?"
41 Docherty, "To Run or Not to Run?," 19.
42 Loat and MacMillan, *Tragedy in the Commons*, 73.
43 Joe Sornberger, "'Unspeakably Lonely' for Women MPs; Long Hours, Distance from Home Take Toll on Female Politicians," *Ottawa Citizen*, November 29, 1992, A7.
44 Jaime Watt, "The Unglamorous Life of a Member of Parliament," *Toronto Star*, September 25, 2016, https://www.thestar.com/opinion/commentary/2016/09/25/the-unglamorous-life-of-a-member-of-parliament-watt.html.
45 Michael Morden, Jane Hilderman, and Kendall Anderson, *The Real House Lives: Strengthening the Role of MPs in an Age of Partisanship* (Toronto:

Samara Centre for Democracy, 2018), 14, https://www.samaracanada.com/docs/default-source/reports/the-real-house-lives-by-the-samara-centre-for-demoracy.pdf?sfvrsn=b893062f_2.
46 John Geddes, "In Conversation: Peter Milliken," *Maclean's*, June 7, 2011.
47 Morden et al., *The Real House Lives*, 16.
48 Amanda Connolly, "New MPs Are Getting Up to Speed in Orientation. Here Are Some of the Perks of the Job," *Global News*, October 29, 2019, https://globalnews.ca/news/6096243/member-of-parliament-expenses-allowances/.
49 Michael M. Atkinson and Dustin Rogers, "Better Politicians: If We Pay, Will They Come?" (Paper prepared for presentation at the Annual Meeting of the Canadian Political Science Association, Edmonton, AB, June 2012), https://cpsa-acsp.ca/papers-2012/Atkinson.pdf.
50 Canadian Taxpayers Federation, "2019 Election Pension and Severance Payments," http://www.taxpayer.com/media/2019_pensions.pdf; "Taxpayers Federation Releases Pension and Severance Figures for 2021 Federal Election," https://www.taxpayer.com/newsroom/taxpayers-federation-releases-pension-and-severance-figures-for-2021-federal-election.
51 One of the few comprehensive studies of post-parliamentary life is a study of former legislators in the Australian state of Victoria: Amy Nethery, Peter Ferguson, Zim Nwokara, and Matthew Clarke, *Transitioning to Life after Parliament* (Burwood, Australia: Deakin University, 2021), https://new.parliament.vic.gov.au/49e8f9/globalassets/images/news/library-papers/transitioninglifeafterparliament.pdf.
52 Daniel Dickin, "Organizing the Halls of Power: Federal Parliamentary Staffers and Members of Parliament's Offices," *Canadian Parliamentary Review*, Summer 2016, 8–16, http://www.revparl.ca/english/issue.asp?param=227&art=1692.
53 MacLeod, "How to Organize an Effective Constituency Office," 9. Accounts of who established the first constituency offices differ, though Flora MacDonald and Ed Broadbent are often identified as early innovators.
54 Paul Wilson, "The Impact of the COVID-19 Pandemic on Canadian Parliamentary Political Staffers," *Canadian Parliamentary Review*, November 2020, http://www.revparlcan.ca/en/the-impact-of-the-covid-19-pandemic-on-canadian-parliamentary-political-staffers/.
55 Feodor Snagovsky and Matthew Kerby, "Political Staff and the Gendered Division of Political Labour in Canada," *Parliamentary Affairs* 72, no. 3 (July 2019): 616–37; Meagan Cloutier and Melanee Thomas, "Representation on the Front Line: Gender and MP Staff in Canadian Politics" (paper presented to the Canadian Political Science Association annual conference, Vancouver, BC, June 2019), 6, https://www.cpsa-acsp.ca/documents/conference/2019/540.Cloutier-Thomas.pdf.

56 Majid Jowhari, "Life as a New MP: How to Create Order in a Chaotic Office," *Hill Times*, October 10, 2018, https://www.hilltimes.com/2018/10/10/life-new-mp-create-order-chaotic-office/171833.
57 Watt, "The Unglamorous Life of a Member of Parliament."
58 Richard E. Matland and Donley T. Studlar, "Determinants of Legislative Turnover: A Cross-National Analysis," *British Journal of Political Science* 34, no. 1 (2004): 87–108, https://www.jstor.org/stable/4092401.
59 Matthew Kerby and Kelly Blidook, "It's Not You, It's Me: Determinants of Voluntary Legislative Turnover in Canada," *Legislative Studies Quarterly* 36 (2011): 621–43, 628, https://doi.org/10.1111/j.1939-9162.2011.00029.x.
60 Matland and Studlar, "Determinants of Legislative Turnover," 91.
61 Kerby and Blidook, "It's Not You, It's Me," 624.
62 Franks, *The Parliament of Canada*, 7.
63 Michael M. Atkinson and David C. Docherty, "Moving Right Along: The Roots of Amateurism in the Canadian House of Commons," *Canadian Journal of Political Science* 25, no. 2 (1992): 295–318, 299, https://www.jstor.org/stable/3229447.
64 Docherty, *Mr. Smith Goes to Ottawa*, 9.
65 Kerby and Blidook, "It's Not You, It's Me."
66 Josh Dehaas and Rachel Aiello, "Who's Not Running in 2019? A Look at the Many MPs Leaving the House or Their Party," *CTV News*, March 4, 2019, https://www.ctvnews.ca/politics/who-s-not-running-in-2019-a-look-at-the-many-mps-leaving-the-house-or-their-party-1.4322412?.
67 Kerby and Blidook, "It's Not You, It's Me," 622.

5 House of Commons Business

1 The most current, authoritative, and accessible resource on House of Commons procedure is Marc Bosc and André Gagnon, *House of Commons Procedure and Practice*, 3rd ed., published in 2017 and available on the House website at https://www.ourcommons.ca/procedure/procedure-and-practice-3/index-e.html. This follows in a long history of guides on House procedure published under the name of the current Clerk of the House, dating back to John George Bourinot's *Parliamentary Procedure and Practice in the Dominion of Canada*, first published in 1884. Another recent general resource is Rob Walsh, *On the House: An Inside Look at the House of Commons* (Montreal and Kingston: McGill-Queen's University Press, 2017). Walsh was formerly Law Clerk of the House of Commons.
2 Ian Brodie, *At the Centre of Government: The Prime Minister and the Limits on Political Power* (Montreal and Kingston: McGill-Queen's University Press, 2018), 46.
3 Lisa Young, "Value Clash: Parliament and Citizens after 150 Years of Responsible Government," in *Taking Stock of 150 Years of Responsible*

Government in Canada, ed. Louis Massicote and F. Leslie Seidle (Ottawa: Canadian Study of Parliament Group, 1999), 106.

4 W.F. Dawson, *Procedure in the Canadian House of Commons* (Toronto: University of Toronto Press, 1962), 98.

5 Jack Stillborn, "An Alternative Approach to Canadian House of Commons Reform," *American Review of Canadian Studies* 47, no. 1 (2017): 46, https://doi.org/10.1080/02722011.2017.1292534.

6 Michael Chong, "Yes, We Can Fix Question Period. We Already Know How," *iPolitics*, January 22, 2016, https://www.ipolitics.ca/news/yes-we-can-fix-question-period-we-already-know-how.

7 Elizabeth May, "Westminster Parliamentary Democracy: Where Some MPs Are More Equal Than Others," in *Turning Parliament Inside Out: Practical Ideas for Reforming Canada's Democracy*, ed. Michael Chong, Scott Simms, and Kennedy Stewart (Vancouver: Douglas+McIntyre, 2017), 28.

8 In a 2013 ruling, responding to disputes within the Conservative Party, then-Speaker Andrew Scheer affirmed that the Speaker still had ultimate discretion to call on any member. Scheer stated that "I myself have seen fit from time to time to deviate from the lists, usually in an effort to preserve order and decorum during Statements by Members and Question Period. Accordingly, the Chair has to conclude, based on this review of our procedural authorities and other references, that its authority to decide who is recognized to speak is indisputable and has not been trumped by the use of lists, as some Members seemed to suggest." https://www.ourcommons.ca/Content/Misc/ebook/ScheerDecisions-e.pdf, 168.

9 May, "Westminster Parliamentary Democracy," 28.

10 Michael Chong, Libby Davies, Marlene Jennings, Mario Laframboise, and Tom Lukiwski, "What to Do about Question Period: A Roundtable," *Canadian Parliamentary Review* 33, no. 3 (Autumn 2010): 2–8, http://www.revparl.ca/english/issue.asp?param=199&art=1391.

11 For a compilation of all votes by the Speaker, see Bosc and Gagnon, *House of Commons Procedure and Practice*, Figure 7.1, https://www.ourcommons.ca/about/procedureandpractice3rdedition/ch_07_1-e.html.

12 John Earnshaw and Maurice Vellacott, "The Casting Vote," *Canadian Parliamentary Review* 26, no. 4 (2003): 16–18, http://www.revparl.ca/26/4/26n4_03e_vellacott.pdf.

13 Elizabeth Thompson, "The 106 Things You Can't Say in Parliament," *iPolitics*, December 14, 2011, https://www.ipolitics.ca/news/the-106-things-you-cant-say-in-parliament. For more general rules on parliamentary language see Bosc and Gagnon, *House of Commons Procedure and Practice*, "Rules Regarding Content of Speeches," https://www.ourcommons.ca/about/procedureandpractice3rdedition/ch_13_3-e.html.

14 Campbell Clark, "Trudeau's Sunny Ways Image Takes a Major Hit," *Globe and Mail*, May 19, 2016, https://www.theglobeandmail.com/news/politics/globe-politics-insider/trudeaus-sunny-ways-image-takes-a-major-hit/article30089339/.
15 Michael Cooper, "How to Fix Question Period: Ideas for Reform," in *Turning Parliament Inside Out: Practical Ideas for Reforming Canada's Democracy*, ed. Michael Chong, Scott Simms, and Kennedy Stewart (Vancouver: Douglas+McIntyre, 2017), 38.
16 Samara Canada, "Cheering or Jeering: Members of Parliament Open Up about Civility in the House of Commons" (Toronto: Samara Centre for Democracy, 2016), https://www.samaracanada.com/research/cheering-or-jeering.
17 Mackenzie Grisdale, "Heckling in the House of Commons," *Canadian Parliamentary Review*, Autumn 2011, 38–45, http://www.revparl.ca/english/issue.asp?param=205&art=1447.
18 Cooper, "How to Fix Question Period," 40.
19 Rob Lundie, "'That's It, You're Out': Disorderly Conduct in the House of Representatives from 1901 to 2016" (Canberra: Parliament of Australia, 2016), https://www.aph.gov.au/About_Parliament/Parliamentary_Departments/Parliamentary_Library/pubs/rp/rp1617/Disorderly Conduct.
20 Michael Morden, Jane Hilderman, and Kendall Anderson, "Flip the Script: Reclaiming the Legislature to Reinvigorate Representative Democracy" (Toronto: Samara Centre for Democracy, 2018), 10, https://www.samaracanada.com/research/political-leadership/mp-exit-interviews/volume-ii/flip-the-script; see also Bosc and Gagnon, *House of Commons Procedure and Practice*, "Appendix 11: Parliaments Since 1867 and Number of Sitting Days," https://www.ourcommons.ca/about/procedureandpractice3rdedition/App11-e.html.
21 Jeff Gray and Tom Cardozo, "Provincial and Territorial Legislatures Spend Fewer Days in Session than a Decade Ago, Globe Analysis Finds," *Globe and Mail*, July 4, 2019, https://www.theglobeandmail.com/canada/article-provincial-and-territorial-legislatures-spend-fewer-days-in-session/.
22 Jonathan Malloy, "Why Trudeau's Self-serving Prorogation of Parliament Should Be Canada's Last," *The Conversation*, August 21, 2020, https://theconversation.com/why-trudeaus-self-serving-prorogation-of-parliament-should-be-canadas-last-144892.
23 Walsh, *On the House*, 112.
24 C.E.S. Franks, *The Parliament of Canada* (Toronto: University of Toronto Press, 1987), 145.
25 Nathan Cullen, "Speaking in Parliament," in *Turning Parliament Inside Out: Practical Ideas for Reforming Canada's Democracy*, ed. Michael Chong, Scott Simms, and Kennedy Stewart (Vancouver: Douglas+McIntyre, 2017), 99.

26 Samuel H. Beer, "The British Legislature and the Problem of Mobilizing Consent," in *Lawmakers in a Changing World*, ed. Elke Franke (Englewood Cliffs, NJ: Prentice-Hall, 1966), 30–48.
27 Charlie Feldman, "Unfinished Business: A Snapshot of Recent Government Bill Practice," *Canadian Parliamentary Review*, Winter 2021, 14–19, 14, http://www.revparlcan.ca/en/unfinished-business-a-snapshot-of-recent-government-bill-practice-2/.
28 Brodie, *At the Centre of Government*, 84.
29 Louis Massicotte, "Omnibus Bills in Theory and Practice," *Canadian Parliamentary Review* 36, no. 1 (2013), 13–17, http://www.revparl.ca/english/issue.asp?param=214&art=1517.
30 In private correspondence with me on research related to social conservatism in Canadian politics, a senior Harper government official confirmed this and said, "We had no idea that was in there," even though it was a government bill, because many aspects were simply brought forward and recycled from the previous government.
31 Andre Barnes and Michel Bédard, "Omnibus Bills: Frequently Asked Questions," Library of Parliament Research Branch Publication (2012; revised 2022), https://lop.parl.ca/sites/PublicWebsite/default/en_CA/ResearchPublications/201279E.
32 C.E.S. Franks, "Omnibus Bills Subvert Our Legislative Process," *Globe and Mail*, July 14, 2010, https://www.theglobeandmail.com/opinion/omnibus-bills-subvert-our-legislative-process/article1387088/.
33 "Justin Trudeau Needs to Stop Borrowing Stephen Harper's Omnibus Trick," *Maclean's*, May 13, 2019, https://www.macleans.ca/opinion/justin-trudeau-needs-to-stop-borrowing-stephen-harpers-omnibus-trick/.
34 Canada. Parliament. House of Commons. *Debates*, 35th Parliament, 1st Session, vol. 133, no. 072 (May 26, 1994), 4443.
35 John Ivison, "How Stephen Harper Learned to Love the Omnibus Bill," *National Post*, May 3, 2012, https://nationalpost.com/opinion/john-ivison-how-stephen-harper-learned-to-love-omnibus-bills.
36 Jenny Uechi, "Justin Trudeau Releases 32-Point Plan for Restoring Democracy, Including End to Omnibus Bills," *National Observer*, June 16, 2015, https://www.nationalobserver.com/2015/06/16/news/justin-trudeau-releases-32-point-plan-restoring-democracy-including-end-omnibus.
37 Donald J. Savoie, *Democracy in Canada: The Disintegration of Our Institutions* (Montreal and Kingston: McGill-Queen's University Press, 2019), 332.
38 Canada. Parliament. House of Commons. *Standing Orders of the House of Commons* (Consolidated Version as of June 23, 2022), s. 69.1, https://www.ourcommons.ca/procedure/standing-orders/Index-e.html.
39 Yves Y. Pelletier, "Governing by Time Allocation: The Increasing Use of Time Allocation in the House of Commons, 1971 to 2021," *Canadian Parliamentary Review*, Winter 2021, 3–13, http://www.revparlcan.ca/en/governing-by-time-allocation-the-increasing-use-of-time-allocation-in-the-house-of-commons-1971-to-2021/.

40 Brodie, *At the Centre of Government*, 85.
41 Franks, *The Parliament of Canada*, 147.
42 Stuart Soroka, Olga Redko, and Quinn Albaugh, "Television in the Legislature: The Impact of Cameras in the House of Commons," *Parliamentary Affairs* 68 (2015): 203–17, https://doi.org/10.1093/pa/gst017.
43 Andrea Ulrich, "A Question of Accountability: Is Question Period in Canada Working?," *Queen's Policy Review* 2, no. 2 (Fall 2011): 5.
44 Bosc and Gagnon, "Private Members' Business," chap. 21 in *House of Commons Procedure and Practice*.
45 Bosc and Gagnon, "Private Members' Business," in *House of Commons Procedure and Practice*.
46 For general discussion of the bill and its history, see Lyne Casavant et al., "Legislative Summary of Bill C-3: An Act to Amend the Judges Act and the Criminal Code" (Ottawa: Library of Parliament Research Branch, December 2020, last revised February 2021), https://lop.parl.ca/sites/PublicWebsite/default/en_CA/ResearchPublications/LegislativeSummaries/432C3E#:~:text=Bill%20C%E2%80%913%2C%20as%20amended,assault%20law%20and%20social%20context.
47 Amanda Connolly, "Rona Ambrose's Judicial Sex Assault Law Training Bill Gets 2nd Shot as Liberals Retable," *Global News*, February 4, 2020, https://globalnews.ca/news/6504372/rona-ambrose-judicial-sex-assault-law-training-bill/.
48 Bruce Campion-Smith, "Abortion Will Never Be Eliminated, Tory MP Says," *Toronto Star*, April 26, 2012, https://www.thestar.com/news/canada/2012/04/26/abortion_will_never_be_eliminated_tory_mp_says.html.
49 I want to thank Michael Donison for pointing out this exceptional event.
50 Kelly Blidook, "The Changing Use of Standing Order 31 Statements," *Canadian Parliamentary Review* 36, no. 4 (Winter 2013): 25–9, http://www.revparl.ca/english/issue.asp?param=217&art=1560.
51 Kady O'Malley, "Process Nerd: All about Opposition Day Debates in a Minority House," *iPolitics*, December 9, 2019, https://www.ipolitics.ca/news/process-nerd-all-about-opposition-day-debates-in-a-minority-house.
52 For discussion see Andrew Heard, "Just What Is a Vote of Confidence? The Curious Case of May 10, 2005," *Canadian Journal of Political Science* 40, no. 2 (2007): 395–416, https://www.jstor.org/stable/25166104; Donald Desserud, *The Confidence Convention under the Canadian Parliamentary System* (Ottawa: Canadian Study of Parliament Group, 2006); Aucoin et al., *Democratizing the Constitution* (2011), http://cspg-gcep.ca/pdf/Parliamentary_Perspectives_7_2006-e.pdf.
53 Rachel Aiello, "Trudeau Government Survives Confidence Vote," *CTV News*, October 21, 2020, https://www.ctvnews.ca/politics/trudeau-government-survives-confidence-vote-1.5154159?cache=kmdeuabt.

54 Bosc and Gagnon, "Committees," chap. 20 in *House of Commons Procedure and Practice*, note 28, https://www.ourcommons.ca/procedure/procedure-and-practice-3/ch_20_1-e.html.
55 C.E.S. Franks, "The Dilemma of the Standing Committees of the House of Commons," *Canadian Journal of Political Science* 4, no. 4 (December 1971): 461–76, https://www.jstor.org/stable/3235534.

6 Diversity

1 H. Pitkin, *The Concept of Representation* (Berkeley: University of California Press, 1967).
2 Len Marchand and Matt Hughes, *Breaking Trail* (Prince George, BC: Caitlin Press, 2000), 86.
3 Marchand and Hughes, *Breaking Trail*, 88.
4 Information derived from Library of Parliament online database at https://lop.parl.ca/sites/ParlInfo/default/en_CA/People/parliamentarians.
5 Some individuals have served both as MPs and as senators, such as Len Marchand, elected to the House of Commons in 1968 and appointed to the Senate in 1984. They are counted separately for each chamber here.
6 Alice Chen, "'We have drive': Indigenous MPs on Their Election and Their Future," *Hill Times*, September 29, 2021, https://www.hilltimes.com/2021/09/29/we-have-drive-indigenous-mps-on-their-election-and-their-future/319877.
7 Statistics Canada, "Aboriginal Peoples in Canada: Key Results from the 2016 Census," https://www150.statcan.gc.ca/n1/daily-quotidien/171025/dq171025a-eng.htm?indid=14430-1&indgeo=0.
8 Jody Wilson-Raybould, *"Indian" in the Cabinet: Speaking Truth to Power* (Toronto: Harper Collins, 2021), 261.
9 Robert Falcon-Ouellette, "Honouring Indigenous Languages within Parliament," *Canadian Parliamentary Review* 42, no. 2 (Summer 2019): 3–5, http://www.revparl.ca/english/issue.asp?param=239&art=1850.
10 House of Commons Proceedings, June 15, 2021, 2513. See also "Nunavut MP Mumilaaq Qaqqaq on Leaving Politics, and Why She Feels No Pride in Canada," *CBC Radio*, June 16, 2021, https://www.cbc.ca/radio/asithappens/as-it-happens-the-wednesday-edition-1.6067864/nunavut-mp-mumilaaq-qaqqaq-on-leaving-politics-and-why-she-feels-no-pride-in-canada-1.6068158.
11 Michael D. Morden, "Parliament and the Representation of Indigenous Issues: The Canadian Case," *Parliamentary Affairs* 71, no. 1 (January 2018): 124–43, https://doi.org/10.1093/pa/gsx009.
12 Falcon-Ouellette, "Honouring Indigenous Languages within Parliament"; see also "The Use of Indigenous Languages in Proceedings of the House of Commons and Committees," *Report of the Standing Committee on Procedure and House Affairs* (June 2018), 42nd Parliament,

1st Session, https://www.ourcommons.ca/DocumentViewer/en/42-1 /PROC/report-66/.
13 Marchand and Hughes, *Breaking Trail*, 119.
14 Peter O'Neil, *I Am a Metis: The Story of Gerry St. Germain* (Madeira Park, BC: Harbour Publishing, 2016).
15 See Michael Morden, "Indigenizing Parliament," *Canadian Parliamentary Review* 39, no. 2 (Summer 2016): 24–33, http://www.revparl.ca/english /issue.asp?param=227&art=1694.
16 Though see Bill Flowers, "Indigenous Seats in Parliament," *Policy Options*, January 26, 2017, https://policyoptions.irpp.org/magazines /january-2017/indigenous-seats-in-parliament/.
17 Stephen Fletcher, Jennifer Howard, Mario Levesque, Kevin Murphy, and David Onley, "Roundtable: Disability in Parliamentary Politics," *Canadian Parliamentary Review* 38, no. 1 (Spring 2015): 6–13, 12, http:// www.revparl.ca/english/issue.asp?param=222&art=1628.
18 Brynne Langford and Mario Levesque, "Symbolic and Substantive Relevance of Politicians with Disabilities: A British Columbia Case Study," *Canadian Parliamentary Review* 40, no. 2 (Summer 2017): 8, http://www .revparl.ca/english/issue.asp?param=231&art=1744; see also Mario Levesque, "Searching for Persons with Disabilities in Canadian Provincial Office," *Canadian Journal of Disability Studies* 5, no. 1 (January 2016): 73–106, https://cjds.uwaterloo.ca/index.php/cjds/article/view/250/434.
19 Langford and Levesque, "Symbolic and Substantive Relevance of Politicians with Disabilities," 13.
20 Fletcher et al., "Roundtable: Disability in Parliamentary Politics," 8.
21 Richard Medugno, *Deaf Politician: The Gary Malkowski Story* (CreateSpace, 2020).
22 Fletcher et al., "Roundtable: Disability in Parliamentary Politics," 12.
23 Fletcher et al., "Roundtable: Disability in Parliamentary Politics," 10.
24 Fletcher et al., "Roundtable: Disability in Parliamentary Politics," 12.
25 D. Poulter, N. Votruba, I. Bakolis, F. Debell, J. Das-Munshi, and G. Thornicroft, "Mental Health of UK Members of Parliament in the House of Commons: A Cross-sectional Survey," *BMJ Open* 9, no. 7 (2019): e027892, https://doi.org/10.1136/bmjopen-2018-027892.
26 Joanna Everitt, Manon Tremblay, and Angelia Wagner, "Pathway to Office: The Eligibility, Recruitment, Selection, and Election of LGBT Candidates," in *Queering Representation: LGBTQ People and Electoral Politics in Canada*, ed. Manon Tremblay (Vancouver: UBC Press, 2019), 252; Erica Lentl, "Canada, Meet Your New LGBTQ2S+ MPs," *Xtra**, September 21, 2021, https:// xtramagazine.com/power/lgbtq2s-federal-election-queer-mps-209072.
27 Joanna Everitt and Michael Camp, "In versus Out: LGBT Politicians in Canada," *Journal of Canadian Studies* 48, no. 1 (2014): 244, https://doi .org/10.3138/jcs.48.1.226.
28 Libby Davies, *Outside In: A Political Memoir* (Toronto: Between the Lines, 2019), 123.

29 Davies, *Outside In*, 127.
30 Truelove, "Afterword: The Champion," in *Queering Representation: LGBTQ People and Electoral Politics in Canada*, ed. Manon Tremblay (Vancouver: UBC Press, 2019), 314–15. See also Graeme Truelove, *Svend Robinson: A Life in Politics* (Vancouver: New Star, 2013).
31 Truelove, "Afterword: The Champion," in *Queering Representation*, 322.
32 Manon Tremblay, "Representation: The Case of LGBTQ People," in *Queering Representation*, 221.
33 Tremblay, "Representation," in *Queering Representation*, 222.
34 Flora MacDonald and Geoffrey Stevens, *Flora! A Woman in a Man's World* (Montreal and Kingston: McGill-Queen's University Press, 2021), 149.
35 Ellen Fairclough, *Saturday's Child: Memoirs of Canada's First Female Cabinet Minister* (Toronto: University of Toronto Press, 1995), 73.
36 Judy LaMarsh, *Memoirs of a Bird in a Gilded Cage* (Toronto: McClelland and Stewart [Pocketbook Edition], 1969 [1970]), 301.
37 Monique Bégin, *Ladies, Upstairs! My Life in Politics and After* (Montreal and Kingston: McGill-Queen's University Press, 2018), 97.
38 Margaret Mitchell, *No Laughing Matter: Adventure, Activism & Politics* (Vancouver: Granville Island Publishing, 2008), 149.
39 Sydney Sharpe, *The Gilded Ghetto: Women and Politics in Canada* (Toronto: Harper Collins, 1994), 48.
40 Davies, *Outside In*, 179.
41 Sylvia Bashevkin, *Women, Power, Politics: The Hidden Story of Canada's Unfinished Democracy* (Toronto: Oxford University Press, 2009), 78.
42 Bashevkin, *Women, Power, Politics*, 79.
43 Bashevkin, *Women, Power, Politics*, 11.
44 Michelle Rempel, "Michelle Rempel: Confront Your Sexism," *National Post*, April 18, 2016, https://nationalpost.com/opinion/michelle-rempel-confront-your-sexism.
45 Stephanie Mullen, "'Way Past That Era Now?' Women in the Canadian Senate," in *Stalled: The Representation of Women in Canadian Governments*, ed. Linda Trimble, Jane Arscott, and Manon Tremblay (Vancouver: UBC Press, 2013), 280. I have updated Mullen's data to 2015 to cover all of Stephen Harper's appointments.
46 Mullen, "'Way Past That Era Now?,'" 282.
47 Elizabeth McCallion, "Feminist Senators Are Critical Actors in Women's Representation," *Policy Options*, November 11, 2019, https://policyoptions.irpp.org/magazines/november-2019/feminist-senators-are-critical-actors-in-womens-representation/.
48 Elizabeth McCallion, "The Canadian Senate Briefly Reached Gender Parity – Here's Why It Matters," *The Conversation*, March 3, 2021, https://theconversation.com/the-canadian-senate-briefly-reached-gender-parity-heres-why-it-matters-153525.
49 Mullen, "'Way Past That Era Now?,'" 284–5.

50 Lisa Young, "Fulfilling the Mandate of Difference: Women in the Canadian House of Commons," in *In the Presence of Women: Representation in Canadian Governments*, ed. Jane Arscott and Linda Trimble (Toronto: Harcourt Brace Jovanovich, 1997), 92.
51 Jackie Steele, "An Effective Player in the Parliamentary Process: The Liberal Women's Caucus, 1993–2001" (Parliamentary Internship Programme/ Institute on Governance, 2001).
52 Canada. Parliament. House of Commons. *Debates*, 35th Parliament, 1st Session, vol. 133, no. 032 (March 8, 1994), 1968.
53 Chris Rands, "The Daycare Caucus: How the Commons Is Coping with a Baby Boom," *CBC News*, March 11, 2018, https://www.cbc.ca/news/politics/commons-babies-mps-trudeau-1.4570416.
54 Rachel Aiello, "Gould Says Parental Leave for MPs Should Be a Priority, after Promise Stalled," *CTVNews.ca*, March 20, 2019, https://www.ctvnews.ca/politics/gould-says-parental-leave-for-mps-should-be-a-priority-after-promise-stalled-1.4344224?cache=yes%3FclipId%3D89926.
55 Joanna Smith, "NDP MP Details Harassment Allegations: 'It Was Sex without Explicit Consent,'" *Toronto Star*, November 26, 2014, https://www.thestar.com/news/canada/2014/11/25/ndp_mp_details_harassment_allegations_it_was_sex_without_explicit_consent.html.
56 Joanna Smith, "MPs Reveal Experiences with Sexual Misconduct on Parliament Hill in Survey," *Globe and Mail*, January 2, 2018, https://www.theglobeandmail.com/news/politics/mps-reveal-experiences-with-sexual-misconduct-on-parliament-hill-in-survey/article37472308/.
57 Laura Stone and Erin Anderssen, "Sexual Harassment Commonplace for Women on Parliament Hill, MPs Say," *Globe and Mail*, November 10, 2017.
58 Cheryl N. Collier and Tracey Raney, "Canada's Member-to-Member Code of Conduct on Sexual Harassment in the House of Commons: Progress or Regress?," *Canadian Journal of Political Science* 51, no. 4 (2018): 795–815, https://doi.org/10.1017/S000842391800032X.
59 Meagan Campbell and Catherine McIntyre, "Sexual Harassment Has Long Festered on the Hill. Now, Female MPs from All Parties Are Saying 'Enough,'" *Maclean's*, March 7, 2018, https://www.macleans.ca/politics/ottawa/sexual-harassment-on-parliament-hill/.
60 Tracey Raney and Cheryl N. Collier, "Privilege and Gendered Violence in the Canadian and British Houses of Commons: A Feminist Institutionalist Analysis," *Parliamentary Affairs* 75, no. 2 (2022): 382–99, 392, https://doi.org/10.1093/pa/gsaa069.
61 Sheila Copps, *Nobody's Baby: A Survival Guide to Politics* (Toronto: Deneau, 1986), 88.
62 "'Nicey-nicey' Trudeau Should Toss Wilson-Raybould and Philpott from Caucus, Says Sheila Copps," *CBC Radio*, March 8, 2019 [Transcript], https://www.cbc.ca/radio/asithappens/as-it-happens-tuesday

-edition-1.5043490/nicey-nicey-trudeau-should-toss-wilson-raybould-and-philpott-from-caucus-says-sheila-copps-1.5049122.
63 Sylvia Bashevkin, *Toeing the Lines: Women and Party Politics in English Canada* (Toronto: University of Toronto Press, 1985).
64 Samantha Wright Allen, "Parliamentarians Form Feminist Association, Say Getting Recognized 'Won't Be Easy,'" *Hill Times*, December 5, 2018.
65 Sarah Childs and Mona Lena Krook, "Should Feminists Give Up on Critical Mass? A Contingent Yes," *Politics & Gender* 2, no. 4 (2006): 522–30, https://doi.org/10.1017/S1743923X06251146; Sarah Childs and Mona Lena Krook, "Critical Mass Theory and Women's Political Representation," *Political Studies* 56 (2008): 725–36, https://doi.org/10.1111/j.1467-9248.2007.00712.x; Sarah Childs and Mona Lena Krook, "Analysing Women's Substantive Representation: From Critical Mass to Critical Actors," *Government and Opposition* 44, no. 2 (2009): 125–45, https://doi.org/10.1111/j.1477-7053.2009.01279.x.
66 Erica Rayment, *Women in the House: The Impact of Elected Women on Parliamentary Debate and Policymaking in Canada* (PhD dissertation, Department of Political Science, University of Toronto, 2020), 82.
67 Rayment, *Women in the House*.
68 Young, "Fulfilling the Mandate of Difference."
69 Joan Grace, "Presence and Purpose in the Canadian House of Commons: The Standing Committee on the Status of Women," *Parliamentary Affairs* 69, no. 4 (October 2016): 841, https://doi.org/10.1093/pa/gsw008.
70 Grace, "Presence and Purpose," 842.
71 Celina Caesar-Chavannes, *Can You Hear Me Now? How I Found My Voice and Learned to Live with Passion and Purpose* (Toronto: Random House Canada, 2021), 245.
72 Lincoln Alexander, *"Go to School, You're a Little Black Boy": The Honourable Lincoln M. Alexander; A Memoir*, with Herb Shoveller (Toronto: Dundurn Press, 2010), 121.
73 Alexander, *"Go to School, You're a Little Black Boy,"* 98.
74 Laura Jean Kwak, *Asian Conservatives in Canada's Parliament: A Study in Race and Governmentality* (PhD dissertation, Department of Social Justice Education, University of Toronto, 2016), 87.
75 Alexander, *"Go to School, You're a Little Black Boy,"* 98.
76 F. Abbas Rana, "Punjabi Is Now Fourth Language in the House," *Hill Times*, July 26, 2004.
77 Jerome H. Black and Andrew Griffith, "Do MPs Represent Canada's Diversity?," *Policy Options*, January 7, 2022, https://policyoptions.irpp.org/magazines/january-2022/do-mps-represent-canadas-diversity/.
78 2021 election data provided by Andrew Griffith (personal email). See also Jerome H. Black and Andrew Griffith, "Do Canada's Most Powerful Federal Posts Reflect the Country's Diversity?," *Policy Options*, June 29,

2020, https://policyoptions.irpp.org/magazines/june-2020/do-canadas-most-powerful-federal-posts-reflect-the-countrys-diversity/.
79 Abbas Rana, "Punjabi Now Third Language in the House," *Hill Times*, November 1, 2015.
80 Andrew Griffith, "Diversity in the Senate," *Policy Options*, February 14, 2017, https://policyoptions.irpp.org/fr/magazines/fevrier-2017/diversity-in-the-senate/.
81 Jerome Black, "Ethnoracial Minorities in the 38th Parliament: Patterns of Change and Continuity," in *Electing a Diverse Canada: The Representation of Immigrants, Minorities, and Women*, ed. Caroline Andrew et al. (Vancouver: UBC Press, 2008), 229–54.
82 Kwak, *Asian Conservatives in Canada's Parliament*.
83 Jerome Black, "Entering the Political Elite in Canada: The Case of Minority Women as Parliamentary Candidates and MPs," *Canadian Review of Sociology and Anthropology* 3 (2000): 143–66.
84 Caesar-Chavannes, *Can You Hear Me Now?*, 246.
85 Caesar-Chavannes, *Can You Hear Me Now?*, 172.
86 Don Oliver, *A Matter of Equality: The Life's Work of Senator Don Oliver* (Halifax: Nimbus Press, 2021), 128.
87 Oliver, *A Matter of Equality*, 129.
88 Karen Bird, "Patterns of Substantive Representation among Visible Minority MPs: Evidence from Canada's House of Commons," in *The Political Representation of Immigrants and Minorities*, ed. Karen Bird, Thomas Saalfeld, and Andreas M. Wüst (London: Routledge, 2010), 207–29.
89 Bird, "Patterns of Substantive Representation," 219.
90 Karen Bird, "'We Are Not an Ethnic Vote!' Representational Perspectives of Minorities in the Greater Toronto Area," *Canadian Journal of Political Science* 48, no. 2 (2015): 249–79, 270, https://doi.org/10.1017/S0008423915000256.
91 Bird, "'We Are Not an Ethnic Vote!,'" 262.
92 Canadian Press, "Black MPs, Senators Call for Government Action against Systemic Racism," June 16, 2020, https://www.ctvnews.ca/politics/black-mps-senators-call-for-government-action-against-systemic-racism-1.4986171.
93 "Statement by the Parliamentary Black Caucus," June 22, 2020, https://gregfergus.libparl.ca/2020/06/22/statement-by-the-parliamentary-black-caucus/?lang=en.
94 Bird, "Patterns of Substantive Representation," 220.
95 Kwak, *Asian Conservatives in Canada's Parliament*, 38–9.
96 Canada. Parliament. House of Commons. *Debates*, 41st Parliament, 2nd Session, vol. 147, no. 091 (May 28, 2014), 5786; Ryan Maloney, "Deepak Obhrai to Chris Alexander in C-24 Debate Last Year: 'A Canadian Is a Canadian,'" *Huffington Post*, October 23, 2015, https://www.huffpost.com/archive/ca/entry/deepak-obhrai-chris-alexander-billc-24_n_8370424.
97 Alexander, "*Go to School, You're a Little Black Boy*," 96.

7 The Senate

1 Emmett Macfarlane, *Constitutional Pariah:* Reference re Senate Reform *and the Future of Parliament* (Vancouver: UBC Press, 2021), 4.
2 David Smith, "Bicameralism: A Concept in Search of a Theory," chap. 1 in *The Canadian Senate in Bicameral Perspective* (Toronto: University of Toronto Press, 2003).
3 Robert A. MacKay, *The Unreformed Senate of Canada*, 2nd ed., rev. and reprinted (Toronto: McClelland and Stewart, 1963), 38; quoted in Senate of Canada, Committees and Private Legislation Directorate, "A Legislative and Historical Overview of the Senate of Canada" (May 2001), https://sencanada.ca/en/Content/Sen/committee/381/pub/legislative-e.
4 Senate of Canada, Committees and Private Legislation Directorate, "The Canadian Senate in Focus 1867–2001" (May 2001), https://sencanada.ca/en/Content/Sen/committee/391/pub/focus-e.
5 As an example of declining activism, "[i]n the first sixty years after Confederation (1867–1927), approximately 180 bills were passed by the House of Commons and sent to the Senate that subsequently did not receive Royal Assent either because they were rejected by the Senate or were passed by the Senate with amendments that were not accepted by the Commons. In contrast, less than one-quarter that number of bills was lost for similar reasons in the sixty-year period from 1928 to 1987." Senate of Canada, Committees and Private Legislation Directorate, "The Canadian Senate in Focus 1867–2001" (May 2001).
6 Robert Jackson and Michael M. Atkinson, *The Canadian Legislative System*, 2nd ed. (Toronto: Gage, 1980), 112.
7 R.A. Mackay, *The Unreformed Senate of Canada*, 1st ed. (London: Oxford University Press, 1926).
8 Jack Stillborn, "Forty Years of Not Reforming the Senate: Taking Stock," in *Protecting Canadian Democracy: The Senate You Never Knew*, ed. Serge Joyal (Montreal and Kingston: McGill-Queen's University Press, 2003), 31–66.
9 Stillborn, "Forty Years," 32.
10 David Smith, *The Canadian Senate in Bicameral Perspective*, 48.
11 Macfarlane, *Constitutional Pariah*, 35.
12 Mackay, *The Unreformed Senate of Canada*, 2nd ed., 9.
13 Colin Campbell, *The Canadian Senate: A Lobby from Within* (Toronto: Macmillan of Canada, 1978).
14 Campbell, *The Canadian Senate*, 11.
15 Campbell, *The Canadian Senate*, 147.
16 Jackson and Atkinson, *The Canadian Legislative System*, 111.
17 Campbell, *The Canadian Senate*, 160–2.
18 Canada, Task Force on Canadian Unity, *A Future Together: Observations and Recommendations* (Ottawa: Minister of Supply and Services Canada, 1979).
19 David Smith, *The Canadian Senate in Bicameral Perspective*, 52–3.

20 Reform Party of Canada, *Platform and Statement of Principles*, 1988, https://www.poltext.org/sites/poltext.org/files/plateformesV2/Canada/CAN_PL_1989_RP_en.pdf.
21 Loleen Berdahl and Roger Gibbins, *Western Visions, Western Futures: Perspectives on the West in Canada*, 2nd ed. (Toronto: University of Toronto Press, 2003), 53.
22 Serge Joyal, "Conclusion: The Senate as the Embodiment of the Federal Principle," in *Protecting Canadian Democracy*, 284–5.
23 Records from the parliamentary website show that prior to 2016, fifteen senators in Canadian history were First Nations, Inuit, or Métis, compared to thirty-four MPs. Given the much larger size of the House of Commons (which has increased over the years, making exact calculations difficult), this suggests Indigenous representation in the Senate was equal or somewhat higher than the House. This does not incorporate higher rates of representation in both chambers since 2016. https://lop.parl.ca/sites/ParlInfo/default/en_CA/People/parliamentarians.
24 Allison Dunfield, "Senators-in-waiting Likely to Stay That Way, PM Says," *Globe and Mail*, November 17, 2004, https://www.theglobeandmail.com/news/national/senators-in-waiting-likely-to-stay-that-way-pm-says/article1144159/.
25 Macfarlane, *Constitutional Pariah*; for discussion of earlier proposals see Jennifer Smith, *The Democratic Dilemma: Reforming the Canadian Senate* (Kingston: Queen's University School of Policy Studies, 2009).
26 Independent Advisory Board for Senate Appointments, "Mandate and Members," https://www.canada.ca/en/campaign/independent-advisory-board-for-senate-appointments/members.html.
27 Calculated based on press releases on IAB website, https://www.canada.ca/en/campaign/independent-advisory-board-for-senate-appointments/allnews.html.
28 Elizabeth McCallion, "The Canadian Senate Briefly Reached Gender Parity – Here's Why It Matters," *The Conversation*, March 3, 2021, https://theconversation.com/the-canadian-senate-briefly-reached-gender-parity-heres-why-it-matters-153525. The decline back to 49 per cent was due to the resignation and death of two women senators and the lack of new appointments by the Trudeau government.
29 Jason VandenBeukel, "Revolution in the Red Chamber? The Senate of Canada in the 21st Century" (PhD dissertation, Department of Political Science, University of Toronto, 2022), 96, https://tspace.library.utoronto.ca/bitstream/1807/123333/3/VandenBeukel_Jason_Robert_202206_PhD_thesis.pdf.
30 Information taken from parliamentary website, https://lop.parl.ca/sites/ParlInfo/default/en_CA/People/parliamentarians.
31 Peter Zimonjic and Rosemary Barton, "Andrew Scheer Says He Will Not Appoint Independent Senators If Elected Prime Minister," *CBC News*,

June 28, 2017, https://www.cbc.ca/news/politics/andrew-scheer-interview-barton-1.4182567.

32 J. VandenBeukel, C. Cochrane, and J. Godbout, "Birds of a Feather? Loyalty and Partisanship in the Reformed Canadian Senate," *Canadian Journal of Political Science* 54, no. 4 (2021): 830–49, https://doi.org/10.1017/S0008423921000548.

33 Elizabeth McCallion, "From Private Influence to Public Amendment? The Senate's Amendment Rate in the 41st, 42nd and 43rd Canadian Parliaments," *Canadian Journal of Political Science* 14 (FirstView edition, 2022): 583–99, https://doi.org/10.1017/S0008423922000488.

34 Emmett Macfarlane, *The Renewed Canadian Senate: Organizational Challenges and Relations with the Government* (Institute for Research on Public Policy), May 29, 2019, 7, https://irpp.org/research-studies/renewed-canadian-senate-organizational-challenges-relations-government/.

35 McCallion, "From Private Influence to Public Amendment?," 15.

36 VandenBeukel, "Revolution in the Red Chamber?," 145.

37 Macfarlane, *Constitutional Pariah*, 132.

38 McCallion, "The Canadian Senate Briefly Reached Gender Parity."

8 Scrutiny

1 Janet Ajzenstat, "Modern Mixed Government: A Liberal Defence of Inequality," *Canadian Journal of Political Science* 18, no. 1 (March 1985): 123, https://www.jstor.org/stable/3227912.

2 Brent Rathgeber, *Irresponsible Government: The Decline of Parliamentary Democracy in Canada* (Toronto: Dundurn, 2014), 231.

3 Office of the Auditor General of Canada, *Report of the Auditor General of Canada for the Fiscal Year Ended March 31, 1976*, 9.

4 S.L. Sutherland, "Responsible Government and Ministerial Responsibility: Every Reform Is Its Own Problem," *Canadian Journal of Political Science* 24, no. 1 (1991): 91–120, 92, https://www.jstor.org/stable/3229633.

5 S.L. Sutherland, "The Role of the Clerk of the Privy Council," Research Studies of the Commission of Inquiry into the Sponsorship Program and Advertising Activities (2006), 102.

6 Sutherland, "Responsible Government and Ministerial Responsibility," 118.

7 Kevin Page, *Unaccountable: Truth and Lies on Parliament Hill* (Toronto: Viking, 2015), 193.

8 David C. Docherty, "Citizens and Legislators: Different Views on Representation," in *Value Change and Governance in Canada*, ed. Neil Nevitte (Toronto: University of Toronto Press, 2002), 165–206.

9 "Critics Blast Oda's Swanky Hotel Stay, $16 Orange Juice," *CTVNews.ca*, April 23, 2012, https://www.ctvnews.ca/critics-blast-oda-s-swanky-hotel-stay-16-orange-juice-1.799961.

10 See Alex Smith and Shaowei Pu, "The Parliamentary Financial Cycle," Background Paper (Library of Parliament Research Branch, 2015; rev. 2019, 2021), https://lop.parl.ca/sites/PublicWebsite/default/en_CA/ResearchPublications/201541E.
11 Rob Walsh, *On the House: An Inside Look at the House of Commons* (Montreal and Kingston: McGill-Queen's University Press, 2017), 126.
12 Robert Jackson and Michael M. Atkinson, *The Canadian Legislative System*, 2nd ed. (Toronto: Gage, 1980), 101.
13 C.E.S. Franks, *The Parliament of Canada* (Toronto: University of Toronto Press, 1987), 171.
14 "Year 7: A Review of the McGrath Committee Report on the Reform of the House of Commons: Proceedings" (Ottawa: Canadian Study of Parliament Group, 1992), 18.
15 Jack Stillborn, "Parliamentary Review of Estimates: Initiatives and Prospects," *Canadian Parliamentary Review* 29, no. 4 (2006): 22–7, 22, http://www.revparl.ca/english/issue.asp?param=179&art=1217.
16 Ian Brodie, *At the Centre of Government: The Prime Minister and the Limits on Political Power* (Montreal and Kingston: McGill-Queen's University Press, 2018), 105.
17 Walsh, *On the House*, 126.
18 I would like to thank one of the reviewers for noting this distinction.
19 Geneviève Tellier, *Canadian Public Finance: Explaining Budgetary Institutions and the Budgetary Process in Canada*, trans. Käthe Roth (Toronto: University of Toronto Press, 2019), 4.
20 Donald J. Savoie, *Democracy in Canada: The Disintegration of Our Institutions* (Montreal and Kingston: McGill-Queen's University Press, 2019), 189.
21 Paul G. Thomas, "The Past, Present and Future of Officers of Parliament," *Canadian Public Administration* 46, no. 3 (September 2003): 287–314, https://doi.org/10.1111/j.1754-7121.2003.tb01171.x.
22 Andre Barnes, Laurence Brosseau, and Elise Hurtubise-Loranger, "Appointment of Officers of Parliament" (Library of Parliament Background Paper, 2009; rev. 2019, 2021), https://lop.parl.ca/staticfiles/PublicWebsite/Home/ResearchPublications/HillStudies/PDF/2009-21-e.pdf.
23 Donald Savoie, *Court Government and the Collapse of Accountability in Canada and the United Kingdom* (Toronto: University of Toronto Press, 2008), 166.
24 S.L. Sutherland, "The Unaccountable Federal Accountability Act: Goodbye to Responsible Government?," *Revue Gouvernance* 3, no. 2 (2006): 3, https://www.erudit.org/en/journals/gouvernance/2006-v3-n2-gouvernance02970/1039120ar.pdf.
25 Jonathan Malloy, "An Auditor's Best Friend? Standing Committees on Public Accounts," *Canadian Public Administration* 47, no. 2 (Summer 2004): 165–83, https://doi.org/10.1111/j.1754-7121.2004.tb01182.x.

26 Kathryn May, "Embattled Budget Officer's Funding Frozen; Page Stalled in Efforts to Recruit and Hire Financial Analysts," *Ottawa Citizen*, December 19, 2008, A1.
27 "Budget Watchdog Operating 'Outside' Mandate: Government Ready to Take Matter to Court, Tony Clement Says," *CBC News*, October 6, 2012, https://www.cbc.ca/news/politics/budget-watchdog-operating-outside-mandate-1.1152959.
28 Page, *Unaccountable*.
29 Neil Macdonald, "What Happened to Transparency? Parliament's Budget Office Wants to Know," *CBC News*, April 6, 2016, https://www.cbc.ca/news/politics/pbo-budget-finance-letter-macdonald-1.3523421; Susana Mas, "Bill Morneau Disagrees with PBO Report That Budget Was Not 'Fully Transparent,'" *CBC News*, April 7, 2016, https://www.cbc.ca/news/politics/bill-morneau-budget-pbo-parliamentary-budget-office-1.3524851.
30 Barnes, Brousseau, and Hurtubise-Loranger, "Appointment of Officers of Parliament."
31 Sutherland, "Responsible Government and Ministerial Responsibility," 99.
32 Donald J. Savoie, *Breaking the Bargain: Public Servants, Ministers, and Parliament* (Toronto: University of Toronto Press, 2003), 280.
33 C.E.S. Franks, "Not Anonymous: Ministerial Responsibility and the British Accounting Officers," *Canadian Public Administration* 40, no. 4 (December 1997): 626–52, https://doi.org/10.1111/j.1754-7121.1997.tb02178.x.
34 David E. Smith, "Clarifying the Doctrine of Ministerial Responsibility As It Applies to the Government and Parliament of Canada" (Research Studies of the Commission of Inquiry into the Sponsorship Program and Advertising Activities, 2006), 132.
35 Philippe Lagassé, "Accountability for National Defence Ministerial Responsibility, Military Command and Parliamentary Oversight" (Institute for Research on Public Policy, 2010), 5–6, https://irpp.org/research-studies/accountability-for-national-defence. See also Philippe Lagassé and Patrick A. Mello, "The Unintended Consequences of Parliamentary Involvement: Elite Collusion and Afghanistan Deployments in Canada and Germany," *British Journal of Politics and International Relations* 20, no. 1 (February 2018): 135–57, 679, https://doi.org/10.1177/1369148117745681.
36 Lagassé, "Accountability," 5.
37 Jean-Christophe Boucher and Kim Richard Nossal, *The Politics of War: Canada's Afghanistan Mission, 2001–14* (Vancouver: UBC Press, 2018), 81.
38 Philippe Lagassé, "Parliament Should Scrutinize, Not Have a Say, on Military Deployments," pmlagasse.com (personal blog), October 17, 2016.
39 Norman Hillmer and Philippe Lagassé, "Parliament Will Decide: An Interplay of Politics and Principle," *International Journal* 71, no. 2 (2016): 328–37, 335, https://doi.org/10.1177/0020702016638679.
40 Brodie, *At the Centre of Government*, 50.
41 Brodie, *At the Centre of Government*, 50.

42 Walsh, *On the House*, 143.
43 Heather MacIvor, "The Speaker's Ruling on Afghan Detainee Documents: The Last Hurrah for Parliamentary Privilege?," *Constitutional Forum* 19, no. 1 (2010): 135, https://journals.library.ualberta.ca/constitutional_forum/index.php/constitutional_forum/article/view/17258.
44 Peter Zimonjic, "PHAC President Iain Stewart Reprimanded in House by Speaker for Failing to Produce Documents," *CBC News*, June 21, 2021, https://www.cbc.ca/news/politics/winnipeg-lab-house-bar-iain-stewart-1.6050835.
45 Robert Fife and Steven Chase, "Liberals Take House Speaker to Court to Block Release of Unredacted Records about Fired Scientists," *Globe and Mail*, June 23, 2021, https://www.theglobeandmail.com/politics/article-liberal-government-asks-court-to-stop-commons-obtaining-full-records/; Joan Bryden, "Commons Speaker Reflects on Dispute over Secret Documents on Scientists' Firing," *Toronto Star*, December 20, 2021, https://www.thestar.com/politics/2021/12/20/commons-speaker-reflects-on-dispute-over-secret-documents-on-scientists-firing.html.
46 Nicholas A. MacDonald, "Parliamentarians and National Security in Canada," *Canadian Parliamentary Review*, Winter 2011, 33–41, http://www.revparl.ca/english/issue.asp?param=208&art=1460.
47 Andrew Defty, "From Committees of Parliamentarians to Parliamentary Committees: Comparing Intelligence Oversight Reform in Australia, Canada, New Zealand and the UK," *Intelligence and National Security* 35, no. 3 (2020): 367–84, https://doi.org/10.1080/02684527.2020.1732646.
48 Ryan Tumilty, "Documents on Firing of Scientists at Top Lab Pit Liberals against Parliament," *National Post*, June 24, 2021, https://nationalpost.com/news/politics/documents-on-firing-of-scientists-at-top-lab-pit-liberals-against-parliament.

9 The Future of Parliament

1 Jonathan Malloy, "The Adaptation of Parliament's Multiple Roles to COVID-19," *Canadian Journal of Political Science* 53, no. 2 (2020): 307, http://doi.org/10.1017/S0008423920000426.
2 Paul E.J. Thomas, "Parliament under Pressure: Evaluating Parliament's Performance in Response to COVID-19" (Toronto: Samara Centre for Democracy, 2020), https://www.samaracanada.com/democracy-monitor/parliament-under-pressure.
3 James R. Robertson, "Television and the House of Commons" (Library of Parliament Research Branch, March 1990, Revised December 1998), http://www.publications.gc.ca/Collection-R/LoPBdP/BP/bp242-e.htm#(2).
4 Richard G. Price and Harold D. Clarke, "Television and the House of Commons," in *Parliament, Policy and Representation*, ed. Harold D. Clarke,

Colin Campbell, F.Q. Quo, and Arthur Goddard (Toronto: Methuen, 1980), 58–83.
5 Price and Clarke, "Television and the House of Commons," 70.
6 C.E.S. Franks, *The Parliament of Canada* (Toronto: University of Toronto Press, 1987), 157.
7 Robertson, "Television and the House of Commons."
8 John Paul Tasker, "Ready for Their Closeup: Senate Begins Broadcasting Proceedings for First Time," *CBC News*, March 18, 2019, https://www.cbc.ca/news/politics/tasker-senate-tv-first-time-1.5060943.
9 Franks, *The Parliament of Canada*, 157.
10 Stuart N. Soroka, Olga Redko, and Quinn Albaugh, "Television in the Legislature: The Impact of Cameras in the House of Commons," *Parliamentary Affairs* 68, no. 1 (January 2015): 203–17, https://doi.org/10.1093/pa/gst017.
11 Darin David Barney, "Push-button Populism: The Reform Party and the Real World of Teledemocracy," *Canadian Journal of Communication* 21, no. 3 (1996): 381–413, https://www.utpjournals.press/doi/full/10.22230/cjc.1996v21n3a956.
12 Paul Thomas, "The Future of Representative Democracy: The Impact of Information Technology," in *Modernizing Governance: A Preliminary Exploration* (Ottawa: Canadian Centre for Management Development, 2000), 87–8.
13 Thomas, "The Future of Representative Democracy," 88.
14 A. Chadwick and C. May, "Interaction between States and Citizens in the Age of the Internet: 'e-Government' in the United States, Britain, and the European Union," *Governance* 16 (2003): 271–300, 293, https://doi.org/10.1111/1468-0491.00216.
15 Jonathan Malloy, "To Better Serve Canadians: How Technology Is Changing the Relationship between Members of Parliament and Public Servants" (Toronto: Institute of Public Administration of Canada, 2003).
16 Amanda Clarke, *Opening the Government of Canada: The Federal Bureaucracy in the Digital Age* (Vancouver: UBC Press, 2019).
17 Jeffrey Roy, "The Rise of Networked Governance Everywhere but in Westminster Democracy," *Policy Options*, September 2010, 57–8, https://policyoptions.irpp.org/wp-content/uploads/sites/2/assets/po/making-parliament-work/roy.pdf.
18 Alex Marland, *Whipped: Party Discipline in Canada* (Vancouver: UBC Press, 2020).
19 J.P. Lewis, "Identities and Ideas: Participation of Young Legislators in the Canadian House of Commons," *Canadian Parliamentary Review* 29, no. 2 (Summer 2006): 12–20, http://www.revparl.ca/english/issue.asp?param=174&art=1188.
20 David C. Docherty, *Mr. Smith Goes to Ottawa: Life in the House of Commons* (Vancouver: UBC Press, 1997).
21 Jean-François Godbout, *Lost on Division: Party Unity in the Canadian Parliament* (Toronto: University of Toronto Press, 2020).

22 Docherty, "It's Awfully Crowded in Here Adjusting to the Five-Party House of Commons" (Ottawa: Canadian Study of Parliament Group, 1998), http://cspg-gcep.ca/pdf/David_Docherty_Paper-e.pdf.
23 Neil Nevitte, *The Decline of Deference: Canadian Value Change in Cross-National Perspective* (Toronto: University of Toronto Press, 1996).
24 Lisa Young, "Value Clash: Parliament and Citizens after 150 Years of Responsible Government," in *Taking Stock of 150 Years of Responsible Government in Canada*, ed. Louis Massicote and F. Leslie Seidle (Ottawa: Canadian Study of Parliament Group, 1999), 105.
25 Environics Institute for Survey Research, "Confidence in Democracy and the Political System: An Update on Trends in Public Opinion in Canada," September 11, 2019, https://www.environicsinstitute.org/docs/default-source/default-document-library/ab-democracy-report-revised-sept11_209.pdf?sfvrsn=bda257b6_0.

Index

abortion bills and motions, 120, 130, 159, 162, 169–70, 190
accountability. *See* Question Period; scrutiny, Parliamentary
adversarial decision-making, 9–10, 13, 159, 224
Afghanistan missions, 108, 204, 220, 224–5, 227, 230
Aiken, Gordon, 77
air travel, 97, 98, 235
Ajzenstat, Janet, 18–19, 22, 203
Alberta, 73, 186, 193
Alexander, Lincoln, 73, 83, 172, 179, 194
Alleslev, Leona, 60
Alternative Vote (AV), 63
amateurism, 27, 55, 78, 98–101
Ambrose, Rona, 129–30
Arab-Canadian representation, 73
Ashton, Niki, 82
Association of Feminist Parliamentarians (AFP), 169
Association of Former Parliamentarians, 69–70
Association of Women Parliamentarians (AWP), 162–3, 164

Atkinson, Michael M., 2, 6, 92, 99, 189–90, 192, 212
Aucoin, Peter, 29, 31, 54
Auditor-General of Canada, 142, 207, 215, 216–17, 218, 244
Augustine, Jean, 73, 194
Australia
  1975 government deadlock, 133, 192–3, 200–1
  bicameralism in, 183, 188
  electoral systems, 63
  heckling, 113
  leadership selection, 42, 44, 45, 46
  minority governments, 61, 137, 243
  political parties, 34, 37, 46, 47, 48
  prorogation, 35, 115
  Senate, 182
Axworthy, Thomas, 3, 5

Badanai, Hubert, 73
Bagehot, Walter, 19–21, 183
Baker, Dennis, 19
Barnes, Andre, 120
Bashevkin, Sylvia, 159
Bastedo, Heather, 82
Bédard, Michel, 120
Beer, Samuel, 118

Bégin, Monique, 3, 158
Bennett, Carolyn, 49, 54
Benoit, Leon, 82
Bergen, Candice, 56
Bernier, Maxime, 220
Bhaduria, Jag, 73
bicameralism, 183–5, 191
Bill of Rights (1689), 16
bills, government
  closure and time allocation, 122
  debate, 117–19, 123–4
  omnibus bills, 119–22
  sessions and prorogation, effects on, 114–15
  ways and means motion, 211
  See also private members' business
Birch, Anthony, 8
Bird, Karen, 177–8, 179
Black, Jerome, 173, 174, 175
Black, Martha, 72
Black Canadian representation, 73, 175
Blidook, Kelly, 82, 99, 100, 131
Bloc Québécois
  2008 parliamentary crisis, 30–1, 134
  creation and rise of, 43, 59, 242–3
  diversity and representation, 168–9, 179
  party discipline and dissent, 58, 59, 60
  Reform Act (2014) and, 56
Blondin-Andrew, Ethel, 149
Board of Internal Economy, 94, 108
Bosc, Marc, 128
Bouchard, Lucien, 153
Boucher, Jean-Christophe, 225
Brison, Scott, 60
British North America Act, 18, 160
Brodie, Ian, 19, 31, 52, 103, 119, 124, 212, 225
brokerage parties, 36, 57–8, 65
Brosseau, Ruth Ellen, 71–2, 112
Brown, Bert, 193
budgets, 211–15
  See also Parliamentary Budget Officer (PBO)

cabinet, 79, 154–5, 164, 205
Caesar-Chavannes, Celina, 3, 171, 176–7
calendar, parliamentary, 25, 113–16, 133, 139, 208, 211, 212
Camp, Michael, 156
campaigns. *See* elections
Campbell, Barry, 69
Campbell, Colin, 191–2
Campbell, Kim, 89, 161
Canadian Alliance, 43, 55, 59, 60, 152, 239
  See also Conservative Party of Canada (CPC); Reform Party of Canada
Canadian Council of Public Accounts Committees, 142
Canadian Senate: A Lobby from Within, The (Campbell), 191–2
Canadian Taxpayers Federation, 93
Carty, Kenneth, 41, 44
Casey, Bill, 60
caucuses, 41–2, 45–6, 50
Chadwick, A., 238
Charlottetown Accord, 152
Charter of Rights and Freedoms, 37, 210
Chief Electoral Officer, 215
Chinese-Canadian representation, 73, 175
Chong, Michael, 27, 55, 56, 106–7, 230
Chrétien, Jean, 29, 35, 45, 51–2, 92, 115, 161
citizen attitudes and Parliament, 243–6
civil service, merit-based, 42
Clark, Joe, 136
Clarke, Amanda, 239
Clerk of the House of Commons, 108–9
clerks and professional staff, 109–10
closure, 122

Collier, Cheryl N., 167
Commissioner of Lobbying, 215, 217
Commissioner of Official Languages, 215, 216
committee chairs and vice-chairs, 79–80
committees. *See* legislative committees; special committees; standing committees
confidence/non-confidence motions, 30, 108, 134–5
Conflict of Interest and Ethics Commissioner, 215, 217
consensus legislatures, 32–3, 39
 See also Indigenous peoples
Conservative Party of Canada (CPC)
 creation of, 43
 diversity and representation, 159, 168–9, 178–9
 member demographics, 74
 on post-2016 Senate appointees, 196, 198, 199
 Reform Act (2014), 45, 56
 See also Harper, Stephen; O'Toole, Erin; Scheer, Andrew
Conservative Senators Group, 197
constituencies, 81–5
Constitution Act, 1867, 18
conventions, party, 42, 45
Cools, Anne, 177, 194
Cooper, Michael, 112, 113
Co-operative Commonwealth Federation (CCF), 42, 58, 191, 242–3
Copps, Sheila, 158–9, 168
COVID-19 pandemic, 89, 96, 132, 204, 220, 233–4, 243
Criminal Law Amendment Act (1967), 120
Croll, David, 189
Cross, William, 44
Crown, 13, 14–15, 16, 20, 148
Cullen, Nathan, 118

Dallaire, Roméo, 155
Davies, Libby, 10, 156–7, 159, 181
Dawson, W.F., 104
Day, Stockwell, 59
deBane, Pierre, 73
debate in House of Commons, 117–19, 123–4
"decline of deference, the" 244–5
"democratic deficit," 7, 29, 245
Democratic Representative Caucus (DRC), 59
Democratizing the Constitution (Aucoin; Jarvis; Turnbull), 54
Depauw, Sam, 47
Deputy Speakers, 80, 105
Desjarlais, Bev, 60
Desjarlais, Blake, 157
Dhaliwal, Herb, 73
Dhalla, Ruby, 172–3
Dion, Stéphane, 30, 31
disabilities, people with, 4, 153–6
diversity in Parliament
 approach to, overview, and conclusions, 3–4, 9–10, 24, 145–8, 180–1
 disabilities, people with, 4, 153–6
 ethnicity and representation, 72–3, 171–2, 175
 Indigenous peoples, 3, 4, 12–15, 148–53, 157, 196
 intersectional people, 146, 147, 171, 179
 LGBT representation, 4, 156–8, 180
 Pitkin's framework of representation, 145–6, 147–8
 racialized representation, descriptive, 173–5
 racialized representation, introduction to, 3, 4, 171–2
 racialized representation, substantive, 176–80
 racialized representation, symbolic, 3, 73, 172–3
 Senate diversity, 194, 196, 201

diversity in Parliament (*cont.*)
  women, 3, 4, 72, 160–2, 167, 169–70, 175
  women's *vs.* feminist representation, 159, 168–70, 178
divorce bills, 127–8, 162
Docherty, David, 2, 5–6, 26, 54–5, 70, 78–9, 99, 242
Dockrill, Michelle, 165
Durham, First Earl of (John George Lambton), 17, 18, 21, 22
Durham Report, 17, 18
Dusseault, Pierre-Luc, 75

elections, 13, 14–15, 18–19, 21, 148
Elections Canada reform (1972), 27
electoral system reform, 63–5
Emerson, David, 71
enfranchisement, 13–14, 148
English Constitution, The (Bagehot), 19
equity-seeking groups. *See* diversity in Parliament
Erskine-Smith, Nathaniel, 50
ethnic representation. *See* diversity in Parliament
Everitt, Joanna, 156

F-35 fighter jets purchase, 228, 232
Fairclough, Ellen, 158
Falcon-Ouellette, Robert, 149–51
Famous Five, 160
federalism, 35, 36–7, 192, 210
Feldman, Charlie, 119
feminism, 159, 168–70, 178, 201
Filipino-Canadian representation, 73, 175
financial accountability. *See* scrutiny, Parliamentary
First Nations, 13–14, 148
"first-past-the-post" electoral system, 63–5
Fitzpatrick, Brian, 83
Flanagan, Tom, 30–1
Fletcher, Stephen, 154, 155

floor-crossers, 60
Franks, C.E.S.
  on British accounting officers, 223
  on budget implementation acts, 121
  on committees, 138
  on debate, 118
  on estimates process, 212
  on MPs, 78, 99
  on Parliament reform, 2, 57
  on television in the House, 236, 237
  on ways of understanding parliament, 8, 22
Fraser, John, 220
Fraser, Malcolm, 192
Fry, Hedy, 73

Gagnon, Andre, 128
gender, 72, 147, 196, 201
George III, King, 13
Germany, 45, 183, 184, 192
Ghebretecle, Terhas, 84
Glover, Shelly, 149
Godbout, Jean-François, 40, 42–3, 58, 243
Goldsmith-Jones, Pamela, 100
Gould, Karina, 165
governance. *See* logics of governance and representation
government. *See* Parliament; representative government; responsible government
Government House Leader, 110
Government Operations and Estimates Committee, 139, 142, 214
Governor General, 20, 114, 186
Grace, Joan, 170
Gradual Civilization Act, 13
"grants and contributions" scandal, 221–2
Green Party of Canada, 43, 64, 136, 169, 242–3
Greene, Barbara, 159
Grey, Deborah, 164

Grey, Third Earl of (Henry George Grey), 17
Griffith, Andrew, 174, 175
Grisdale, Mackenzie, 112–13
Guppy, N., 74

Hajdu, Patty, 167
Hansard, Thomas, 109
Hansard service and record, 108–9, 112
Harder, Peter, 197–8
Harder, Rachael, 159
Harper, Stephen
  2008 parliamentary crisis, 30–1, 134
  abortion bills and motions, 130–1, 159
  accountability reforms, 217–18, 223
  Bev Oda incident, 208
  CPC foreign policy issues, 108, 134, 224, 225–6, 227–8
  David Emerson, parachute candidate, 71
  minority governments, 61, 62, 136
  omnibus bills, 121
  prorogation, 35, 115
  Question Period, 125
  Senate reform attempts, 186, 194–5
  Senate vacancies and appointments, 161, 187, 193, 196
  See also Conservative Party of Canada (CPC)
Hassainia, Sana, 165
Heaps, A.A., 73
heckling, 111–13
Hill Times newspaper, 174
Hillmer, Norman, 225
House Leaders, 110–11
House of Commons
  approach to and conclusions, 102–5, 116–17, 144
  budget speech, 212–13
  chambers and seating, 111
  Clerk of the House of Commons, 108–9
  clerks and professional staff, 109–10
  closure and time allocation, 122
  debate in, 117–19, 123–4
  decorum in, 111–13
  functions of, 5–6
  House Leaders, 110–11
  independent candidates, 59–60, 256n35
  minority governments, 41, 61–3, 135–7, 243
  obstruction, 122–4
  omnibus bills, 119–22
  parties, recognition of, 43
  relevance, 30
  Sergeant-at-Arms, 109
  sessions and prorogation, 114–15
  Speakers of the House, 25, 80, 105–8, 113
  viewpoints on process, malleability of, 2–3, 10, 103–4, 121, 122, 219
  ways and means motion, 211
  See also Members of Parliament (MPs); opposition parties; Parliament; parties, political; private members' business; Question Period; reforms, Parliamentary; scrutiny, Parliamentary; sexism in Parliament; standing committees
House of Commons (UK)
  accounting officers, 223
  chamber, 111
  committees, 33, 55, 138, 139, 210
  leadership selection, 45
  minority governments, 61, 243
  MPs, 33, 55, 111, 126, 155, 210
  Question Time, 33, 126, 210
  sessions and prorogation, 115
  single-member plurality (SMP) electoral system, 63
  Speakers, 105, 107, 126

House of Commons (UK) (*cont.*)
  supply, power to deny, 133
  three-line-whip system, 47
House of Lords (UK), 20, 21, 182, 183, 184, 189
Høyland, Bjørn, 42–3
Hsu, Ted, 83

Independent Advisory Board for Senate Appointments (IAB), 195–6
independent candidates, 59–60, 256n35
Independent Senators Group (ISG), 187, 197, 200
Indian Act (1876), 13, 148, 162, 201
"Indian" in the Cabinet (Wilson-Raybould), 149
Indigenous peoples
  consensus, preference for, 13, 15, 32
  First Nations, 13–14, 148
  Inuit, 13, 14, 148, 149, 152
  Métis, 14, 148, 149, 152
  Parliament, representation in, 3, 12–15, 148–53, 157, 196
  See also consensus legislatures
Information Commissioner, 215
internet, 5, 237–40
  See also social media; technology's effects on Parliament
intersectional parliamentarians, 146, 147, 171, 179
Inuit, 13, 14, 148, 149, 152
Irresponsible Government (Rathgeber), 60
Italian-Canadian representatives, 73
Ittinauar, Peter, 14, 149

Jackson, Robert, 2, 6, 189–90, 192, 212
Jaffer, Rahim, 73
Japanese-Canadian representation, 175
Jarvis, Mark, 54
Jean, Michaëlle, 30
Jewish-Canadian representatives, 73

Johnson, Boris, 35
Jowhari, Majid, 95
Joyal, Serge, 193–4
Jung, Douglas, 73, 172

Kerby, Matthew, 99, 100
Keretak-Lindell, Nancy, 149
King, W.L.M., 36
Koop, Royce, 46, 82
Korean-Canadian representation, 73
Kwak, Laura Jean, 172, 175, 179

Labrador, 152
Lagassé, Philippe, 224, 225
LaMarsh, Judy, 158
Lametti, David, 129
Lamoureaux, Lucien, 105
Langford, Brynne, 153
Lankin, Frances, 196
leaders, selection and removal, 42, 45–6
Lefebvre committee, 25
legislative assemblies, colonial, 13, 16–18
legislative committees, 139
legislatures, 6–7, 9, 32–3, 39
Levesque, Mario, 153
Lewis, J.P., 241
LGBT representation, 4, 156–8, 180
Liberal Party of Canada
  2008 parliamentary crisis, 30–1, 134
  2021 Conservative motion on China, 134
  Catholics, preference for, 42–3
  conscription and, 36
  Indigenous members in Parliament, 151
  leadership challenges, 29
  leadership selection by convention, 42, 45
  member demographics, 75
  minority governments, 61
  provincial-federal separation, 37
  Reform Act (2014), 56

sponsorship scandal, 115, 142, 217
standing, post-1993, 43
WE Charity, 115, 136
women's *vs.* feminist representation in, 168–9
See also Trudeau, Justin
Liberal Women's Caucus, 164
Library of Parliament, 139, 143, 207, 218
Liu, Lauren, 166
Loat, Alison, 46, 69, 76, 80, 84
Loewenberg, Gerhard, 9, 24
logics of governance and representation
  in Canada *vs.* similar countries, 33–5, 36, 38, 232
  as frame for understanding Parliament, 7–8, 9–11, 38
  governance, logic of, overview, 18–21
  representation, logic of, overview, 21–5
  See also diversity in Parliament; House of Commons; Members of Parliament (MPs); Parliament; Parliament, future of; parties, political; reforms, Parliamentary; scrutiny, Parliamentary; Senate
loose fish, 42, 58
Lower Canada, 16, 17
Luchkovich, Michael, 73

MacDonald, Flora, 158
Macdonald, Lyn, 129
Macdonell, J.J., 204
Macfarlane, Emmett, 190–1, 199
MacIvor, Heather, 228
Mackay, R.A., 190, 191
Mackenzie, Alexander, 189
MacMillan, Michael, 46, 69, 76, 80, 84
MacPhail, Agnes, 72, 158
Malhi, Gurbax Singh, 73
Malkowski, Gary, 154

Mallory, J.R., 5, 25
Manitoba bicameralism, 188
Manning, Preston, 28, 54
Marchand, Len, 14, 73, 148–9, 151
Marland, Alex, 47, 48–9, 51–2, 240
Marleau, Robert, 212
Martin, Keith, 60
Martin, Paul, 29, 45, 55, 61, 161, 186, 194
Martin, Shane, 47
May, C., 238
May, Elizabeth, 107
McCallion, Elizabeth, 162, 198–9, 201
McCreath, Peter, 85
McGrath committee, 25, 242
McLeod, Peter, 27, 82, 84
Members of Parliament (MPs)
  approach to and conclusions, 67–8, 101
  ages of, 75–6
  backbenchers, 50–2
  career opportunities, 78–81
  constituency responsibilities, 81–5, 259n32
  daily routines, 96–8
  expectations of the job, 72, 77–8, 83
  floor-crossers, 60
  job descriptions, lack of, 67, 86, 101
  job orientation for, 76–7
  job security, 88, 93, 99
  motivations for running for office, 68–70, 92
  nominations and appointments, 44, 70–1
  party caucus meetings, 50
  private lives, managing, 88–91
  roles, 7–8, 9, 22, 23, 24, 68, 85–8
  salary and benefits, 91–3
  socio-economic and occupational backgrounds, 74–5, 78
  staffing, 93–6
  turnover, 55, 98–101, 139–40, 242

Members of Parliament (MPs) (*cont.*)
  whips, 52, 79, 106–7, 110–11, 139, 167
  See also diversity in Parliament; House of Commons; parties, political; party cohesion; party discipline; Senate
Members' Statements, 107, 131–2
Ménard, Réal, 156
Métis, 14, 148, 149, 152
Milliken, Peter, 90, 106, 108, 227–8
minority governments, 41, 61–3, 135–7, 243
Mitchell, Margaret, 158
"mixed government," 18, 22
mixed-member proportional electoral system (MMP), 63, 64–5
modern state, 4–5, 6
money. *See* bills, government; budgets; scrutiny, Parliamentary
Morden, Michael, 150, 151
motions. *See* bills, government; private members' business
Mr. Smith Goes to Ottawa (Docherty), 242
Mullen, Stephanie, 161, 162
Mulroney, Brian, 50–2, 58–9, 161, 186, 190, 193
Murphy, Kevin, 154

Nathan, Henry, 73
National Energy Program, 122–3
National Security and Intelligence Committee of Parliamentarians (NSICOP), 229–30
national security and Parliamentary scrutiny, 229–31
Nevitte, Neil, 244
New Brunswick, 16, 188
New Democratic Party (NDP)
  1921 election, 242–3
  1993 election, 163
  2008 parliamentary crisis, 30–1, 134
  Orange Wave (2011 surge), 71–2, 75–6, 100, 164–5
  party discipline in, 58
  party status, 43
  Reform Act (2014) vote, 56
  staffing practices for MPs, 94
  stance on the Senate, 184, 191
  WE Charity motion vote, 136
  women's *vs.* feminist representation in, 168–9
New Zealand
  bicameralism, end of, 183, 188, 191
  leadership selection, 42, 45
  Maori representation, 152
  minority governments, 61
  mixed-member proportional electoral system (MMP), 34, 41, 63, 64–5
  prorogation, 35, 115
Newfoundland, 16
Nisga'a treaty, 152
non-confidence/confidence motions, 30, 108, 134–5
Northwest Resistance of 1885, 14
Northwest Territories, 15, 32–3, 39, 152
Nossal, Kim Richard, 225
Nova Scotia, 16, 17, 188
Nunavut, 15, 32–3, 39, 152
Nunziata, John, 60

Obhrai, Deepak, 179
obstruction, 122–4
Oda, Bev, 208
Office of the Auditor-General (OAG), 142, 207, 215, 216–17, 218
officers of Parliament, 215–19
Okanagan Nation, 14
Oliver, Donald, 177, 194
O'Malley, Kady, 134
Ontario referendum (2007), 64–5
opposition motions, 134
opposition parties
  competition among, 9, 103, 124–5
  cooperation agreement (2008), 30–1

in minority governments, 62, 135–7
opposition days (supply days), 25, 26, 133–4, 211
party views, malleability of, 2–3, 10, 103–4, 121, 122, 219
role in Parliament, 19, 21
shadow ministers, 79, 127
tactics in Parliament, 117, 118–19, 122–3, 124–5
See also Members of Parliament (MPs); parties, political; Question Period; scrutiny, Parliamentary
Orange Wave (2011 NDP surge), 71–2, 75–6, 100, 164–5
O'Toole, Erin, 45, 46, 56
Ouellet, Martine, 59

Page, Kevin, 206, 218
Pagtakhan, Rey, 73
parachute candidates, 70–1
paradox of Parliament
 approach to, overview, and conclusions, 1–2, 6–11, 246–7
 See also logics of governance and representation; Parliament
Parliament
 bicameralism, 183–5, 191
 cabinet, 79, 154–5, 164, 205
 calendar, 25, 113–16, 133, 139, 208, 211, 212
 in Canada *vs.* similar countries, 33–7, 98
 consent, mobilization of, 118, 119
 criticisms of, 1–2
 Crown, relationship with, 20–1
 frames for understanding, 7–8
 functions of, 5–6
 as gendered institution, 165–7
 legislatures, expectations of, 6–7
 minority governments, 41, 61–3, 135–7, 243
 officers of, 215–19
 origins, 15–18, 145
 problems, reasons for, 4–6, 10
 prorogation in, 30, 34–5, 114–15, 134
 sessions, 114
 "strong executive" model, 18–19, 21, 22–3, 203, 211
 time allocation, 41–2, 58, 77, 103, 117, 129
 underrepresented groups, 3–4, 153, 155, 157, 171, 173–5, 180
 US political system's influence on, 22–3
 weaknesses of, 34–8
 See also bills, government; diversity in Parliament; Governor General; House of Commons; logics of governance and representation; Members of Parliament (MPs); Parliament, future of; parties, political; reforms, Parliamentary; scrutiny, Parliamentary; Senate; television
Parliament, future of
 adaptation to change, 233–4, 246–7
 citizen attitudes and, 243–6
 membership, changes in, 241–3
 technology's effects, 235–40
Parliament Act (1911), 189
Parliamentary Black Caucus, 178
Parliamentary Budget Officer (PBO), 216, 217–19
parliamentary secretary, 79
parliamentary systems, 6–7
parties, political
 benefits of, 39–40
 brokerage parties, 36, 57–8, 65
 caucuses, 41–2, 45–6, 50
 diverse representation in, 151–2
 federal *vs.* provincial, 37
 lack of, in NWT and Nunavut, 32
 leaders, selection and removal, 42, 45–6
 membership, 44
 in minority governments, 41, 61–3

parties, political (*cont.*)
  multi-party system, 242–3
  nominations and appointments, 44, 70–1
  party system, three eras of, 41–3
  policy setting, 44–5
  private members' business, 130–1
  recognition of in House of Commons, 43
  rise of, 21
  women's *vs.* feminist representation in, 159, 168–70, 178
  See also Bloc Québécois; Canadian Alliance; Conservative Party of Canada (CPC); Co-operative Commonwealth Federation (CCF); Green Party of Canada; Liberal Party of Canada; New Democratic Party (NDP); party cohesion; party discipline; Progressive Conservative Party (PCs); Progressive Party; Reform Party of Canada
partisanship, 5, 23, 42–3, 90–1, 131, 195
party cohesion, 47–8, 57–8, 65
party discipline
  in Australia, 34
  British *vs.* Canadian, 33, 55
  brokerage parties, 36, 57–8, 65
  concerns around, 1, 2, 22, 25, 29, 31
  dissent, approaches to, 49–53, 58–9
  excessive *vs.* acceptable, 54–5
  floor-crossers, 60
  independent candidates, 59–60, 256n35
  in minority governments, 41, 61–2
  persistence of, 40–1, 42, 43, 46–7, 61
  Reform Act (2014) and, 56–7
  as system of support for MPs, 48–9
party whips. *See* whips
patronage, 3, 41–2, 58, 189
Persons case, 158, 160
petitions, presentation of, 132–3

Philpott, Jane, 60
Pitkin, Hannah, 145–6, 147
Poilievre, Pierre, 75
policy-making, 23–4, 44–5, 141
political parties. *See* parties, political; party cohesion; party discipline
Portuguese-Canadian representatives, 73
premiers
  colonial, 17–18
  provincial, 32, 36–7
presidential systems, 6
Prince Edward Island, 16
Privacy Commissioner, 215, 216
private members' business
  confidence/non-confidence motions, 30, 108, 134–5
  Members' Statements, 107, 131–2
  opposition days (supply days), 25, 26, 133–4, 211
  parliamentary time for, 129–30
  parties, role of, 130–1
  petitions, presentation of, 132–3
  private bills, 127–8
  private members' bills and motions, 128–9, 130
  time available for, historically, 41, 42, 58, 116, 127–8
  See also Reform Act (2014)
Progressive Conservative Party (PCs), 43, 163, 242
Progressive Party, 28, 42, 58, 242–3
Progressive Senators Group, 197
prorogation, 30, 34–5, 114–15, 134
Public Accounts Committee (PAC or PACP), 139, 142, 214, 215
Public Health Agency of Canada, 229
Public Sector Integrity Commissioner, 215, 217

Qaqqaq, Mumilaaq, 3, 150
Qualtrough, Carla, 154–5
Quebec bicameralism, 183, 188
Québec Debout, 59

Quebec Parliamentary Group, 59
Question Period
    changes and reforms, 26–7, 55,
        106–7, 116, 126, 237, 262n8
    interruptions during, 112–13
    purpose and value of, 8, 103,
        124–7, 205
Question Time (UK), 33, 126, 210

racialized people. *See* diversity in
    Parliament
Railway Committee, 138
Raney, Tracey, 167
Rathgeber, Brent, 60, 204
Rayment, Erica, 169–70
Reform Act (2014), 45, 56
Reform Party of Canada
    citizen discontent and, 244–5
    constituency-based voting, 54–5,
        237–8
    creation and purpose of, 28–9,
        58–9, 242–3
    diversity issues, 164, 179
    heckling, 113
    "O Canada," regular singing of, 116
    reunification with Progressive
        Conservatives, 43
    "Triple E Senate" as goal, 3, 193, 201
    See also Canadian Alliance;
        Conservative Party of
        Canada (CPC); Progressive
        Conservative Party (PCs)
reforms, Parliamentary
    1960s–1980s, 2, 5, 25–7, 133, 244
    1990s and 2000s, 28–9
    2004–2011 minority era, 29–32
    cyclical calls for, 2–3, 4, 5, 35
    demands for in Canadian
        colonies, 16–17
    electoral system reform, 63–5
    evaluation of, 6
    Question Period, 26–7, 55, 106–7,
        116, 126, 237, 262n8
    See also Senate

Regan, Geoff, 80, 106
regionalism and regional issues, 3,
    35–7, 42, 185–6, 192–3, 201
    See also Bloc Québécois; Reform
        Party of Canada
Reid, Scott, 49–50, 55
Rempel, Michelle (later Michelle
    Rempel Garner), 160, 164
representative government, 7–8, 16,
    17–18
responsible government, 8, 15–18
Riel, Louis, 14, 43, 149, 251n4
Robertson, James R., 236
Robinson, Svend, 4, 156, 157
Rogers, Dustin, 92
Roy, Jeffrey, 240
Royal Assent, 20
Royal Commission on Aboriginal
    Peoples, 152
Royal Proclamation of 1763, 13
Russell, Peter, 30, 61–2, 65

Samara Canada, 68, 90–1, 112
Sauvé, Jeanne, 106–7
Savoie, Donald, 36, 121, 213–14,
    217, 223
Scheer, Andrew, 75, 80, 106, 198,
    262n8
scrutiny, Parliamentary
    approach to and conclusions,
        203–5, 231–2
    collective responsibility, 205
    financial, 211–15
    information, access to, 227–30
    of military and foreign policy
        issues, 223–7
    ministerial responsibility, 205,
        220–3
    officer roles created for, 215–19
    as political process, 209–10
    standing committees and, 141–2
    theory and practice, balancing,
        205–9
    two principles of, 231

Seats and Regional Formula, 185–6
Seidle, Leslie, 46
Senate
　activism, 189, 272n5
　appointment process, 3, 7, 182, 186–7, 195–7
　bicameralism and, 183–5, 191
　as chamber of "sober second thought," 3, 183, 184, 188, 189
　futures, possible, 200–2
　gender parity, 196, 201
　history of, 40, 182, 184, 188–90, 272n5
　organization and process of, 187
　reform debate, early 20th century to 2016, 190–5
　reforms of 2016 and outcomes, 195–9
　turnover in, 161
　unaccountability, air of, 185
Senate Public Bills, 187
Sergeant-at-Arms, 109
sessions, 114
　See also calendar, parliamentary
Sévigny, Pierre, 153
sexism in Parliament
　assaults, 159
　sexual misconduct, 56, 165–6, 185
　systemic issues, 147, 164–5, 166–7
　toxic work environment, 147, 158, 159–60, 166
　See also Association of Feminist Parliamentarians (AFP); Association of Women Parliamentarians (AWP)
sexual assault training legislation (Bill C-337), 129–30
shadow ministers, 79
Sheeple (Turner), 53
Shin, Nelly, 73
Sieberer, Ulrich, 47
Siksay, Bill, 156
Simms, Scott, 83
Single Transferable Vote (STV), 63

single-member plurality (SMP) electoral system, 63–5
Sloan, Derek, 56, 132
Smiley, Donald, 36–7
Smith, David
　on critiques of Parliament, 2, 35–6, 37, 183, 223
　on dominance of parties, 59
　on the Senate, 190, 192, 201
　on "the invisible Crown," 20
Smith, Jennifer, 22, 28
Social Credit and Creditistes, 242–3, 244
social media, 5, 53, 132, 166, 209, 237–8, 240
South Asian representation, 73, 174, 179
Speakers of the House, 25, 80, 105–8, 113
special committees, 139
Speech from the Throne, 20, 114, 135
sponsorship scandal, 115, 142, 217
St. Germain, Gerry, 152
St. Laurent, Louis, 122, 161
staffing for MPs, 93–6
Standing Committee on Finance, 139, 214, 228
Standing Committee on Government Operations and Estimates, 214
Standing Committee on Health and Welfare, Social Affairs, Seniors, and the Status of Women, 170
Standing Committee on Justice, 140
Standing Committee on Public Accounts, 214
Standing Committee on the Status of Women, 159, 164, 170
standing committees
　chairships, 79–80, 140
　committee assignments, 139–40
　committee-officer relationships, 217
　creation and evolution of, 25, 26, 55, 137–8, 139
　functions of, 141–4, 214

special committees, 139
See also Members of Parliament (MPs); scrutiny, Parliamentary
Standing Orders, 121, 122, 123, 131, 133, 151, 213
Stanfield, Robert L., 5
Steele, Jackie, 163
Stewart, Jane, 221–2
Stewart, Kennedy, 46
Stillborn, Jack, 104, 190, 212
Stronach, Belinda, 60, 137
"strong executive" model, 18–19, 21, 22–3, 203, 211
Sub-Committee on the Status of Women, 170
supply days (opposition days), 25, 26, 133–4, 211
Sutherland, Sharon, 27, 206, 207, 209, 217, 222–3

Task Force on Canadian Unity (the Pepin-Robarts Commission), 192
technology's effects on Parliament, 235–40
See also social media; television
telephones, 235, 238
television
   House of Commons, introduction into, 5, 25
   national news broadcasts, 235
   in Parliament, effects of, 5, 26, 96–7, 112, 118, 124, 236–7
   in the Senate, 237
   standing committees on, 139
   and third party system, 43
Tellier, Geneviève, 213
Thi Lac, Ève-Mary Thaï, 73
Thibeault, Louise, 60
Thomas, Paul G., 26, 238
time allocation, 122
Tragedy in the Commons (Loat; MacMillan), 46
treaties with the Crown, 13, 14–15
Tremblay, Manon, 157
"Triple-E Senate," 3, 193

trucker convoy (2022), 243
Trudeau, Justin
   2020 prorogation, 35, 115, 129–30
   backbenchers, managing, 51
   governments, stability and disruption under, 31, 242
   omnibus legislation, 121
   reforms, Parliamentary, 2–3, 64, 126, 187, 194, 195–6, 197–8
   sanctioning party members, 167
   shoving incident, 112
   WE Charity, 115, 136
   See also Afghanistan missions; Liberal Party of Canada; Senate
Trudeau, Pierre, 25, 120, 122–3, 158, 161, 186, 192
Turnbull, Lori, 29, 54
Turner, Garth, 52–3, 60
Turning Parliament Inside Out, 4, 46
turnover in Parliament, 55, 98–101, 139–40, 161, 242

Ukrainian-Canadian representatives, 73
Ulrich, Andrea, 125
Unaccountable (Page), 218
United Kingdom
   Brexit referendum, 35, 47, 245
   Crown, 13, 14–15, 16, 20, 148
   devolution of power, 36
   House of Lords, 20, 21, 182, 183, 184, 189
   political parties, 33, 42, 44–5, 47, 48, 55
   See also House of Commons (UK); Westminster system of parliamentary democracy
United States of America
   attack on US Capitol, 243, 245
   political influence on Canada, 22–3, 27
   political system, 6, 19, 21, 63, 98–9, 111, 183–4

Unreformed Senate of Canada, The
(Mackay), 190, 191
Upper Canada, 16, 17

VandenBeukel, Jason, 196, 198, 199
Vickers, Kevin, 109
Victoria, Queen, 20–1
voting rights and participation, 13, 14–15, 148, 155, 158
See also "first-past-the-post" electoral system

Walsh, Rob, 117, 211–12, 227
Waters, Stan, 193
ways and means motion, 211
WE Charity, 115, 136
Western alienation and Senate reform, 192, 193
Westminster system of parliamentary democracy, 15–17, 36, 39, 108–9, 111, 240, 246–7
See also Australia; House of Commons; New Zealand; "strong executive" model
whips, 52, 79, 106–7, 110–11, 139, 167
Whitlam, Gough, 192

Wilks, David, 53, 240
Williams, John, 142
Wilson, Cairine, 160
Wilson, Paul, 94
Wilson-Raybould, Jody, 60, 77, 140, 149, 168
Winnipeg government lab controversy, 228–30
women
adversarial nature of Parliament and, 24, 112, 159–60, 180–1
early experiences in Parliament, 158–9
expressions of ambition, 69
in the House, 161, 162–7
parliamentary careers, challenges of, 67, 88–91, 100, 165–6
in the Senate, 160–2
underrepresentation in Parliament, 3, 4, 72, 157
women's *vs.* feminist representation, 159, 168–70, 178

Young, Lisa, 104, 163, 244
Yukon, 32